TRAIL WAYS, PATH WISE

Books by John Illig

Trail Ways, Path Wise
Pacific Dream
Man In The Middle

TRAIL WAYS, PATH WISE

JOHN ILLIG

ELDERBERRY PRESS, INC.
OAKLAND

Events in this story were real, but are subject to interpretation. Perspectives will
differ for the people who have lived through these events. This is simply the
story as I saw it, and no harm is wished upon anyone else.

ELDERBERRY PRESS, INC.

1393 Old Homestead Drive, Second floor
Oakland, Oregon 97462—9506.
E MAIL: editor@elderberrypress. com
TEL/FAX: 541.459.6043
www.elderberrypress.com

Elderberry Press books are available from your favorite bookstore, amazon.
com, or from our 24-hour order line: 1.800.431.1579

Library of Congress Control Number: 2005929049
Publisher's Catalog—in—Publication Data
Trail Ways, Path Wise/John Illig
ISBN 13: 978-1-932762-42-6
ISBN 10: 1932762426
1. Hiking.
2. Nature.
3. Through-Hiking.
4. Thru-Hiking.
5. Appalachian Trail
6. Adventure.
I. Title
This book was written, printed and bound in the United States of America.

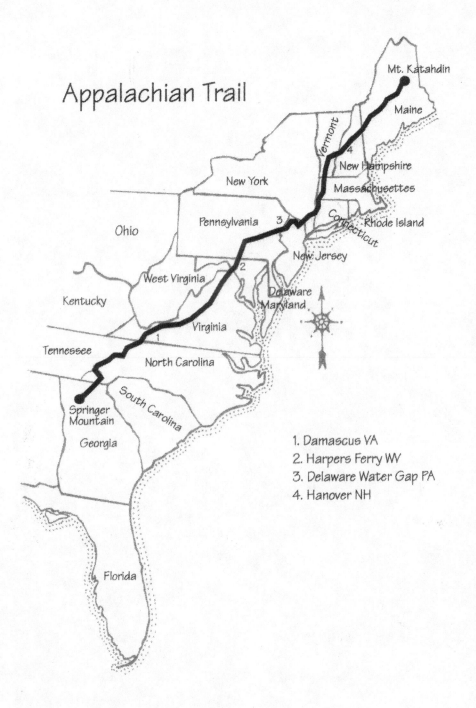

Appalachian Trail

1. Damascus VA
2. Harpers Ferry WV
3. Delaware Water Gap PA
4. Hanover NH

CONTENTS

1
The Hardest Thing

Late in the night when the fires are out,
Why does he gallop and gallop about?

—Robert Louis Stevenson, *"Windy Nights"*

Primordial Urge.

The hardest thing about through-hiking the Appalachian Trail is getting to the start. To through-hike, you must walk the entire trail, end-to-end, in one calendar year; and because this can take four to six months and earns you no paycheck, you must first carefully shuffle your life, remove yourself from whatever existence you lead and convince your beloveds and others that this is a worthy endeavor before you actually find yourself at the start (on top of Springer Mountain in Georgia, or on top of Katahdin in Maine). Perhaps you will do anything for the chance—quit your job or retire early. Or with luck you will find a convenient pocket of time in your life.

I found a pocket of time and I hiked the whole trail. This is the story. My through-hike took 137 days, including a vacation halfway, several nights in a hospital, and an off-the-trail job interview less than two weeks from the end. I hiked the whole trail wearing running shoes (trail name: *Sneakers*). I followed the white blazes and never took a short cut. I kept a fast pace and carried not a single map until I reached New Hampshire. I used fifteen mail drops for food that I'd carefully planned in advance. But I was no expert. Just the opposite: I began my hike with a seventy-five-pound pack carrying ridiculous things—an Abdomonizer, snowshoes, chess set, saw, shampoo, canned tomatoes, books and more. I was poorly equipped and inexperienced, yet still I believed I would reach my goal.

I was a twenty-nine-year-old northbound novice hiker when I stood at The Start, on Springer Mountain in Georgia, in the spring of 1993. Springer's summit is the trail's southern terminus while the northern terminus is the summit of Maine's Mt. Katahdin. The Appalachian Trail is the path which connects the summits of these two mountain peaks. At 2,147 miles, the AT is the longest continually marked footpath in the world. You can begin your through-hike at either end (on either summit). Most common is to start in the south in the spring and hike north. *"Northbounders"* follow the cool weather, enjoy great camaraderie and reach Katahdin before it closes in late October. A much smaller number start in the north in midsummer and hike south. These few *"southbounders"* are often late-May college graduates who have little choice but for this. I was with the majority, northbounders, headed for Katahdin. Unlike most through-hikers, I'd had no previous connection to the trail. I hadn't grown up near the trail, hadn't hiked on it as a kid. But I had grown up climbing mountains, at a summer camp in northern New York.

The first time I had ever heard of the trail, I sat in my car driving east on the Massachusetts Turnpike while moving to Maine at age twenty-five. I looked up and saw a footbridge overpass marked by a small sign: APPALACHIAN TRAIL. That was the spark—just the sight of a small sign on a bridge on my way to Maine. Once in Maine, word of the trail kept reaching me. I heard it as a powerful call, too, as up to that point in my life a growing yearning to work hard and commit myself to a challenge continually left me empty because for years I had discovered little out there which compelled me to latch myself to it.

I had always been restless. The week after my college graduation I bought a round-trip bus ticket to California and I rode six thousand miles from east coast to west and back again, hopping from bus to bus, sleeping five straight nights without layover, slumped against people and windows and bags. That was odd, and unpleasant; and there was the time after that, odder still, which I'll simply call *"Riding Freight Trains to Texas."* RFTT never got far off the ground, and to be wise I should not even mention it further. By twenty-nine, I had mellowed. Hiking the Appalachian Trail was orthodox, after all. Somewhat normal people did it. And for me, the hike fit. I was employed then as a college squash coach who worked through the winter and had summer months free. That previous summer had meant a season of team tennis in Germany. This summer I would fulfill a primordial urge to get up and go—*and go, and go…!*

Personal Ads.

My winter coaching job placed such a demand on my time that I just wasn't able to fully prepare for my through-hike. Actually, the truth is that I didn't *want* to prepare. I'm one who simply likes to go and do things. I had run my first marathon without training. It nearly ruined me, but I had known I could do it. And I knew I could do this. I didn't want to read all the books out there anyway. I didn't want to be versed in solutions to all possible situations. I didn't want to read other people's perceptions. I refused to prepare to the millionth degree. I aimed to be open to accidents and surprises. I wanted to experience the trail for myself, learn myself, find out for myself. I just wanted to go down and do it. Whether good or bad, it has always been that way for me. I had spent my childhood outside climbing trees.

First thing, you take inventory of the equipment you own, and determine what you will need. Next, you join the Appalachian Trail Conference (ATC), which is the trail's governing body, located in Harpers Ferry, West Virginia. Membership earns you their quarterly ATC magazine (published since 1939), as well as their ATC catalogue through which you buy the *Data Book, Wingfoot's Thru-Hiker's Handbook,* and the *Workbook.* Also for sale are AT bandannas, T-shirts, coffee mugs, video tapes, postcards, placemats, pendants, posters and maps, section by section, of the entire trail. I did not buy the maps because they were expensive, and I knew that I could do without them. Only the data book and the hiker's handbook would accompany me on the trail. The workbook helped me plan fifteen mail drops to which my family would send me food in advance so that I could eat along the way.

The remainder of my planning meant determining what day to start, figuring out how to reach Springer, and deciding at what rate I would hike (I planned to average 16.5 miles a day the first half of the trail, and 20 miles a day for the second). Of course, there are no guarantees. Books say the attrition rate for through-hikers is 90 percent, but that didn't scare me. I realized that unforeseeable events could pop up and derail me, but I also felt sure that if nothing went drastically wrong, I would finish. Still, I lacked camping knowledge. I didn't know what to bring in my pack or what to leave behind. I had never used a stove. I had so many questions. Should I pack a knife for protection? Where would I use the bathroom? How often would I get into town, and what would I wear when I got there? What would I use for money? What if I needed a doctor? Would there be water? Would I be warm enough? Would I have free time? Would I be lonely?

My greatest concern was that I had no hiking partner. My friends worked; my girlfriend—the Y—had commitments; everyone had a job; no one was free. But I couldn't imagine hiking alone, so I did what many aspiring through-hikers do: I took out a personal ad in the back of the ATC magazine: VEGETARIAN ATHLETE SEEKS THROUGH-HIKING PARTNER. I got strange responses:

I am not some couch potato with a half-crazed idea about taking
a long walk.
Good Lord! 16.5 miles a day right at the start? Why?
I'm an experienced hiker but not a hell-bent one.
I spent six years as a Girl Scout, second through seventh grades.
I'm a thirty-nine-year-old housewife who would like to get out of
the city for a while.
Without dashing your hopes too much, we think you are crazy to
try to do 16.5 miles a day, day after day after day, because
to us the hike is a hike of a lifetime and it should not be
rushed.
About wearing running shoes on the trail: I talked to a
backpacking instructor at William and Mary. The instructor
told me that hiking in running shoes can be dangerous.
She explained that a person she was hiking with got stress
fractures in both feet while wearing boots.

An old man wrote that the best way to hike the trail is for someone to follow along in a car. A man from out west, retired from the military, wrote about assembling a team of hikers, each person with a duty, as if we would make an attack. I contacted a few people, but in the end nothing came of my ad. I couldn't find a hiking partner. It was just as well. I had begun to sense that. Most northbounders begin solo, but you are seldom alone on the AT. Northbound solo hikers need never worry about being alone. There are scores of people. Amidst hundreds of northbounders, you get swept up in constant, varying companionship. Groups form, break apart, and new groups form. There is great camaraderie. Friendships form easily. Unless you have a spouse or a partner whose life you are intricately tied to, it is easier for northbounders to start solo. The alternative is promising a partnership to someone you don't really know. That can be tricky.

Two old men once agreed by mail to hike the trail together. They wrote back and forth months in advance, planning. Departure time drew near and their anticipation heightened. They rejoiced when they finally met for the first time in Georgia's Amicalola Falls State Park. They set out, but one of the men was weak and he couldn't make it up Springer. He turned back and went home. The other continued without him and hiked all the way to Katahdin. They had planned for months, but they hiked together for hours. I took heart. I was finally glad that I would be starting alone. I hadn't committed to anybody or made any promises that would be difficult to keep.

When my winter work ended, I searched for a backpack in a hiking store. But I knew very little about backpacks. I owned just a small pack which had sufficed on the day climbs I had made returning occasionally to the

Adirondack Mountains those past years. But this was a trip of the greatest magnitude imaginable. For this I believed I would need the biggest backpack ever built. So I chose the biggest backpack in the store. It wasn't the most expensive backpack, but it was the biggest. The thing was, I thought that not even it would be large enough to hold all the supplies I would need to bring. I carried the backpack to the counter along with two large AT posters showing the entire East Coast with a red line tracing the trail's route. One poster was for my parents to hang on a wall back home to chart my progress. The other poster was for me, to save and later frame upon my completion. I told the register worker that I was on my way down to hike the Appalachian Trail. He looked at me. He looked at the posters. He said: *"They have smaller maps, you know."* I left the store with my new backpack, got in my car, left Maine, and drove nine hours home to my parents' house in upstate New York for final preparation.

Mad Scientist.

The first thing I did, back home in New York, was take scissors outside, turn my head upside down and cut off all the hair that hung down. I gave myself the shortest haircut of my life. I liked my scalped head, it was low maintenance. I felt like a different me. That is one thing about the trail, it gives you the chance to try something new. If you have never had long hair, you can let it grow. If you have never had short hair, you can shave it all off to try that. Men grow beards; women also stop shaving.

Five months in the woods with strangers? Anything goes. You can even experiment with a new personality—more generous, daring, engaging, accepting. Through-hikers use pseudonyms—trail names. These largely determine your trail ego. Others name you, or you can name yourself. You can treat yourself to an empowering name: *Mercury Mark, Mighty Mike, Ironman, Venomous, Unleashed.* Or perhaps your own brand of self-deprecating humor will release the pressure from your hike like a pin to a hot air balloon: *Slow Boots, Slacker, Mozyin', Easy Stryder, Easy Steps, Baby Steps.* Or pick an obscure name from some private source: *Kilgore Trout, Ook-Piolook, Chinook, Peripidus, Horse Badortes, Cotactin Nomad, Alexander Supertramp.* Couples use joint names: *Bonnie and Clyde, Beauty and the Beast, Garlic and Basil, Mixed Doubles, Sesame Seeds.* On the trail you are no longer Jennifer Peterson who went to Evanston High School, who lives on Elm Street in Peoria and works in sales. On the trail that identity vanishes. On the trail you are *Mountain Do,* living in the woods, eating out of a pan. No past, no future; only what you do, how you behave. Still, it is wise to remember that the old saying rings true: *No matter where you go, you'll always be there.*

I turned my parents' basement poolroom into my headquarters for planning, sorting, and packing. I filled fifteen cardboard boxes with food for my parents to mail to me all summer in advance to predesignated post office stops at predesignated times. It is possible to buy your food along the way in little trailside stores. *(Heel and Toe* said they believe there is a moral imperative to do just that— *"We hike through their neighborhoods, we enjoy their hospitality, we should purchase their goods.")* But those stores are infrequent with limited selections, limited hours.

More common is to mail yourself food through the United States Post Office. There are PO branches close to the trail all the way from Georgia to Maine. Each one will save your package for months if need be. Just address your box to the PO branch labeling it with your name, and "General Delivery, Through-Hiker." I filled each of my fifteen drop boxes with food to last seven days so that each time I reached a box I would get what I'd need to carry me to the next box. In that way I would hop from PO to PO, from drop box to drop box, the entire length of the trail. The workbook makes planning that easy. It lists every post office on or near the trail from Georgia to Maine. It tells how far off the trail each PO lies; it even has boldfaced recommendations for the most convenient places to stop.

Meals meant following my vegetarian diet. On the trail I would eat a PowerBar every morning for breakfast, peanut butter for lunch, and nightly dinners of pasta. Snacks were dried fruit, nuts, candy bars, vegetarian beef jerky, noodle soups, and almond-flavored cereal. I would eat fruit and vegetables in town whenever I had the chance. I had confidence in my diet until I read that through-hikers should eat over four thousand calories a day, and that the average weight loss on the trail is forty pounds per person (what I didn't know then was that most hikers have that much to lose). I read that and panicked, imagining myself as a one-hundred-and-ten-pound stick figure teetering through the woods. It scared me so much that I rushed out and spent a fortune on a grand solution: high-potency drink mixes with names like Ultra Fuel, Metabolol III). I took those powdered drinks home and divvied them out like a mad scientist into dozens of separate ziplock bags. But the sad reality was that those drinks tasted bad. I would carry them two-thirds of the trail, yet I would drink them just a few times all summer. While fine in theory, carrying those drinks was a rotten mistake. In the end, I began the trail weighing 150 pounds and I ended the trail weighing 150 pounds, without drinking those mixes and without paying the slightest attention to calorie intake. With my PO drop boxes packed and labeled, all that finally remained was to fill my backpack and head to Georgia.

Back then I had a strange belief, my Energy Philosophy. I believed that I had such limitless energy that I would have to bring along diversions. I thought that *just* hiking the trail wouldn't be enough to stimulate me, so on the trail I would tackle some projects. I hoped to sharpen my German, so I packed a book of German to study. I loved chess so, I packed a small set with a folding board. My abs needed work, so I strapped to the back of my pack a blue, plastic sit-up sled called *The Abdominizer* (the only item I had ever bought off a television commercial in my life). I brought *Walden* because I had always wanted to read it, and I placed other books at home on reserve. That was my Energy Philosophy. I imagined that I would arrive at a shelter at the end of a day's hike to find time on my hands, so I would play a leisurely game of chess; then perhaps I would study some German, do a few sit-ups, and maybe read before going to sleep. I thought I couldn't *just* hike the trail. Back then I had no idea.

Pack weight is best kept below one-third of your body weight, according to hiking books. Foolishly, I ignored the advice. After all, there were so many things that I *wasn't* bringing—first aid kit, foldable pliers, short-wave radio, miniature binoculars. On initial weighing my pack registered seventy-five pounds. And that didn't bother me. I had no conception of what it meant. I thought that the books were only trying to scare people. I thought the advice was only for short trips. My trip was longer and I would need more things. I would later learn the reality, that carrying monstrous weight is so painful it can drain the fun from your hike. When light, you are free to observe, detour; when heavy you are wracked with pain. If you load yourself down with food, tools, and gadgets, you end up traveling so slowly that you spend extra days in the woods between towns and you end up having emergencies. You end up needing that tube of cream for your pack strap rash, that knee brace for your knee pains, that first aid kit for your blisters, and those extra five days of food for those extra five days you'll spend between stops. Packing heavy becomes a self-fulfilling prophecy. I began as a heavy packer because I lacked the experience to know any better. I didn't believe there was any conceivable way I could pack under seventy-five pounds (and packing under fifty pounds was unthinkable). But if only I'd had a crystal ball, I could have looked into the future to see myself hiking through Maine near the end of my hike, entering the longest stretch of wilderness on the entire trail—one hundred miles without a road of any kind—carrying food for three days in a pack whose total weight was twenty-four pounds. But that was another lifetime.

Chaos Theory.

The worst East Coast snowstorm in one hundred years hit on the day that I planned to depart. The Storm of the Century dumped some states with eight feet of fresh snow. I postponed my departure and watched on television as rescue workers airlifted trapped hikers out of the Appalachian Mountains by helicopter. It was the only time in my life that I'd ever seen news coverage of the Appalachian Mountains and it was for crippling weather conditions on the day I was supposed to go there. I wondered what the storm would mean for my hike. Would the snow melt? When could I start? I called the ATC. They

15

told me to wait a week. They said that trees had blown down everywhere from Georgia to Pennsylvania making the hike slow, tedious, and in some spots impassable. They said that the trail was buried in snow down south and that I would need snowshoes to hike it. Dutifully, I drove to an outfitter store and bought snowshoes. The saleswoman laughed when I told her that I would be hiking in running shoes. Really, that one-hundred-year storm served a purpose for me. It reaffirmed my understanding of Chaos Theory, a thought I'd first read of in a dinosaur novel years earlier.

Chaos Theory recognizes the infinite complexity of things: how trillions of factors come together and lie behind every event. Small differences in input can create vast differences in output. Some happenings occur on such small scales that we don't bother to measure them or consider them, yet they do factor in and can shape the outcome of larger, visible, tangible events. You plan for something to occur in a certain way, yet such complexity exists that you cannot possibly take everything into consideration. A through-hike attempt gives an excellent example. They say two thousand aspirants set out each year planning to hike the whole trail, but only two hundred actually make it.

A ninety percent attrition rate. What happens to all those hikers? Things happen that you can't anticipate: you set out on the trail; then you get hit by the worst snowstorm in one hundred years. The message is not that it's pointless to plan, research, and prepare (preparation surely increases your chance for success). The point is simply that even a lifetime of the most careful preparation imaginable is no guarantee. Things happen outside your control which even the most insightful planner could not have foreseen.

On a broad scale, we claim to care how we treat other humans, but we don't care as much how badly we mistreat other parts of earth's living and nonliving environment. Chaos Theory proves that how we treat all things affects us—we are part of the environment, not removed from it. The Web of Life. All our actions matter. That is the beauty of Chaos Theory; it does not offer an excuse to give up, as if the future is predestined and events are outside our control. Instead it is a call to action, a reason for hope. Because every little thing factors in, we know that everything we do, say, use, eat, and wear matters. Each person's actions *will* factor in; each person's actions *do* matter. Our actions matter, and thus by our actions we can change things. I knew I would never quit my hike, but I also knew that things could happen and that I might not complete my through-hike through no fault of my own. And I knew I would be able to live with that; my life would not end. I felt a calm peace of mind. I felt pressure relieved. I held no going-away celebration, sought no glamour article in the local paper.

2

The Approach

I would rather sit in the open air.

—Henry David Thoreau, *Walden*

Bus Ride South.

I rode the bus south to Georgia, but stopped halfway down, in Washington, DC, to visit my old friend, Toot. We played tennis at Georgetown and jogged around the Mall at night, lamppost lights reflecting off the water. We jogged around the Washington Monument, ran up the stairs of the Lincoln Memorial. Trail books advise you to train by walking around with your backpack on before you begin your hike. *Easy Stryder* trained for his hike by running bleachers at the U. Georgia football stadium, in his hiking boots, with his backpack on. I found that a little extreme. But I finally decided that I would test my pack. I walked outside up Macomb street with my pack on, and that day made a horrible discovery—my new backpack was defective; it offered no waist support; my shoulders alone bore the full weight of seventy-five pounds. And the pack flopped about with every step.

The street rose slightly. I struggled up it, yet I could barely stand upright. I suffered in shuffling a block and a half. I staggered back to Toot's. I thought I would cry. Trail books say that bearing weight is difficult at first, but that you soon get used to it. I didn't mind the weight as much as I minded the broken pack. No waist support. I was a mess. I called the hiking store and spent an hour pleading to three different workers who all tried to help. I twisted, turned, poked, and prodded the pack, adjusting every strap ten times. I fastened shoelaces and safety pins every place imaginable, but I could not jury-rig an adjustment to shift weight to my waist to relieve the pressure from my shoulders. On my last day in DC, I drove to an REI camping store and bought a synthetic sleeping bag which stuffed down to half the size of my original so that it fit inside my backpack. Expenses were mounting, but this purchase marked a turning point for me. It turned out to be one of the wisest things I would do all trip. Still, I never looked at new backpacks in the REI store; I just wasn't prepared at that moment to shell out more money.

"You're carrying that backpack?" Toot had teased me about it all week. My pack sat like a used car in a corner of his apartment. *"You can barely pick it up off the floor,"* he said. *"It will kill you. You'll be back up on a bus in a week. I'm going to leave the blanket out on the sofa so it will be here for you. Is there anything you want to do next week after you quit your hike and come back? You want to play some more tennis? You want to see that new movie?"* It was only a joke. He knew me. He knew that I wouldn't return on a bus. He knew that I would never give up. My visit over, I said good-bye and I staggered away down the street toward the Metro wearing my defective backpack and carrying a box as well as my snowshoes. The last familiar voice that I heard on my trip to the trail was Toot calling out after me, mocking: *"See you in a week!"*

They say the hardest part about hiking the trail is getting to the start. It is meant figuratively, but ironically it is literally true: nothing about gaining Springer would be easy. I had a desperate time reaching it. From the very start it had taken great effort to even find out how to do it. I'd had to search diligently through the trail books to divine the great secret that Gainesville, Georgia, is the nearest town you can ride a bus to. Washingtonians stared at me as I rode the subway to the bus station. I couldn't blame them, for I looked like a sideshow. I wore an enormous backpack with crap hanging haphazardly off it like tent poles, sneakers, water bottles. I held two snowshoes under one arm and a box full of papers and books under the other. I could barely stand straight. At the bus station, I purchased a ticket south to Gainesville, Georgia. (*"Not Gainesville, Florida?"*) I rode the bus all night, reaching Atlanta at 4 AM. Next, I rode a 7 AM bus up to South Carolina, waited outside a diner and then boarded another bus back to Gainesville.

The tiny Gainesville bus station is a box of a building off a quiet, rural road. Two taxis sat parked out front with drivers waiting to shuttle hikers to Amicalola Falls State Park, forty minutes away. I was glad about that. It was the first little bit of convenience. I loaded my things in a taxi, and we drove off. The driver asked what my snowshoes were for. I glanced out the window. There was no snow on the ground, not a flake. What had happened to the

18

worst snowstorm in one hundred years? I was lugging the snowshoes for nothing. We reached the Amicalola Falls State Park Visitor Center, a clean ranch building with a row of cars parked outside, each car with a different state license plate—Tennessee, Florida, Michigan, Pennsylvania. It was a bright, promising morning, but I felt numb from the bus fumes, shaken from traveling. Springer Mountain's summit (the start of the AT) is 8.1 miles from the visitor center up an access trail. Supposedly roads exist in the park over which jeeps and smart locals can drive to within two miles of Springer's peak, but like most I couldn't arrange a ride like that. My taxi driver claimed ignorance, then drove off, and I stood alone. Then a sudden realization swept over me. It was just me alone at that point, standing on my feet. I was down in Georgia, far from home, and two feet were all that I had to take me step after step all the way to Maine.

A Dime A Dozen.

I entered the Amicalola Visitor Center hoping to find a postal service so that I could mail home my snowshoes, but there was none. I was stuck with them. I signed a hiker register off in a corner, filling in blanks with my trail name, real name, home address, and the date. A worker stood behind a counter where patches, maps, and postcards were sold. People in street clothes milled about. I greeted the worker who seemed not the least bit interested in my affairs. That surprised me, as I guess I'd been under some strange assumption that he would have been thrilled to meet an aspiring through-hiker. I had traveled so far to get there and stood on the threshold of a great adventure. *(Didn't he see the AT patch I'd sewn onto my pack?)* Well, the truth is that of course he knew and he just didn't care. I was nothing he didn't see everyday, day after day. What a shock.

It was my first lesson learned—that most Southerners by the trail are nonplused by through-hikers because we are many. On every inch of the trail, north and south, almost every person you meet is exceedingly generous, helpful, and friendly. Down South they are friendly, but they are just not terribly impressed because the truth is at that point northbounders haven't done anything yet. That's a difficult realization for a needy ego self-thrilled by it all. But soon you get used to the treatment. You concentrate on your hike and cease being self-impressed. By the time you actually reach the north, you walk modestly along intent on your hike, changed by so many thoughts and emotions, not caring or thinking a bit about such matters—but by that time northbounders actually have done something impressive. It is about that time when you begin to meet people who are absolutely, positively, utterly amazed that, say, you reached New Hampshire from Georgia by walking there. You meet people who have never heard of the trail and are stunned by the answers you give to their questions. Some take pictures. Others practically ask for autographs. But by then northbounders have long since stopped feeling special and aren't accustomed to the treatment. A strange phenomenon. Down South is where you want the treatment because it's all new, you are anxious, nervous, and could use a boost; but that is precisely the place where aspiring through-hikers, who have barely begun, are a dime a dozen.

The Amicalola Falls State Park Visitor Center is your last chance to stop to collect your thoughts. It is your last chance to sit on a toilet, look in a mirror, drink water out of a fountain, watch people step into and out of cars. Actually, you do get these things on the trail very often; still the visitor center is the demarcation point. The wilderness begins out back behind the building, beyond its mowed lawn and picnic tables, where there is a break in the trees and a sign marked EAST RIDGE ACCESS TRAIL. The access trail leads 8.1 miles through the woods and up to the top of Springer Mountain where the AT begins. I didn't hurry. I had chores to finish first. I carried my pack out behind the visitor center and emptied its contents out on a picnic table. I spent the next hour there sorting, repacking. "Are you okay?" someone asked me. Through-hikers arrive at the visitor center in varying degrees of preparedness. I was a zero. A group earning a perfect ten was *The Portland-Four,* from Maine. They were two young couples with lightweight gear who stepped nimbly out of a parent's car, pecked little kisses good-bye, then skipped lightly, annoyingly, away into the woods. I was jealous and impressed. Little did I know then what a very odd trip was in store for the Portland-Four.

I labored along, my competitive juices beginning to flow. The result of a lifetime bent on competition is thoughts like these: *Those people are getting ahead. I will catch up, I want to start!* But I fought those feelings until they subsided. Then I was glad to relax and take my time. I used the bathroom. I shaved, brushed my teeth, and filled my water bottles. When would I shave again? When would I have a mirror again? How would I know what I looked like? What if I had dirt on my face? I wouldn't even know to clean it off.

I tied my snowshoes onto the back of my pack. I stuck my water bottles onto the ridiculous metal garden poles that I'd rigged to the top of my pack to carry them. Somehow I taped, strapped, and crammed everything into and onto that pack. Everything flopped, thunked about, hung loosely, drooped down like the animals on the antlers of Dr. Seuss' Thidwick the Big-Hearted Moose. There was a hanging scale behind the visitor center, and I staggered over to weigh in. I had full water bottles, snowshoes, books, papers, and everything I owned on that pack with the full weight on my shoulders, no support from my hips. I hooked my pack up on the scale—seventy-five pounds! I could not believe it. I suddenly understood that I was gravely ill-prepared, perhaps even in trouble, and there was no post office handy to remedy the situation. In that sad state, at twelve noon, March 25, I turned my back on the visitor center, stepped into the woods, and walked north up the access trail, uphill, climbing toward Springer Mountain. I was glad to be alone. I needed to go slow. I would not have been good company. I could not have kept up; my pack weighed too much. I needed to be alone, to take my time and to think.

East Ridge Access Trail.

After such a long buildup it was finally happening. I was approaching the AT, hiking in toward it on the access trail. It felt good to be moving, to be out in the woods, free for the first time in a long while, far from bus fumes and the noise of the highway, from Washington and the Metro. There was no more waiting, no more nerves. I actually had a fine time that morning, bearing up reasonably well under the strain of my pack. It was a clear, beautiful day. I snuck a peek where a sign marked FALLS OVERLOOK. Twice, I stopped to rest and drink water. But then suddenly I crashed. Four miles in, beyond a dirt road up in the woods, I was hit by fatigue and couldn't take another step. I took off my pack and flopped down in the trail. All the strain from the jostling around on the bus overnight and the driving up and down Georgia on buses all morning had rushed over and decked me. I sank down in the trail, exhausted. I lay with my backpack beside me. Perhaps I was delirious. I'm not sure what I was thinking, but all of a sudden I had to have soup.

I had no system for packing, so in order to get out my food almost everything else had to come out, too. I looked like Death sprawled out on the ground just a few pathetic miles from the visitor center with all my junk spread out all around me—clothes, papers, tent, poles, books, flashlight, pots and pans—and a little pot bubbling over with soup on an uneven patch of grass. Just then a mother and daughter in day packs walked south down the trail coming toward me heading down to the visitor center below. They had probably never seen such a sorry sight. They were gracious about it. They asked if I was testing my gear. I laughed to myself and shook my head. I was so tired. I said: *"Something like that."*

I reached Black Gap shelter, late afternoon, at 7.1 miles on the day. A short, Einstein-haired, fifty-year-old wild man ushered me over. His trail name was *Maddog*. He was a funny man, obviously a lunatic. He bustled about talking rapidly. He was from southern California. He had ridden east by train, man. One hundred relatives had seen him off including various ex-wives, their children and all.

"This is my *dream*, man. It's my *dream*."

I told him my trail name was Sneakers, and I pointed down to my running shoes.

"Sneakers? Ha-ha! Hey, that's all right! That's really different. I like that! Look, you gotta' stay here tonight. You can't go up to the next shelter. It's suicide. That shelter is filled to the brim."

The next shelter was only one mile farther, on top of Springer. Staying here meant that on my first day hiking I would not even reach the AT. But I didn't care; there was no need to continue. We had room here and I was glad for the chance to set down my pack. This lean-to was just like the hundreds of other shelters that sit by the trail from Georgia to Maine. It was twelve feet wide, seven feet deep, made of logs with three walls, a high open face, and a down-slanting roof back toward the recess. Variation exists in the size and design of the shelters along the trail, but they remain essentially the same— safe havens that get you out of the rain. In the South they are called shelters, in the north they are called huts and lean-tos.

I took out my sleeping bag and organized my things. I got water from a spring across the trail. Maddog related the difficulties he'd had in getting here. They sounded worse than mine. His taxi driver had dropped him off at the end of a dirt road 3.5 miles from Springer's summit. He was off alone on some mysterious corner of the mountain and blowdowns from the storm blocked his path from there to this shelter. He'd had to climb over and under fallen trees of every size, often having to take off his pack to pass it through gaps. It had taken him two days to hike 2.5 miles to the shelter, and he had ruined his back in the process.

"I'm changing my trail name to *Tree-Climber*," he said.

"No, don't do that," I said. "You have to stay Maddog; definitely Maddog."

A middle-aged couple came in. Maddog recounted his tree-climbing story verbatim. They didn't say much. They whispered to each other. They seemed apprehensive. I felt wired myself. Two teenagers arrived, surprised and disappointed that none of us were within ten years of their age. Perhaps they worried if it was just old fogies on the trail. These two set up not one but two tents outside the shelter and they hung their food from a high tree limb in impressive fashion. At one point they sat close together on a log, heads bent, locked in serious discussion. Maddog whispered that he believed they were discussing aborting their trip. It turned out he was right. But I hoped those early days of the trail wouldn't be like that—people sizing each other up, calculating who would and wouldn't make it. Thankfully, it isn't like that. You are too busy wrestling with your backpack and experimenting with your gear to care about anything else. I pulled out my can opener and opened a can of tomatoes. I hadn't been able to find spaghetti sauce mix for the trail, so I'd brought canned tomatoes. I hadn't sampled them before, and now I found them inedible. I felt ridiculous. But I wasn't the only beginner. Maddog's backpack apparently weighed as much as mine. We laughed at ourselves. He pulled out a pack of cigarettes and began smoking. I thought that didn't speak well for his chances. He took a drag and said:

"I've got to have my leafy brown vegetables...I've been trying to quit, though. I'm going to use my time on the trail to finally do it."

Yeah? Hey, good start, I thought to myself. Had he realized the shape

I was in, he'd have been shocked. I was skinny, I was a mess, and I was dragging, but that was only exterior. Truly, inside I was in tournament form. I had spent the past six months with daily weight lifting, tennis, and squash. Six point seven percent body fat, a postexercise heart rate of sixty-four beats-per-minute—my stats were off the charts and I was quickly going to sort things out and make a go of it. But Maddog could never have guessed that. He emptied his backpack. Out dropped a carton of cigarettes, each pack sealed in its own ziplock sandwich bag (he had really taken care of those cigarettes!). Next he pulled out a shortwave radio. My mother had tried giving me one as a gift, but I had refused it. We listened to the weather report, although I would have preferred not to. I like to take the weather as it comes. Once, while we were hiking in the Adirondacks, Toot had explained that he didn't like hiking in the rain. He said that he liked the woods and thus wanted to hike on nice days when he could see them. I answered that to truly enjoy the woods, one should appreciate them as they are and for what they are. It rains in the woods, that is part of it all. If one wants to be in the woods, learn the woods, know the woods, experience the woods, one must hike in the rain, in the sun, in the snow. There is a definite special beauty in the woods when it rains; all is darker and more profound (there were to be plenty of dark and profound days ahead of us). I laughed wondering if Maddog had also brought binoculars and foldable pliers. Maddog laughed at my Abdominizer. He laughed even harder at my snowshoes.

"You brought snowshoes? What for?"

"Hey that's nothing, look at these canned tomatoes. Check out how heavy *these* are."

"You want to see something heavy? Feel this shovel."

"Man, that weighs a ton! Look, check out this saw."

"What do you have a *saw* for?"

And on and on.

No, I didn't do any sit-ups that night. It was a momentous evening, my first night spent in the woods on my long trip. I'd had some doubts wondering what it would be like always sleeping with strangers, but that evening eased all my fears. I slept soundly that night with a grin on my face dreaming of Maddog running around like a crazy man.

3
White Blazes

Once a journey is designed, equipped, and put in process, a new factor enters and takes over. A trip, a safari, an exploration, is an entity, different from all other journeys. It has personality, temperament, individuality, uniqueness. A journey is a person in itself; no two are alike. And all plans, safeguards, policing and coercion are fruitless. We find after years of struggle that we do not take a trip; a trip takes us.

—John Steinbeck, *Travels With Charlie*

Mantra: *Neels Gap!*

Hiking the trail, you constantly dangle incentives before yourself. And Neels Gap, my friend, is one giant carrot. You hear about Neels Gap almost immediately, within one or two conversations with hikers. Everyone talks about it. Neels Gap is on everyone's mind. Lying just thirty miles north of Springer, Neels Gap is the place that saves novice hikers—if we can just make it there. It's what the place does. Neels Gap is the name of a pass between mountains. A road runs through the pass and a great stone mansion there called Walasi-Yi Center holds a backpacking store, grocery store, bunkhouse, Laundromat, and post office. The trail passes under a building archway. It is the only spot on the entire AT where the trail passes *through* a building.

I rejoiced over that for it meant I could not miss the place; there was no hidden turnoff, no obscure sign to find. If I could just hike thirty miles,

I would slam into the building. It would be difficult hiking there carrying my heavy load in my broken backpack, but the thought of Neels Gap fueled me; it gave me a purpose and a goal, for from there I could mail home my snowshoes and the rest of the junk that I'd brought. Suddenly so little of it seemed necessary. That was because I was no longer sitting at home on a sofa packing the junk; now I was carrying it all through the woods on my shoulders. I walked along and recited my mantra:

"Neels Gap, Neels Gap, Neels Gap..."

Seventy-five pounds. I hated how heavy my pack felt. I plodded through the woods over hills, through ravines, staggering under the broken backpack carrying half my own weight. Had I been a Native American Indian and my tribe seen this, they would have named me *Slowshit*. I kept thinking about that. It bothered me. This was no way to hike. I longed to be *Running Deer;* that was I. I wanted to bound, leap and soar. All my life I'd had to be swift, quick, light on my feet. But I could barely walk with this pack on, let alone skip, hop, jump, jog, or run. This was nothing like that. This was labor; I was doing this wrong. It was obvious like an anvil over my head. Images filled my mind. I could see warriors from an enemy Indian tribe cresting the ridge at my side, racing down the hill at me, darting through trees, bounding over logs and rocks screaming to smash me with tomahawks. I couldn't run away. I couldn't even shuffle away. I was Slowshit, in great pain, suffering with every step.

Following the trail is easy; you just follow the white blazes. White blazes mark the AT from Springer to Katahdin. They are white marks six inches tall and two inches wide painted neatly on the trees along the trail. Where the trail crosses treeless mountaintops, the white blazes are painted on boulders or rocks; and where the trail crosses treeless pastures, the white blazes are painted on wooden posts stuck into the ground; and where the trail follows roads, the white blazes are painted on guardrails and telephone poles; and where the trail winds through towns, the white blazes are painted on building walls, fire hydrants, stop signs, whatever. The deepest river to cross is the Kennebec River in Maine. In recent years workers there have run a canoe service ferrying through-hikers across. Those workers understand the bond that an AT hiker has with the white blaze, for they have painted a single white blaze on the bottoms of their two canoes, so that hikers who ride across won't even briefly be far from the blaze.

Standing beside a blaze, you can often look out and see the next one. The most blazes I ever saw looking one direction from a single point was five, and I saw that twice. Five blazes visible from one spot seems excessive. Usually it isn't that bad. Blazes are more ubiquitous in some places than others, like all through the Smoky Mountains. Other places, you might have to walk hundreds of feet between blazes before you can see the next one. Your feelings toward blazes changes from week to week. Sometimes you feel glad and reassured by a constant string of them. Other times you feel cheated by them, considering them a needless bother intruding upon your sense of the woods as untamed wilderness. It is possible to mistakenly wander off the trail, as I can attest, but the truth is you must work extremely hard to get lost. If the trail is home, then the blazes assure you that yes, you are home. If you can't find a blaze on a tree or a rock or a post, then you aren't on the trail, you aren't home, you aren't where you need to be. Frequently during those early days, I would reach out my hiking stick and touch it to an occasional blaze to pay homage and thank the blazes for marking the trail. In that way I showed my appreciation, for at the instant I touched a blaze I knew that I was not lost but that I was exactly where I wanted to be.

Tired As Hell Philosophy.

Day one, I awoke in Black Gap shelter to the sound of rain, ate my PowerBar breakfast, stuffed my belongings inside my backpack, and said good-bye to Maddog. I believed I would never see him again, and I was very nearly right. I followed the access trail its final one mile up to the summit of Springer Mountain. Upon gaining the peak, I now stood at the start of the AT. It was 10 AM. The quiet couple from the shelter was there. Springer's peak is covered with trees and we had no view in the rain and mist, but we took pictures anyway. There was a bronze hiker plaque on a rock and a mailbox tacked onto a tree with a register inside that I signed with the wet tip of a pencil stub.

The southern terminus is a far less spectacular place than the northern terminus, the summit of Mt. Katahdin. Katahdin is a breathtaking treeless peak offering a 360-degree panorama of hundreds of miles of Maine wilderness, forests, and lakes. There are iron rungs in the rocks leading up Katahdin in some places as parts of that climb are so steep. On its rocky summit stands a wooden signpost and a giant cairn of stones. Springer just isn't the same. It hasn't the feel of a benchmark place. But that was okay. I didn't care. I didn't need trumpets. I turned and faced north. I paused a moment and took a deep breath. There was a white, painted dash on a rock just north of the bronze plaque. It was the first blaze of the trail. I put out my foot and I took a step. At that moment I had begun my hike of the Appalachian Trail.

Rain fell my entire first day on the AT. I wouldn't have wanted it any other way. I learned interesting things that first day, like how my rain cover wouldn't fit over my pack with my snowshoes tied to it. When it rained, I had to carry my snowshoes in my arms. If anything, I was glad for the rain: it helped divert my mind from my pain. I passed a hiker on the trail who looked over and said: *"No Rain, no Pain, no Maine."* One mile later I passed another hiker who looked over, smiled, and said: *"You gotta hike in the Rain if you wanna get to Maine."* It was dark in the woods. My body hurt. I thought that if anyone else made a rhyme, I would slap them.

I kept my windbreaker hood down over my head and shuffled along continuing to recite my newfound mantra: *Neels Gap, Neels Gap, Neels Gap...* You don't mind getting wet, so long as you keep your pack contents dry. I wore polypropylene long underwear beneath a nylon windbreaker shell. It's what I'd once worn running ten miles daily through a Maine winter two years earlier, so I knew these clothes were right. There was much I didn't know, and my pack weighed too much, but I was in shape, I was mentally strong, and I knew what to wear. Georgia's mountain air was cold, but I kept moving and stayed warm and comfortable. I reached Hawk Mountain shelter by midafternoon, at 8.6 miles on the day. The next shelter was another 8.5 miles farther, so continuing wasn't an option. It was too late, I was too tired, and my back ached too badly.

I set down my backpack in the lean-to. I had no system, no idea what to do first. I observed to learn. Other hikers soon arrived and joined me inside. By day's end there were seven of us side by side in the wet shelter with two more sleeping just outside in a tent. We were headfirst in the lean-to with our feet sticking out toward the open air. We each had our own narrow lane to lie in, the width of a sleeping bag. We hung our wet clothes and food bags up on the nails that were tacked into the log ceiling and walls. Our food bags and wet socks and shirts, hung from nails, were stalactites dangling from the roof of our cave, creating a wonderful sculpture. It was difficult to stand because of the low, sloped ceiling and our hanging bags. If we had to use the bathroom, we crawled on our hands and knees out our enormous, wide-open front door. All this while trying to stay warm and dry. There was no chess, no German, no sit-ups, no book reading that first trail night. It was awkward for me just lying there. Besides, I was too tired for any of that. After just two days my Energy Philosophy dissipated into a *Tired-As-Hell Philosophy.*

This was a young shelter crowd. I was the oldest by five years. I recognized a few of the others as those I'd seen start up the access trail the day before. They'd all slept together on Springer Mountain while I'd slept a mile below them in my shelter with Maddog. There was the Portland-Four (one couple slept inside the lean-to while the other couple slept out in a tent). There was a tall, lanky boy with a dense black beard whose trail name was *Chicago Kid.* There was a shorter young man who struggled in deciding to name himself either *Purple Man* or *Lord of the Flies,* who mused aloud, weighing the relative merits of each. There was a giant named *Coyote* who sat cross-legged and spoke not a word to any of us. And there was a young married couple who were making their second attempt at a through-hike. Their first attempt the previous spring had failed when the guy had injured his knee 150 miles in. He had a full beard, and she had a trail name after some kind of butterfly. At one point, I was alone in the shelter with the butterfly wife. The others were out getting water or using the outhouse. The woman turned her back and changed out of her wet clothes taking off her shirt and sports bra. I stared at her bare back thinking, *So this is what it's like on the trail.* I imagined there would be frequent nudity in such tight, communal living. *Mozyin's* introduction would be vastly different. I would meet Mozyin' only much later, and he would tell me the story of how on his second night an overweight woman in his shelter changed in front of him, completely undressing without turning around. Then later that night, the woman urinated in a can in a corner of the shelter.

Novice hikers are amazed by veterans. That repeating butterfly couple astounded us by their ability to settle in, unpack, dry out, and cook dinner so effortlessly in such a tiny space. They shared a stove. They had silent communication, perfect coordination. It seemed as if they'd been born on the trail. Probably none of us imagined that we would ever be anything like the butterfly couple. We took our cues from them to see when to change, when to cook, when to eat. One day, far down the line, I myself would amaze people. If I'd had a crystal ball to look into the future to see myself on the trail months away, I would have been startled by the ease and grace with which I could enter a shelter wet or dry and rapidly get things done in a small space without so much as a single movement wasted. But here it was slow going. We novices observed. We asked subtle questions. Everyone seemed more experienced than I. Everyone seemed a bit more organized, a bit more confident. Bits of conversation wafted up from the corners of the lean-to and echoed in my ears:

"These three-quarter pads are awesome."

"Is that a ten-degree bag?"

"I'm taking it nice and slow all the way to Virginia."

"Did you hear, that guy brought snowshoes..."

"Yeah? Check his pack. He's probably got a ratchet set, too!"

To cook dinner, I pulled out my stove with its blue fuel can. To my surprise, all five other stoves that appeared were identical Whisperlite stoves with tall and narrow red fuel cans marked MRS on the side. I was not afraid to be different, but I had known all along that my stove was junk. My old stove took blue butane fuel canisters which, once punctured, couldn't be separated from the stove, so as I walked along, I had a fully assembled stove shoved into my pack behind my head. I hated that. I kept waiting for it to explode and my head to blow off and wind up in a tree. Worse was that I couldn't buy replacement blue butane fuel cartridges anywhere on the trail. I had known that, yet I'd brought the stove anyway. But the Whisperlite stoves used Coleman fuel which was sold in practically every hotel, hostel, convenience store, or roadside vegetable stand the entire length of the trail. I wrote WHISPERLITE STOVE on the shopping list I was making for Neels Gap. To light my stove, I proudly produced my hurricane matches from out of their rainproof storage spot inside a Glad sandwich bag that was itself tucked ingeniously inside an impenetrable plastic film case. These were indeed

Hurricane Matches. Very impressive—they could not be destroyed! You could light them in a hurricane. The thing was, on my entire hike I never once had to light my stove in a hurricane. Everyone else in the shelter pulled out a lighter and flicked on their stoves. I added CIGARETTE LIGHTER to my shopping list.

We ate noodle dishes, rice dishes, Kraft macaroni and cheese. After dinner the married couple rolled two joints and we passed them around. Maddog had lit up with cigarettes my first night in the woods, and now here was pot on my second night. Neither shocked me. Again, I simply thought, *So this is what it's like on the trail—people smoke cigarettes on the trail; people smoke pot on the trail.* I had that response for everything that happened. I didn't know what the trail was like so I observed, and whatever happened *on* the trail *was* the trail. A rock could have fallen on my head and I wouldn't have cared. I would have thought, *So this is what it's like on the trail—rocks fall on your head on the trail.*

I wrote some notes in my journal. Everyone kept a journal. There was a register in the shelter, as there are notebook registers in every lean-to all the way to Maine. Inside you write poems, stories, quotes, or even draw pictures. I signed the register and read what others had written. There were entries dating back a month to the season's through-hiking early birds. There was great camaraderie in the shelter. There were jokes. There were mice inside, too. I knew that because I could hear them scampering around at night, and I felt one climb over me. I fell asleep having left out on a little shelf beside me a knife covered with peanut butter, and when I awoke the next morning the knife was sparkling clean, licked clean by little mice tongues. At least it was either mice or else one of the other through-hikers who climbed over me as I slept and licked the peanut butter off the knife. Based on what I now know about through-hikers, I almost tend to believe the latter was true.

Skateboard-Snowshoes.

You find it hard exiting your warm, comfortable sleeping bag in the cold mountain mornings. Once you make the move, you're okay, but making the move is hard. Rising, shivering, stuffing a sleeping bag into a pouch, packing, maneuvering in the same narrow slot that you slept in is another challenge. I'd never been an early riser, but on the trail it felt natural to live with the sun—to go to sleep exhausted when the sun sets, and to wake up at sunrise. Waking up is one thing, setting out is another. Those early days it took me over an hour to pack up and leave. I hiked alone again on my second trail day. I was suffering greatly. It was drizzly out and I had to carry my snowshoes again. I passed a few people. I met the Chicago Kid at a spot where a few meager patches of snow were visible off in the woods. He said:

"*Dude, you see what I'm looking at over there? There's some snow by*

29

that bush. You see it? Come on Man, now's your big chance to break out those snowshoes."

I came upon The Portland-Four all sitting barefoot in a clearing, surrounded by an impressive collection of medical supplies, including Band-Aid wrappers, bandages, Moleskin, New Skin, knives and scissors everywhere. Such a blister festival I had never seen. I hiked past army reservers—five grown men seated in a wet ditch, armed and camouflaged, slouched down in the dampness and drizzle. There was a base nearby. We had heard mortar fire that previous night. I saw two exploded mortar casings on the ground by the trail. Frozen black snakes lay coiled in the trail waiting for sunlight to heat their bodies. They were lovely to see. No one had to tell me their scientific name, either. They were black, and they were snakes: they were Black Snakes. I nudged one on the side with my hiking stick. It barely moved. Those snakes aren't poisonous; you can tell just by looking at them.

In between conscious moments of pain, I hiked ecstatically through an infinite landscape of birds, twigs, bushes, rocks, trees, sticks and leaves, rises, swales, curves and bends in the trail, distant mountains, hills, gullies, valleys, clouds spread out all around me. I realized then that I'd forgotten whether it was Tuesday or Friday. A liberated feeling settled in. I didn't care what day it was. In the woods you have no appointments, no deadlines. Few responsibilities. The decisions that you make are personal ones: Wear your windbreaker or pack it? Eat your last peanut butter or save it? At first you feel selfish admitting that on the trail you are concentrating on yourself, but you must concentrate. You must sustain yourself with nourishment, hydrate yourself with water, shelter yourself from the elements, step smartly, think clearly, and behave rationally. In order to find peace on the trail, you must come to terms with this necessary selfishness. On the trail you are spoiling yourself, treating yourself, monitoring your thoughts, reading and reacting to the patterns of your body—and you had better be able to relish it for the chance may come once in a lifetime. I once heard a through-hiker answer another's guilt with this question: *"Would you rather be out on the trail spending money or off the trail earning it?"*

At the end of that second day of 8.5 miles of backbreaking labor, I reached Gooch Gap shelter—another milestone in my quest for Neels Gap—which was .3 miles off the trail on a blue-blazed side trail. We were gaining a feel for distances, learning how it felt to hike .3 miles. I was glad to reach the shelter and find new faces there. Two young men had watched me approach. They were Southerners with strong accents who were confident and comfortable. They were friends who were hiking together. As I approached, one called out:

"Hey, what do you got there?"

"These? I've got snowshoes."

"Snowshoes? Oh, hey! I heard about you. You're the guy with the

snowshoes!"

Yeah, I'm the idiot with the snowshoes.

The other said, "Man, I saw you coming down the hill. I thought you were carrying a skateboard!"

I told them my trail name was Sneakers. They said I should change it to *Snowshoes.* They said I should carry my snowshoes all the way to Katahdin. Through-hikers do such things deliberately, just to cement kooky, off-beat reputations. A through-hiker once carried a Pink Flamingo lawn ornament the entire length of the trail. Someone else hiked the entire trail with his cat Ziggy riding on top of his backpack. Another through-hiker carried a spice rack. A woman carried a watermelon up Katahdin in her arms on her last day. In our year already we had heard of a growing legend of Pied Piper fame named *Low Rider* who was carrying a hiking stick named *Despair.* Low Rider picked up garbage off the trail and he tied the refuse to his stick. His stick became a monument to the trail.

These two didn't have trail names and they weren't through-hikers. They hadn't the time. They were soon to begin work. They had started at Springer and were only hiking to the Virginia border. Like me, they had jobs awaiting them. Like me, they weren't at that moment questioning their direction in life. In that regard we were unlike many. That previous night I had listened to myriad conversations about quitting jobs, switching jobs, searching for jobs, needing time to think things over. Such is life on the trail. Many hikers are searching for answers, hoping to gain knowledge—about themselves, about life. But the bond that exists between through-hikers is great. These two would be getting off the trail while the rest of us were in for the longer haul.

Lord of the Flies, Chicago Kid, and finally the Portland-Four showed up. The nearest water was back at the trail split. I walked back and forth carrying water in my little cooking pots, spilling it over the sides with each step like a cartoon character. Everyone else had water bags, weightless when empty yet able to hold ten times the amount in my pots. The others filled their water bags at the stream and hung them on shelter nails so they always had water nearby. I wrote WATER CARRIER on my growing shopping list. Shelter conversation that night touched on hiking pace. None of us were hiking swiftly. We all had aches and pains. The Portland-Four limped in last again after spending half their day sitting by the trail tending blisters. The others mentioned the name of a hiker who had started with them, whom I hadn't yet met, called the *Jersey Coalminer.* He was young, twenty-two, just out of the navy. They were tracking his progress in the registers. They said he was flying, hiking as much as seventeen miles in a day. That seemed a lot to us then.

"Remember how we told him to change his name to *Kangaroo Man?"*

"We should have called him *The Energizer."*

"Yeah, that would have been perfect: *'He keeps going, and going!'"*

"I wonder how far he's gotten by now."

"He's definitely at least in Pennsylvania."

"Pennsylvania? Dude, no way. He's already through Pennsylvania by now. He's into Vermont."

"Yeah, that's right. He'll be climbing up Katahdin next week."

"Are you kidding? He's already climbed Katahdin. He's already back home, watching TV!"

I remained quiet. I knew I would catch the Jersey Coalminer. He sounded like a strong hiker; I thought he might be someone to hike with. It made me consider the others in the shelter. They were mellow, carefree. They were moseying along, and I knew that very shortly I would leave them behind probably never to see them again. I was about to lighten my load, and then I was going to blaze.

You learn these early days what you will need and what you won't. For me, I discovered that brushing my teeth after dinner is the greatest moment of the day. Unfortunately I had sawed my toothbrush in half before leaving. I had done that in what I'd believed was a diligent effort to keep my pack weight down, as if I'd believed that that solitary extra sixteenth ounce of a toothbrush would have mattered while I was busy stuffing in eight-ounce cans of tomatoes. Ironically, I was now left with a death-heavy pack and I could barely brush my teeth while trying to hold on to my tiny toothbrush stub. Soon I would reverse the mistake. Soon, very soon, I told myself, I would have a light pack and a full toothbrush.

Discovering all that you don't need is important, but it can pose problems; overpacked hikers sneakily discard scads of belongings in the early shelters. *The Brothers Karmatzof* lay abandoned in a corner of this shelter. One glance at that Leviathan of books left no doubt why a hiker would ditch it. Whoever had brought it believed they would spend the summer reading it. Instead they ditched it in Gooch Gap shelter just sixteen miles into their hike. That book was too large, too heavy, so they ditched it. Through-hikers don't read novels. Novels take you away, but on the trail you are already away so there is no need. On my entire hike I saw just one through-hiker reading a novel. I myself had abandoned my saw and five cans of tomatoes back at Black Gap shelter with Maddog. Here at Gooch Gap, I ditched half my heavy pots, silverware, a plastic trowel and *Walden*.

People grow angry at we hikers who discard belongings, and rightly so. We must leave the woods as we find them. All agree: *"If you pack it in, pack it out."* But for some like me it seemed a matter of survival. With my broken backpack and seventy-five pounds, I truly thought I might not even make it out of the woods those last fourteen miles to Neels Gap unless I had lightened my pack. Fortunately, this wasn't littering. Georgia mountain residents know that we discard camping gear in these first few shelters along the AT, so many locals patrol the area collecting choice goods for themselves. Boy Scout leaders swing through each spring rounding up camping equipment for their troops. They say you can fill an outfitter store with all the items discarded by through-hikers in the early shelters.

I had learned much in a short time and I was becoming familiar with the trail. We were all slowly growing accustomed to calling each other by our trail names. It took getting used to at first. At first we'd said:

"Hey Pack Rat."

No answer.

"Hey, *Pack Rat.*"

"What? Huh?"

You learn a sense of the trail's routine—wake up, pack, hike to a shelter, set down your mattress pad, lay out your sleeping bag, get water, change into dry clothes, produce your food, sit in your sleeping bag while you cook and eat dinner. After dinner, still seated in your sleeping bag, you write in your journal, read the shelter's register, write in the register, read ahead in the hiker handbook and data book, brush your teeth, tell a few jokes, swap a few stories, sleep, rise, pack and hike. That is the trail. As we lay in the dark ready for sleep, it began to rain. It felt magical lying in the woods, body tired, warm and dry, listening to the endless, steady sound of rain, powerful drops plopping down on the shelter roof, on the ground, on rocks, on the leaves of the trees, pouring down in a rush so loud and yet all at once impossibly so very gentle, soothing, even, steady, and quiet. Thoreau: *"There was never yet such a storm but it was Aeolian music to a healthy and innocent ear."*

Saved.

I woke up my third morning excited because this was the day that I would reach Neels Gap. *Neels Gap*—it was 14.6 miles away, but I was not going to stop until I got there. I was fueled by powerful incentive. It was my third day hiking the trail and it would be my first covering double-digit mileage. I knew I would make it. I hiked all day over hills, down into passes, and up over hills again. In the South passes are called "gaps." They loved naming gaps down there—we had *Gooch Gap, Woody Gap, Lunsford Gap, Jarrard Gap, Bird Gap, Slaughter Gap.* It seemed there was a gap named after just about everything imaginable—*High Gap, Low Gap, Big Gap, Small Gap, Earl's Dead Dog Willy Gap.*

After twelve miles, I reached the next shelter on the trail, just two miles shy of Neels Gap. That shelter was on top of Blood Mountain at 4,460 feet, the highest point on the AT in Georgia, according to the handbook (every speck of the trail all the way to Maine seems worthy of some little distinction or other). There were house-sized boulders and trees on the summit and no view whatever. Blood Mountain shelter is particularly dismal. It is a fully enclosed stone house with one hole for a door and another hole for a window. A rat lives inside. I peeked inside, then resumed my hike, continuing down the far side of the mountain. Just two miles to go; success propelled me.

Walasi-Yi Center came into my view at 4 PM from an open spot on a descending path where a sign by the trail detailed the fierce battle of Blood Mountain fought four hundred years earlier between Creek and Cherokee warriors. The battle was so bloody that it turned the mountain red. The handbook advises you to look for Balance Rock, estimated at 1.5 billion years old. I missed the rock, but I didn't feel bad; something that old wouldn't be going anywhere anytime soon. I reached the road and followed the white blazes across to the Walasi-Yi Center. The building spread out to the right and left. The trail led off to the left underneath the building's stone archway. I walked to the right and climbed the stone steps to the porch. I had carried my snowshoes again that day even though it hadn't rained. I had done so through habit, and perhaps also through anger. I carried them now into the outfitter store. I looked bad, smelled bad—of course nobody batted an eyelash.

There were two shoppers inside and a worker behind the counter who moved about busily bending down checking things. I approached the counter and gently set my three-foot-long snowshoes down on the glass. The worker was a gigantic, heavy man with a full black beard, mustache, and wild hair. He wore overalls. And when he stood up, he kept standing up, and he looked at me and took notice. He then looked down at the snowshoes. Then back up at me. His expression never changed. He said:

"You probably want to mail those home, don't you?"

That was Wayne. That was Neels Gap. I had made it.

4

Neels Gap

Sorrow can take care of itself, but to get the full value of
happiness, it has to be shared.

—Mark Twain

Bunkmates.

Neels Gap is the first spot of civilization for northbounders. The outfitter store sells apples, bananas, candy bars, Gatorade, Coca Cola, doughnuts, bread, frozen dinners, and other groceries. I had hiked only thirty miles, yet I felt as if I'd crossed a great wilderness and come out alive on the other side. Neels Gap changed my hike. By dumb luck I would survive simply because the Walasi-Yi Center is here on the trail just thirty miles from Springer. Neels Gap is a place of many trail firsts: first store, first shower, first laundry, first pay phone, first electricity, first night sleeping in a bed on the trail. Things work differently for southbounders. While northbound novices arrive here and get saved early, southbound novices must take care. Southbounders starting in Maine must hike 320 miles to reach their first trailside outfitter store, at Pinkham Notch, New Hampshire.

If you start in Maine you had better begin with the right gear and know how to use it, for not only is the first trailside backpacking store a long way off, but right off the bat you must hike through the one-hundred-mile wilderness almost immediately after coming down off Katahdin. That's the longest stretch of wilderness on the trail and southbounders begin their trip walking through it. We northbounders don't face such a daunting task.

35

All we do is hike thirty miles and then, be anything wrong, Neels Gap's Walasi-Yi Center saves us. The Neels Gap workers know the routine. Wayne had through-hiked himself. The owners are a married couple who had both through-hiked. The workers know the trail; they answer questions and offer advice. They keep a post office scale in the store. Confused hikers bring in their packs and empty them out on the floor. The store workers review every packed item and discus its merits: *"Keep that, keep that, get rid of that, get rid of that, get a different brand of those."* The gear they sell in that small store is the exact gear needed, no more no less.

I mailed home thirty-five pounds of belongings from Neels Gap (I felt sure I had set the record). Still, I kept my tent and the Abdominizer. Checking items off my shopping list, I bought a toothbrush, a water carrier, a cigarette lighter, a Whisperlite stove, and a nylon ground tarp. I also brought a replacement pot and a replacement spoon. All the items I bought were virtually weightless. The key to success is to pack light. That secret had finally sunk in. I also bought a new backpack. I hadn't intended to, but when I pulled a Gregory internal frame pack down from the shelves and tried it on, the second phase of my trip had begun. The single moment it went on my back could be called the real start of my hike. One instant taught me the difference between internal and external frame backpacks. External frames, like the defective one I'd begun with, felt like some kid down the street twisted metal together, while this internal frame felt like top NASA researchers had spent decades creating a functional wonder toy. I believed this purchase would determine the difference between success and failure. I asked Wayne if I should buy a large Gregory internal frame. Apparently I'd still been grappling with the lingering fallacy that I needed a huge pack to hike a huge trail. Wayne measured me. He measured my back and fitted me with a medium-sized Gregory. I chose the most basic style and the most fitting color: green.

My new Gregory had just two compartments—one small accessible pouch on top for emergency and common-use items like snacks, camera, and rain gear, and one large compartment down into which went 95 percent of my gear—heaviest items on the bottom and close against my back—sleeping bag on the bottom, then tent, ground tarp, fuel can, food bag, clothing bag, jacket, stove, and water carrier. I loaded the Gregory with my new things and I tried it on. It was an indescribable feeling. The pack's comfortable padding fit snugly against my back. I leaned to the right and the pack moved with my body; it was an extension of me; its entire weight was distributed evenly. I felt like I had nothing on. The best feature was elastic side flaps that held my water bottles, so that now I could just reach back for water and drink while I hiked without so much as even breaking my stride. Suddenly I hated that original, defective external frame pack more than ever for the needless pain it had put me through. Of course, I felt bad about spending more money, but I would later receive a full refund for the initial defective pack. The trail does get expensive. The cost of your hike ranges from $50–$5,000 depending on how much equipment you buy, how many hotel rooms you rent. Some hike in full Gortex sweat suits with top-brand equipment while others pull old discarded socks from community bins and wear them. You need not travel high-tech. Important is simply that what you own is lightweight and functional.

I paid $11 for a bunkroom bed in the cellar of the adjoining building beyond the archway, and I carried my things down for my first evening spent indoors on the trail. Walasi-Yi Center has two large cellar bunkrooms. Our room had a stove, sink, refrigerator, and dining room table. I spread out my things and organized my pack on the dry, clean floor. None from that group the previous night had made it this far; they all pulled up short staying two miles back in the Blood Mountain shelter. I walked upstairs to the laundry room. I washed my clothes and took my first hot shower since leaving DC. One of the greatest things about hiking in the woods is how much you appreciate the comforts available once you leave. It's like you have to do this in order not to take modern life for granted. Like you have to do this to know what you truly are. Warm water poured over me.

Clean and refreshed, I returned to the bunkroom to the company of the three new through-hikers whom I'd met there earlier: *Ponder Yonder, the Peaceful Warrior* and Patrick (no trail name yet). All three were quiet, respectful, modest, and friendly. They were all younger than me and they'd all begun solo. Ponder Yonder was just out of college. He was my first trail friend. The Peaceful Warrior had horrible blisters on her feet. Ponder Yonder had hiked with her for two days, helping her limp through the woods to reach Neels Gap. Both agreed now that he should go on from here at his pace while she would linger longer to tend to her blisters and decide whether or not to continue (she wasn't enjoying herself). We took turns answering the million-dollar question: What had brought us to the trail?

"I've been planning this for most of my life," said Ponder Yonder. "I used to hike a lot with my father. I've hiked the trail through the middle states. But now I finally have the chance to do it all at once."

"My older brother through-hiked last year; now I'm hiking this year," Patrick said.

"I'm hiking to overcome my fear of the dark," said the Peaceful Warrior.

Me, I wished I could be like Kerouac's "penniless rake going *anywhere…*" But I could not; I was far too uptight, too nervous and anxious all the time. I needed this trail for structure. But hiking to overcome fear of the dark didn't seem like much of a reason to hike. The Peaceful Warrior was yet another hiker from Portland, Maine. She was the first woman I had met who had begun solo. About one-quarter of all through-hikers are women, but most women begin with partners. The Peaceful Warrior was tall, broad, extremely strong, in her early twenties. She was a competitive power lifter and a distance swimmer. She annually races Maine's Peaks-to-Portland five-mile ocean swim. She showed us the twelve-inch hunting knife that her brother had given her as a gift, which she carried for protection (she didn't look like she needed it). Patrick was a Southerner with relatives who lived nearby and later stopped in to bring us food.

I sat on my bed and sorted through my pack once again. I cooked dinner on the stove, read the hiker register, and wrote my own entry. I read ahead in the handbook and data book to learn what would come next. The store owners brought us a bowl of popcorn and cold Cokes. It was *"Trail Magic."* Trail Magic is when you get a magical, unexpected, fortunate event. I thought of my crystal ball fantasy—how if any of my friends back in Maine had owned crystal balls and could have checked in on me this very second to see what life was like on the trail, they would have been shocked to discover me eating popcorn, drinking Coke, and climbing into a comfortable bed.

Threshold.

I rose at my leisure in the morning. I had no reason to hurry as I planned to hike only 9.5 miles that day. You look ahead in the data book to learn where the nearest shelters lie. You spend the summer looking ahead in the Data Book and in Dan "Wingfoot" Bruce's Thru-Hiker's Handbook, figuring out what's where and deciding what you will shoot for that day and that week. You calculate how long it will take to reach the next lean-to, the next store, your next post office food drop, the next town. Both books are indispensable. The data book gives facts and figures detailing the distance of every object on the trail to everything else, while Wingfoot's handbook has prose essays describing virtually everything about any particular trail place or object you care to research—what stores are in town, what time the stores close, whether or not you can sleep, shower, wash laundry, make phone calls or receive packages there.

My most pressing goal upon leaving Neels Gap would be to reach my first post office drop box in Fontana Dam, North Carolina. There in my drop box would be food, supplies, and hopefully plenty of mail. But Fontana Dam was 130 miles away, and I had thus far averaged just ten miles a day. I could carry food to last seven days, but anything more than that felt too heavy. Clearly I would have to stop to buy food along the way to Fontana Dam— but where would I stop? The data book shows that the first chance for food resupply north of Neels Gap is thirty-three miles farther at a place called Dicks Creek Gap, where a three-mile hitchhike left leads to The Blueberry Patch (an organic farm which hosts hikers), and where an eleven-mile hitchhike right leads to Hiawassee, Georgia (two thousand residents and a Foodland grocery store). Just thirty-three miles? I was traveling light now and I needed a more distant goal to strive for. I made a more ambitious plan. I would hike seventy miles from Neels Gap to a place called Wallace Gap where one mile off the trail was Rainbow Springs Campground with a hiker bunkhouse, grocery store, showers, and laundry. So that was my goal. And with that plan settled, I suddenly had four simultaneous goals: to reach Katahdin; to reach my first post office drop box at Fontana Dam; to reach Wallace Gap and my Rainbow Springs pit stop; and most immediately, to reach Low Gap shelter that evening, just 9.5 miles away.

The trail is like that: it is a series of goals within goals. The Appalachian Trail is a lesson in goal setting. There is the ultimate goal: to hike the whole trail, end to end. There are landmark goals along the way: reaching your first state line (and each subsequent state line), reaching Virginia, reaching the halfway marker, crossing the Mason-Dixon Line, entering New England, reaching the Maine border. There are fifteen or more personally significant post office goals: reaching your first PO drop box, your second, your third. And the smallest subset is the goal of reaching certain points like stores, roads, mountains, rivers, and certain shelters as day's-end destinations. Goals within goals within goals. The goals support, strengthen, reinforce one another. Northbounders are always aware of the ultimate goal of reaching Katahdin. Every step placed on the ground is a step toward fulfilling that goal. But every step is also a step gained in reaching the next shelter, and by reaching that shelter you are approaching Katahdin. If you achieve each modest goal, one by one, you will achieve the grand goal. Inner knowledge that the grand goal exists buoys you. Reach Katahdin. Always the ultimate goal exists.

The nearest shelters north of Neels Gap are 5.1 miles away, 9.5 miles away, and 16.7 miles away. I had final morning business to settle in the store which negated an early exit and thus caused the 16.7-mile shelter to be an unreasonable goal. But I could easily reach the 9.5-mile shelter no matter when I departed, so I took my time. Back then I was utterly dependent on the shelters. Like most novices, I only felt comfortable hopping from shelter to shelter. There are many advantages of stopping at shelters. They are invariably located near water, they offer protection from rain and storms, and most important, they provide companionship and camaraderie. It is fine to hike alone all through the day—I was actually enjoying that very much—but at the end of the day, it feels good to meet people at the shelters and talk and share experiences. Mark Twain: *"Sorrow can take care of itself, but to get the full value of happiness it has to be shared."*

Ponder Yonder and Patrick had left early. The hikers I'd met those previous days trooped down from Blood Mountain shelter and milled around the outfitter store buying candy and sunbathing on the terrace, eating, sorting through their packs, and enjoying the view which overlooks a series of valleys to the east. The store owners brought us together and snapped a photograph. They kept a photo album of all the hikers who pass through. A fit, unassuming man in his midthirties plunked down an extraordinarily minimalist pack and sat on the terrace wall beside me. He smiled. I smiled.

"Hi. I'm Sneakers."

"Eddie-B."

Beside me was Eddie-B, the gentleman who would hike the trail faster than anyone else would that summer, and faster than almost any through-hiker ever had. I couldn't have known it at the time.

"When did you start?" I asked.

"Yesterday."

"Yesterday? From Springer?" I couldn't believe it. I shouted over to Chicago Kid, "Hey, this guy started *yesterday!*"

Eddie-B had hiked twenty-eight miles from the visitor center his first day, and he'd already hiked ten miles this morning on his second day by the time we met him at 10 AM. The rest of us had stumbled, staggered, plodded, crawled, inched, limped, bled, cried, and dragged ourselves to Neels Gap in three, four, or five days while here was a man who had hiked here in one day plus a couple of extra hours. I was intrigued. I suddenly had a hundred questions to ask. I was eager to learn and I feared I would never meet another hiker like this the rest of the summer.

"How far are you going today? What shelter are you shooting for?" I asked, expecting him to name a shelter some tremendous distance away.

"I don't use shelters. I sleep in my tent," he said.

"Well how far are you going?"

"I don't know," he said. "I never plan that. I'll hike until nightfall, then set up my tent. I like to set up my tent in spots where there are beautiful views."

Eddie-B traveled without a stove. He ate cold meals of Ramen noodles thrown into his Nalgene water bottle, soaked, shaken, then drunk. He had raced ultramarathons. He was a freelance computer software designer. He planned to finish the trail in under three months. He wasn't racing; he had merely calculated his arrival date based on his knowledge of the daily distances he knew he could cover. Plus he said that he didn't care to spend too much time in the woods. What I didn't know then was that Eddie-B was good friends with a past through-hiker named *Maniac* who at the time held the trail's unofficial second fastest speed record having through-hiked in fifty-five days a few years back. It is a very controversial distinction, one which raises the ire of the vast majority who feel that there shouldn't *be* a speed record (racing teams taking to the woods in uniforms with camera crews and sponsorship vans parked at all the trailheads).

Me, I wanted to hike long distances. I wanted to test myself to learn where my limits lay. I wondered what it felt like to hike twenty-eight miles in one day. Little did I know, I would find out. I would later hike almost twice that in a single day (but that, too, was another lifetime). Eddie-B was interested that

I was hiking in running shoes. I wanted to ask him about ultra-running, but he slipped away inside the store. He bought two freeze-dried meals; then he was off. I would never see him again, but I would catch wind of his exploits the rest of my hike. People loved to tell Eddie-B stories. Rumors abounded: he was a rocket scientist; he was a physicist; he held two PhD's as a rocket scientist *and* a physicist; he was independently wealthy; he owned a bank; he owned two banks; he had won Hawaii's Ironman Triathlon—*four times!*

Lord of the Flies, Chicago Kid, and the butterfly couple walked to the road to hitchhike to the nearest town for a beer to celebrate. They asked me to go, but it didn't feel right. I had just bought a pack, I had just bought a stove, I had just shed thirty-five pounds. The last thing I wanted was to get off the trail. I wanted to hike and to cruise. I set out at 1 PM. I walked under the stone archway of the Walasi-Yi Center at Neels Gap. I reached up with my hiking stick and touched the white blaze on the stones in homage. I had crossed a threshold; I had crossed *the* threshold. I had mailed home my junk. I had a new backpack. The real start of my trip had begun.

5

Blisters

Eeech, oouch, ooch, I wish I had some hooch.

—Badger Boy, GA-ME

No Shampoo.

I shot from Neels Gap flying down the trail covering nine miles in three hours. It was a new me with my new pack. I was becoming Running Deer, I could feel it. Still, I had residual pain in my feet and back from those past few extraordinarily painful days. At 4 PM, I found Ponder Yonder and Patrick sitting by their tents just shy of Low Gap shelter. They said that fraternity brothers on spring break from some southern college had filled the lean-to. The shelter was over a hill and down in a valley on a rolling, blue-blazed side trail. We could hear a dog bark, and barely audible rising up out of the valley came the out-of-place sound of raucous laughter.

Boisterous crowds were something I hadn't expected. I'd thought that only through-hikers would fill the woods, but instead it was spring break from colleges and high schools, and the woods were packed with day hikers, section-hikers, and weekend warriors. You soon learn that sometimes and in some places the trail is busier than others, and you learn quickly that you will always have to share it. Roughly three million people set foot on the Appalachian Trail every year, and we were just guests like everyone else. I set up my tent for the first time, and we three sat cooking dinner together, discussing our gear, the woods, the weather, our goals. Ponder Yonder showed me how to use my new stove.

"I don't have a trail name," said Patrick.

"No, you don't. But you should definitely get one," we said.

There was silence.

"Yeah, I know," he finally added.

Another silence, lasting several minutes.

"I definitely need one," Patrick repeated.

We just weren't catching his hint. So then finally Patrick came out and spoke his mind, "Hey, do you guys think you could give me a trail name?"

"You want us to give you a name?"

"Yeah."

"Okay, sure. We can do that. Why not?" we said, and we reeled them off like candy: "How about *Chowder Head, Bird Drop, Big Foot, Sloppy Joe?*"

"No, no, no; nothing like that," Patrick said. "Please, don't just rush into it. And it can't be anything like that, either. Those names don't have anything to do with me. How do you get Sloppy Joe? I'm not eating a Sloppy Joe. Do you see me eating a Sloppy Joe? My name isn't Joe. I don't even like Sloppy Joes! It has to be personal. It has to be something about me."

"Okay," we said. "Sorry. Okay, fine. Well, let's see. What do you like? Do you want, like, a tree name or an animal name or a—"

"No! Nothing like *that,* either! You guys just don't get it, do you? It can't be anything like that. Don't you know? Someone has to just name me. You can't ask me how I like it. You have to just do it. It has to be for a *reason.* And I can't go around *asking* people. You should realize that. It isn't something that we should even be *talking* about. It's not something that you discuss."

"But most people name themselves," Ponder said.

"I know. I don't want that," Patrick said.

We all grew quiet and went on with our meals. Ponder Yonder and I studied Patrick, searching for a reason to give him a name, but there just wasn't much we were doing at that moment. Suddenly Patrick looked up, shocked to realize what we were up to. He had caught us staring at him, studying him, watching him, waiting for him to do something stupid.

"Oh forget it!" he finally said (apparently he didn't wish to be called *Pan Dropper, Dinner Burner,* or *Spilled Food on his Shirt*).

Ponder Yonder massaged his feet with rubbing alcohol to soothe them, dry them, toughen them. He stretched for twenty minutes after dinner; then he sat in a yoga position for his breathing exercises. Ponder Yonder stretched every night and every morning to stay limber and prevent injuries. He said that even though he felt strong, he planned to continue a slow hiking pace those first few weeks to ease gradually into his hike. He planned to hike all night under the first full moon. That sounded fine to me. I vowed to free my mind to think up creative ideas like that myself. I had learned much already. I believed I could learn something from every hiker on the trail. I spent those early days observing and asking questions. I remembered how on my second night I had asked Lord of the Flies (or was it Purple Man?) how he carried his shampoo, expecting him to share some trick of the trail or show me some kind of high-tech, weightless, indestructible camping store shampoo vial.

"How do you pack your shampoo?" I had asked.

"What shampoo?" he'd answered.

Ponder's tent was homemade. It looked like a miniature circus tent with a single pole suspending a blue and white striped canvas square under a center point. The sides of the canvas sloped symmetrically down from the center pole toward the ground where its four corners were tied to ground stakes, but the canvas didn't quite reach all the way to the ground, so Ponder could look out underneath all around as he lay inside, and wind, cold, noise, animals and everything else could get in. Ponder Yonder was inside, but connected to the outside. I hated the confinement of my tent. Inside, I was cut off from the world in a tiny nylon shell. In the open-faced lean-tos, we remained outside, wind easily finding us. I longed to be outside, to enjoy a connection with the world. I vowed to find a way. I held in mind a romantic vision of sleeping outside in a desert out West, after coffee, coat for a blanket, hat down over the eyes, full moon and thousands of stars above, coyotes calling in the distance.

Practice Charity.

I left Ponder Yonder and Patrick behind, hiking 14.9 miles to mountaintop Tray Mountain shelter that next day. It was the longest distance I had hiked. Those earlier eight-mile days had been half-day efforts. Fifteen miles was a full day now, and I was aiming for full days every day. I wondered when I'd be able to hike twenty miles in a day. I was impatient for it. The terrain here was steep. I heard that there would be easier stretches in Virginia.

Weekend warriors filled the mountain around this shelter in clusters of tents. Out of the blue, Coyote ambled up. Excluding Eddie-B, it made him the only hiker who had kept up with me thus far. Coyote was tall and powerfully built. He wore glasses. His movements were slower and even more deliberate than Ponder Yonder's. I thought it was David Caradine beside me in a Kung Fu episode. He pulled out of his backpack a twenty-pound gym bag filled with dehydrated beans, grains, and oatmeal. He said that he ate by weight. He ate two pounds of food a day. Coyote was painfully quiet, but we talked a bit now as we were the only two through-hikers in the shelter. Coyote was twenty-three. He had taken a one-month survival-training course out West. I asked what he'd learned. He said that in the end survival all boils down to one thing: *"If you can eat bugs you can survive."*

This shelter was shorter than the others so that our feet nearly stuck out, and the register was filled with complaints from hikers who'd gotten rain blown in on their feet as they slept. We read that a group of hikers had been stranded here for two days during the one-hundred-year snowstorm. They had set up two tents inside the shelter and had played cards for two days while chest-deep snow piled up outside the lean-to. After dark, we looked down at the lights of a small town in a valley below. I went to sleep, but I woke up twice in the middle of the night, my feet burning as hot as coals. Twice that night I had to rise in the darkness, fumble for my water carrier and pour icy cold mountain water over my feet to douse them and cool them off. I sat there, dousing my feet in the dark and feeling alone in the dead of night. I sat looking out, wondering if I was a survivor, wondering if I could ever eat bugs.

Next afternoon, high on a ridge, to my joy for five minutes I hiked through simultaneous sunshine and rain. I followed the ridge through clouds, thunder, wind, lightning. I reached Plum Orchard Gap shelter after a second consecutive day of 14.9 miles (I couldn't break the fifteen-mile mark). Remote in the woods, this lean-to has a cement patio, thermometer, mirror, steel hooks for food bags, and a split-level loft with a window at the top. Extravagant lodging. Already spread out in the top loft was a married couple from Minnesota who were through-hiking with their monstrous chocolate Lab. They were *Four Feet and Four Paws*. Coyote sauntered in and shared the bottom level with me. We went to sleep that night as we did every night on the trail, reflecting and anticipating another day.

Next thing I knew, plaintive whining awoke us all that next morning. Lying on my back, I opened my eyes and looked straight up into the eyes of Four Paws, that colossal seventy-pound monster staring down at me from almost directly above, looking very much like he wanted to jump (using me for a pillow). The dog's whine registered immediately and sent us all scrambling to our feet, becoming rescuers. At first we couldn't think how to get the dog down, but then we decided to lower him down in a sleeping bag. Once on the ground, Four Paws raced into the woods for the nearest bush; then he returned, relieved, and ran around recklessly retrieving rocks that we threw. He was wired, primed for the day. Four Feet finally brought him in and quieted him down. They fed him some breakfast and strapped a small dog pack onto his back so that he could carry his own food. They checked his paw pads which had torn open in the snow weeks earlier (they, too, had gotten caught in the storm). They said their dog loved the trail. Unfortunately, they would have to ship him around the Smoky Mountains because dogs aren't allowed in the park. They worried, too, how he would fare through the sharp rocks which litter the trail in Pennsylvania.

Dogs on the trail have freedom to romp amid endless smells, sights, sounds. I wondered what they think it's about. Do they think there is a reason for the trek? Do they think they are going somewhere? Do they ever expect to reach a destination? Do they care? Do they have an awareness of time? Do they worry those early days whether this sudden magical fun isn't merely a temporary gift? Do they believe that the world is an endless, limitless place? Early on they are anxious, untrusting of constant playtime, believing this too good to be true. So they start every day with a bathroom break, then a run up to their humans: *"Hi! Good morning! Are you awake? Are you awake? I'm awake! I'm Tobey! It's me! It's Tobey! I'm ready! I'm ready! Are you awake? Are you gonna get up? Are we going to go? Are you ready to go?"* But finally through-hiking dogs gain confidence, chill out, and become a bit more relaxed as the weeks go by. Soon they know what's in store. But do they think it will end? They say that it's hard for a human to adjust back to life after the trail; I can only imagine what the heartache is like for a dog.

Coyote left the shelter early, after having first left me a sample of his dried beans. Jack Kerouak: *"Practice Charity without holding in mind any preconceptions about Charity, for charity after all is only a word."* I thought I would never see Coyote again because he was out ahead of me now, hiking fast, and I couldn't keep up. The pain in my feet grew worse. I was limping from blisters, and my feet couldn't take another full day.

April Fool.

I was thirty-five miles shy of Rainbow Springs with its hot showers and bunkroom. Two full days would get me there, but my feet couldn't do it. My back felt better, my pack weight was down, but now my feet hurt with every step. At 4.3 miles on the day, I limped up to reach my first state line. That first border crossing lies deep in the woods and is marked only by a small black pipe nailed onto a tree with small white letters painted on it: GA-NC. It is a modest marker, but you need nothing more. You know what this means. It means that you have hiked seventy-five miles and you have reached the end of a state. You now leave Georgia behind. It is a tangible success, an empowering thought. You walked, on your feet, right out of a state. Reaching this border confirmed a suspicion growing inside me—*I'm doing it!* I stepped across the border into North Carolina. One state down, thirteen states remained. My feet resumed aching immediately. Then a blister on my heel broke open, which hurt so bad that I couldn't continue. I sat by a stream and soaked my feet in its freezing water. My feet numb, I resumed my hike.

I carried no bandages, but that was okay—blisters were no mysterious threat to me. On the contrary, I knew blisters. After twenty years of tennis, blisters were one thing I did know. I'd learned everything about them—how to drain them, air them, soothe them, heal them. I'd known blisters, blood blisters, blisters under calluses, blood blisters under calluses. I'd shaved down calluses with razor blades and drained blood blisters underneath with safety pins. Yes, I knew blisters, and I would tend to these the first chance I had. I truly hadn't expected to get blisters at all, not while hiking in running shoes.

Everyone scoffed at my running shoes, and yet they had always worked well for me. I wear them for hiking because they are light and comfortable. They dry fast, go on easy, and offer excellent traction. Critics insist that they don't offer ankle support, but I'd never found that a problem. They are built to absorb the shock of a marathon runner pounding away mile after mile on hard pavement, and still in them I feel nimble and quick. I can lift my legs, bound around. I had never previously gotten blisters in running shoes, but now I had to admit that they aren't infallible. But gimmick trail-running shoes were on my feet now; that was the problem. I hadn't started my hike with old, comfortable running shoes. A clerk back home had shown me a pair of Asics trail runners, swearing by the advantage of the elastic bands under their tongues which hug feet firmly and are specifically designed for the woods to keep pebbles and twigs from falling inside. So I'd bought them, and now they were giving me fits. I was stuck deep in the woods in blister-inducing trail runners.

The pain grew so bad that after limping just three miles past the border I couldn't go on. At 7.3 miles on the day, I staggered into Muskrat Creek shelter, a dismal, graffiti-filled A-frame shack in a thicket by a swampy creek. It was 1 PM, and I was alone in the most cheerless dump on the AT. It was bitterly cold. The altitude was four thousand feet. I set up my tent inside the shelter for greater warmth and I climbed inside it. I got inside my sleeping bag wearing all my clothes and my polypropylene hat and gloves. Then boredom set in. I wrote in my journal, read the register, and tried to stay warm. Like most of the registers in the shelters these first one hundred miles, this one was filled with entries virtually all about pain—blisters, back aches, knee pain. You could fill a book with all the complaints. We'd always heard that our start-up pains would shortly subside, but what we didn't know was that new problems would arise and we would gripe about those—data book off by .1 mile, restaurant closed, stove breaks, reach a post office on a Sunday. *Hydro* would one day put it best: *"A through-hiker always needs something to complain about."* I wrote my own register entry at Muskrat Creek shelter:

> *April 1, 1993—here alone, in after a painful 7.3. Ponder Yonder, what are you doing back there? Me, am enjoying this wonderful shelter, keeping myself busy by draining the blood out of my shoes. Right foot has an open sore. There's a white patch deep inside which I think is my bone. Have been poking at it through the puss with a twig, but I can't feel anything as the leg has gone numb below the knee. Unfortunately, have also lost hearing in my left ear. A back molar fell out and my gums are bleeding. Everything else is fine except for some blurred vision, dizziness, nausea, head lice, gout, goiters, scurvy, dysentery, and the two straps that*

*broke off my pack. PS—if anyone finds either my sleeping bag or
my stove, would you please bring them up to me as I need them.
Thanks!*

It was April 1—April Fool's Day—and little did I know then, but
Muskrat Creek shelter was about to pull its own joke on me. After writing my
false entry, I fell asleep and napped all afternoon. I awoke and ate dinner, but
nobody had arrived, nor would they. I fell asleep again; then I awoke in the
darkness completely refreshed. I sensed it was early, but I knew that I was
awake for good. I wanted to get up, but it was still dark so I lay and waited for
sunrise, but sunrise never came. After thirty minutes, I fumbled for my watch
and discovered then to my horror that it was only 1 AM. Worse, I had slept so
much already that I was no longer tired. It was the perfect chance for a night
hike, but thick clouds caused utter darkness. No, I was trapped. For the next
five hours I lay awake in my sleeping bag freezing and cursing my fortune.

I crawled out of my tent at the first trace of daylight and beheld outside a
white universe of snow that had fallen overnight. Snow blanketed every inch
of the ground; every tree, leaf, bush, and branch was white powder. It was the
first true snow that I'd seen on the trail. It was an extraordinary sight made
all the more so as it was totally unexpected. I stared in awe—*Snow wraps the
earth like a great God's wide hand.* That long rest at Muskrat Creek helped
my feet enough so that I was able to hike 12.5 miles to Carter Gap shelter,
putting me just a day's hike away from my hot shower at Rainbow Springs.

Carter Gap shelter was also at four thousand feet. A plastic tarp covered
the shelter's roof. The air was so cold that I pulled the tarp down for
protection, covering the shelter's entrance, darkening the inside like a cave.
Four Feet and Four Paws showed up. Later, in walked *The Jersey Coalminer,*
the young man whose hiking prowess I'd heard discussed earlier those first
few nights of the trip. Here was the hiker they'd said would have already
reached Katahdin. I wondered how he had gotten behind me. He said that he'd
given himself a new trail name, *Wounded Knee.* He said that his knee "blew
out" (whatever that meant) and that he'd gotten off the trail to rest. Wounded
Knee was twenty-two, just retired after four years in the navy. He was small,
slight—dark hair, clean-cut, handsome, good-natured. He had been on ships
all over the world. During the last several months, he had longed for the
start of his hike so badly that he had planned with intricate detail, charting in
advance the distance he'd hike every day and the shelters he'd sleep in every
night from Georgia to Maine. Chaos Theory explains the impossibility of
his keeping his schedule (could he have foreseen his knee pain?). That frigid
night, just after dark, a skunk ducked inside our plastic tarp stepping into the
shelter to investigate. Four Paws issued a guttural growl. On cold nights Four
Feet slept with their dog between them to serve as a living hot water bottle.

So they grabbed their dog now and held him tight to avoid a fight. The skunk considered things. He looked about, calmly, then turned and walked away.

Whole Pickle.

You push for a town or a rest-stop through rain, snow, or excruciating pain. You rise at 5 AM just to be sure to make a town one full day's hike away. I needed 14.7 miles to reach my Rainbow Springs pit stop, and I intended to reach it this day. I was first up and on the trail at 7 AM. I walked two hundred yards and came to a view looking down from a high ridge over an endless series of valleys below. Mist had settled in the valley pockets, and mountain peaks jutted up from the mist like shark fins—patterns of gray and white, with bright morning sunshine burning over it all. My breath came out in clouds. It was a glorious moment: I could have been standing on Everest. I snapped some photographs. It was one of the first views that I'd had my whole hike. Anyone thinking that hiking the trail means beholding view after wonderful view is mistaken. Vladimir Nabokov wrote, in Lolita:

> *I remember as a child in Europe gloating over a map of North America that had "Appalachian Mountains" boldly running from Alabama up to New Brunswick, so that the whole region they spanned—Tennessee, the Virginias, Pennsylvania, New York, Vermont, New Hampshire and Maine, appeared to my imagination as a gigantic Switzerland or even Tibet, all mountains, glorious diamond peak upon peak, giant conifers, le montagnard emigre in his bear skin glory, and Felis tigris gold-smithi, and Red Indians under the catalpas. That it all boiled down to a measly suburban lawn and a smoking garbage incinerator, was appalling. Farewell, Appalachia!*

No, hiking the trail means walking through the woods day after day, surrounded by a dense cover of foliage. The foliage is so dense that through-hikers call this trail "The Green Tunnel." This is what you do here: you hike through trees day after day after day. There is no glamour here. This is something you undertake and stick with. Through-hiking the Appalachian Trail is not about breathtaking mountain views. Those exist, but they are rare. On the trail you live lower than that. The AT is about the more mundane. It is about being in the woods. It is about simple routines, natural pleasures, sticking to a goal, journeying far for a purpose, quiet time for thought, reflection, observation. It is not about living high above the fray, climbing above the tree line. It is about existing down in the fray, in the woods, in the dirt, in the mix, sleeping in a bag, listening to the rain. Your daily views aren't postcard views, but they are truly wonderful in their own way.

At six miles I reached the blue-blaze side trail leading .2 miles to the summit of Standing Indian Mountain (5,498 ft). It was our first accessible mountain over five thousand ft. East Coast mountains don't rise much higher. I hadn't previously realized that there were mountains in the south at all, yet I learned. Tennessee's Mt. Mitchell (6,684 ft.) is the highest mountain east of the Mississippi River, and North Carolina's Clingman's Dome (6,643 ft.) is the highest peak on the Appalachian Trail. Standing Indian's summit is just off the trail. I would have turned to climb the extra bit, but my feet hurt too much for a detour, so I declined and continued north.

At Rock Gap road crossing, I got lost. I did not know I was lost. Not immediately, anyway. That is how one gets lost. I turned left off the trail at the first road I came to and walked 1.5 miles to Standing Indian Campground. Once there, however, I realized that this was not where I wanted to be. Standing Indian is a motor home campsite which offers nothing to through-hikers—no bathroom, no bunkhouse, no store, no showers. Instead I should have turned left at the *second* of two roads and walked one mile to Rainbow Springs Campground with its through-hiker bunkhouse, Laundromat, and grocery store. My error was that I hadn't read the data book and the hiker's handbook carefully enough. The data book lists only public sites (Standing Indian), while the hiker's handbook lists only sites that are of value to through-hikers (Rainbow Springs). Because each book listed only one, I'd thought that they were one and the same. I just hadn't read carefully enough. It took awhile, but I finally figured out what had happened. And it came at a bad time. I had known that I was bound to get lost sooner or later, but why now? Why now when my feet hurt so bad I could barely stand? Frustration overcame me. I smashed my hiking stick onto the ground, breaking it into little pieces.

I felt better after my tantrum. I considered the damage. Walking to Rainbow Springs from here meant 1.5 road miles back to Rock Gap, then .6 trail miles to Wallace Gap, and then one road mile to Rainbow Springs. Having already forced a long and painful 16.2 miles on sore feet, I still had 3.1 miles to go! That wouldn't do, so I put my pack in the road and I stopped all cars leaving Standing Indian. A father and son in a truck stopped and drove me the three miles, depositing me at the front steps of the Rainbow Springs Campground general store. In taking the ride I missed a .6 mile stretch of trail between Rock Gap and Wallace Gap that I would have to pick up the following morning. I hadn't skipped an inch of the trail thus far, and I didn't intend to. This obsessive act of hiking every speck of the trail is what some derisively call being a *"purist."*

Rainbow Springs Campground has a general store which sits on a hillside, then drops down into a valley, and has a long front porch graced with strange amenities like plastic wind chimes, and empty tuna fish cans nailed to the porch railing for ashtrays. A long line of little orange flags on the ground marked a path leading down from the gravel turnaround, down a dirt hill to bunkhouses beside the river in the valley below. I struggled up the porch steps, entered the store. I set down my pack at a table where Wounded Knee sat eating a pizza. I told him my story and ordered a pizza and set out shuffling about the little store, wobbling uncontrollably, dancing *The Through-Hiker Shuffle*. The through-hiker shuffle is one of the great oddities of the trail. It happens when you take off your pack at the end of the day. After hiking all day, then removing your backpack, your body still rocks and sways while you walk as if it believes it is still carrying and balancing a heavy load. It is funny to see. You wobble around like a toddler taking its first steps. My dance was made worse with a limp from sore blisters added into the mix. I was ravenous. You crave strange foods while deep in the woods, and your stomach turns virtually bottomless. I waddled through the aisles snatching items off the shelves. I munched and snacked, snacked and munched, and then out came my pizza from a small oven. It was the first meal served to me on the trail. There would be times on the trail when I would eat very well, including gourmet meals at fine restaurants, but truly nothing I ate on the AT those four months from Georgia to Maine tasted as delicious to me as this frozen pizza did in this backward, backwoods camping store. I walked to the counter to pay.

"Okay now. What did you have?" the two old men there asked.

"I had a large pizza and a Coke," I said.

"What else?"

"A box of Cracker Jack, a box of animal cracker cookies, a pickle—"

"Whole pickle or a half a pickle?"

"Whole pickle."

"That it?"

"No. Also a cookie and two pieces of cheesecake," I said. "I think that's all. Can you believe that?"

"Believe it? Sure," one of the old men said. "Through-hiker came in here last week, ate three pizzas and ten Twinkies without getting up from the table. I'll believe anything after that."

We laughed awhile. Then suddenly an old woman emerged from a back room, brushed these two aside, and snapped at me for setting my flip-flop sandals on the counter. I'd had a long day. Didn't she know how tricky it is emerging from the woods and trying to remember civilized manners while tired, sore, and disoriented? I paid for a bed, then staggered down the hill and settled into a tiny hiker bunkhouse by the river. There were rental units and mobile homes parked nearby with children racing around by the river, screeching, laughing. Later, I limped back up the hill to shower and wash laundry. Wounded Knee arrived but then left to have dinner with friends he'd made while off the trail resting his knee. Four Feet and Four Paws made it in. We lit a fire in the wood stove and burned a log. Four Paws slept on a mat outside the screen door.

Ten Commandments.

Early next morning, the two old men drove me back to Rock Gap where I'd left off. I hiked my missing .6 mile stretch, and limped 3.7 miles farther to Highway 64, at Winding Stair Gap. The town of Franklin, North Carolina, lay ten miles down the road. It isn't a common through-hiker stop, but I needed more time off the trail, to rest in a hotel, and to buy supplies to nurse my sore feet, so I stuck out my thumb to hitchhike. Rainbow Springs had helped, but it wasn't the break I'd been looking for. I needed the chance for complete rehabilitation. Wounded Knee approached, well rested, his gear in perfect order. He showed me proper hitchhiking technique with my thumb, and he waited with me for twenty minutes; then he went on, hiking toward Maine, a broad smile on his face. A wizened old man in a rusty orange car picked me up and drove me down the highway dropping me off at the Franklin exit ramp. I shuffled my way into town. Franklin covers a sprawling area. I walked five minutes before I came to a bed and breakfast beside a golf course. Staying there meant sharing a bathroom and eating a community breakfast, neither of which held any appeal as that's how I'd been living daily. I needed a break with some privacy. The B&B owner grasped my fatigue and she gave me a ride down the road to the Franklin Motel, a cheap ranch building with all its rooms facing forward into a parking lot. Nabokov's *Functional Motel.*

My feet burnt like hot coals, but my day wasn't over; I still needed to buy healing supplies. I took a room, dropped my pack; then I limped down the street to a cash machine and a supermarket. I bought Band-Aids, aluminum pans, a carton of Morton salt, vanilla pudding, baked beans, M&M's, and more food to last through the night. Finally back at the hotel, I spent the rest of the day sitting on the edge of my bed soaking my feet in pans of hot salt water. It was a magical time. It was my first hotel room and a joy to be able to lock the door and lie down on my bed to relax. I wrote postcards, telephoned friends, showered, shaved, wrote in my journal, soaked my feet, poked through my gear, and read far ahead in the trail books to learn exactly what to expect.

It was my first night of television on the trail. I watched the *Ten Commandments.* By some incredible stroke of Trail Magic, they showed that entire four-reel movie all in one night. It was heaven to lie there watching Charlton Heston stare down the Egyptians, part the Red Sea, and point his staff all over creation while I ate my M&M's and healed my blisters in hot tubs of salt water. I called home and spoke with my father.

"What a surprise," my father said. "Are you *okay?* Is everything *all right?"*

"Everything's great. I'm fine. Just calling to say hello."

"Where are you?"

"Right now? I'm in Franklin, North Carolina."

"Well, where are you *calling* from? Did you find a phone by the trail?"

"Actually, I'm in a hotel room right now."

"You're in a *hotel?*"

"Yeah, I'm off the trail. I have horrible blisters so I got off in this little town. I'm soaking my feet. It's great—I'm writing letters, watching TV."

"You're watching TV? Can you do that?"

"Can I watch TV?"

"No—I mean, can you get off the trail like that?"

"What do you mean, like, is it against the *rules?*"

"Yeah. Can you just leave the trail like that?"

"Well, there aren't exactly any rules out here," I said. "There isn't a rule book. They don't have trail monitors. People do whatever they want. I'm heading back to the trail as soon as I'm ready."

"Okay. That's great. Here, wait, let me get your mother."

"Hi J!" she says. "So, are you *enjoying* yourself? Are you having *fun?*"

"Hi. Yeah. Sure. Of course. But honestly? It isn't exactly a question of fun. That's probably not the best word to use to describe it."

"Well is it *rewarding?*"

"Extremely so."

"Have you had any problems with *animals?*"

And on, and on…

I awoke that next morning in the Franklin hotel, in my small room, with camping gear spread out all over the floor. I looked out my window at a dismal, rainy day. *"You gotta hike in the Rain if you wanna get to Maine."* I knew it, yet I didn't feel ready to go. I didn't feel rested. It was too soon. I couldn't bear the thought of continuing hiking that day with my feet still sore and the rain and the task of working that long way back to the trail. On the other hand, if I stayed, I'd be following a 3.6-mile day with a *zero day* (hiking zero miles in a day). I was trying to reach Maine, after all, and I wouldn't get there by staying in one place. I didn't know what to do. I only knew that hiking on felt like too much, too soon—and then in an instant I realized that the pressure I was putting on myself to make miles had to disappear. I had to relax and be free to act as I pleased, and I definitely pleased to stay put. So I would stay put; I would enjoy; I would treat myself. I decided to stay a second straight day in the hotel. I had the money. I needed the rest. I needed the break. My feet weren't entirely healed, and my mind wasn't, either.

The way it turned out, taking that zero day was the wisest decision I would make on my hike, and it would turn out to be the single most carefree day I had. My decision made, I opened the window welcoming in a cool breeze and the sound of the rain, and I climbed back into bed with my unzipped sleeping bag as my blanket. I napped through the morning; then I awoke, soaked my feet and poked through my pack examining my things again. I napped, soaked, telephoned, wrote letters, wrote journal entries, and read my trail books all through the day. You have fun reading ahead, learning things about Pennsylvania, Vermont, New Hampshire. It keeps you focused, bonded to the trail, and it gives you lots to look forward to. It was Monday, April 5, 1993. At 2:30 PM, I watched the Miami Marlins expansion team play their first baseball game. They recorded their first hit in the history of the franchise, also their first stolen base, first walk, first strike, first strikeout. The game mirrored my early days on the trail—first rain, first river, first lake, first waterfall, first sunset, first view, first snake, first deer, first slip and fall, first lean-to, first hitchhike, first town, first hotel room, first bed, first shower, first telephone call.

I went shopping that afternoon, lugging home more food to last through the night. I set up my stove in the room to cook dinner. I had a can of baked beans (vegetarian, no pig-piece inside) but no can opener. With no way to open that can, I took it into the shower along with a chair, and I banged one chair leg down onto the can on the tile shower floor with smashing blows, over and over and over. That impenetrable can bent and dented one hundred small places, but it wouldn't break. Finally, with one last blow that Fort Knox of baked bean cans burst open. Sauce sprayed the shower. I washed the shower and I cooked all the beans that had remained in the can. Nothing tasted finer.

That night I watched the NCAA men's college basketball championship game—North Carolina winning by six. I lay with my feet sticking out from under my sleeping bag to let air flow over them to toughen them up. I did everything right for my feet. If Neels Gap had materially healed me, then Franklin had physically healed me. Falling asleep, I considered my crystal ball fantasy; how if before my trip I could have looked into the future to peek at what life was like on the trail, I would have seen myself enacting some of the strangest scenes—lowering a big dog from a shelter loft deep in the woods, lying in bed with remote control watching TV, standing inside a hotel room shower smashing a chair leg down onto a can of baked beans harder and harder, over and over and over.

6
Fontana Dam

They go! They go! I know that they go, but I
know not where they go,
But I know that they go toward the best—
toward something great.

—Walt Whitman, *"Song of the Open Road"*

Pondering Yonder.

Old, retired Jack Coriell picked me up at the Franklin hotel and drove me back to the trail. We'd arranged the meeting by phone the night before. Jack's name and number are listed in the hiker's handbook as one who will drive a hiker to or from the trail for a small price. It was a clear, bright morning. I was healed and eager to walk toward Maine. Staying in Franklin that extra day was the wisest thing I had done. I hadn't forced myself to leave prematurely, apprehensive, in the rain. Now I felt ready. I stood in the same spot where I'd stood two days earlier. Back then I'd felt I just had to get away. Now I felt there was nothing that could stop me. I had fifty-six miles left to reach the Smoky Mountains. I set into the woods and was back on the trail. I hiked over Wayah Bald mountain in a park with its tourist sidewalks, its tall stone tower and Port-O-Let. At ten miles I hiked up behind a familiar figure.

"Hey, Ponder Yonder!"

"Sneakers! I thought you were already in Maine by now. How did you get behind me?"

It was Ponder Yonder—the tortoise meeting the hare. We hiked together

55

the rest of the day. It was my first time hiking with anyone on the trail. I had grown to prefer hiking alone, but after two days alone in Franklin it was nice to have someone to talk to. The trail was crowded. We hiked up behind a gigantic Boy Scout caravan of fourteen kids and five leaders. They were inching along, and when they saw us, they were glad for an excuse to stop. They sent up a call from the back of their group to the front that was repeated in stages along the way,

"Stand Aside!"

"Stand Aside!"

"Stand Aside!"

The entire caravan halted and moved to the side of the trail. The kids had been taught to keep an eye open for through-hikers. They stared at us now to see what we looked like. When we reached the front of the group, their grape-shaped leader there asked us:

"Going the whole way?"

We answered, "Yeah, trying to. Hope so."

He smiled warmly and added conspiratorially: "God willing, right?"

Ponder Yonder and I were both atheists and so there was nothing obvious to say. It's dizzying to find other people assuming that you believe in their dogma. Later, alone, Ponder said: "Yeah, well, I certainly hope *the gods are all* looking out for us."

We stopped for the night at Cold Spring shelter, 15.8 miles on the day for me, the longest distance I had hiked. I was healed; my saltwater soakings had done the trick. This shelter was on the trail. Sometimes when you say that it means that the shelter is so close that you can stand on the trail and look out and see it, but in this case it was literally true—you could stand on the AT path and touch the side of this shelter. Its opening faced north, so we couldn't tell it was empty until we walked past it and peeked around the corner. We settled in. Two young couples entered later. They sheepishly shared the contents of a whiskey flask. A spring flowed from the side of an embankment twenty feet before us. Taped inside the shelter register was a typed copy of a famous 1854 Chief Seattle quote (never mind that a screenwriter named Ted Perry actually wrote large chunks of the passage for a movie script in 1971):

> *What will happen when the buffalo are slaughtered? The wild horses tamed? What will happen when the secret corners of the forest are heavy with the scent of many men and the view of the ripe hills is blotted by telegraph wires? Every part of the Earth is sacred to my people. Teach your children what we have taught our children, that the Earth is our mother. Whatever befalls the Earth befalls the sons of the Earth. This we know—the Earth does not belong to man—man belongs to the Earth.*

We were awakened in the darkness in the middle of the night by the sound of a small party marching by at 3 AM. We went back to sleep.

I hiked with Ponder Yonder all that next day. At ten miles we discovered a group of boys napping in a clearing. They were the teenage surge hikers who had passed us during the night. One hundred feet away, on a hill leading up a gully at the edge of the clearing, was the recently crushed *A. Rufus Morgan Shelter,* complete with fallen tree still lying on it. The fallen tree had split the shelter in half, splintering every inch of it. We had heard the story of a shelter that had been crushed by a tree during the snowstorm, and we suddenly realized that we now stood looking at it. A couple and their two dogs had been inside the shelter the afternoon that the tree fell. *The Family Circus* had settled there for the night when high winds had picked up. The wind had scared them so much that they packed up and hiked one mile farther north to the Nantahala Outdoor Center for safety. The tree had then blown down later that night. We walked over and inspected the damage. The tree wasn't large; still, the shelter hadn't so much as slowed its fall. Anyone inside it would have been gravy. It gave us the willies. How many shelters would we be sleeping in that summer, and how many trees loomed over the shelters? I wondered how The Family Circus could cope with the knowledge that they'd been one decision away from becoming pancakes. We continued on to the outdoor center where tourists milled about. There were restaurants, stores, and a kayaking and rafting center. I ate a garden burger for lunch in a restaurant. We walked to the outfitter store. A flyer posted on the door asked if any hikers had information about a district attorney who'd been found dead in the woods two days earlier. The flyer asked for information on the dead DA, an empty whiskey bottle, two teenage girls, and a French poodle. Strange thoughts filled our minds: *Anyone with information about a dead DA, an empty whiskey bottle, two teenage girls, a French poodle... a wok, a trapeze, two spatulas, rubber gloves, Johnson's baby oil, and a space blanket...*

But this was no joke. Inside, the store workers confronted us.

"Did you read the flyer?"

"Sort of."

"What do you know about it?"

"Excuse me?"

"I said, What do you know? Where have you been the past few days?"

I wouldn't stand for the questioning, so we left the store. We crossed a bridge leading over the river and we sat on the opposite bank petting a large dog that was tied there to a picnic table. We soaked our feet in freezing river water and we watched kayakers navigate the rapids through a course of hanging poles. We finally continued, stopping that late afternoon at Sassafras Gap shelter, 18.4 miles on the day—once again, the longest distance I had ever hiked. Two other through-hikers sat in the shelter. One was quiet, but the other, *Bear,* was an enormous heavy man with a big, lively mouth. His told us that his feet hurt: *"My dogs'll be barking tonight."* The night-hiking teenagers showed up and slept on a ridge above us in their tents. Bear told us that *Grandma Soul* had left the trail with a back injury. I had wanted to meet her. Grandma Soul was a seventy-six-year-old through-hiker who was just up ahead of us. I'd been reading her register entries for days. We would have caught up with her shortly. Bear described how Grandma Soul threw her pack on over her head. She would set her pack on the ground before her, backward, then reach her arms down over its top through its straps. She would grip its sides with her hands and lift the pack by flipping it back up over her head and onto her back in one smooth motion. She claimed it was the only way she could put on her pack unassisted. I took my pack out and tried it. The trick worked wonderfully. I had learned something new. It became the only way that I would put on a backpack for the rest of the trip and the rest of my life.

The teenagers were already up and gone by the time we awoke that next morning. It was my two-week anniversary on the trail. Ponder Yonder and I hiked 16.1 miles to Cable Gap shelter. This put us just six miles short of Fontana Dam, so we knew we would make it there the next morning. Cable Gap shelter was crammed with weekend warriors, so we staked out tent space downhill on an island between two branches of a stream. Remembering the flattened shelter, we looked up at the trees around us studying their height to gauge the length of their reach if they fell. Drifting to sleep that night I heard a very strange noise. It sounded like a helicopter blade twirling faster and faster, building to a powerful crescendo, then tapering off. The noise came again and again, over and over and over. I fell asleep to the sound— *"Thump, thump, thump, Thump-Thump!, THUMP!THUMP!THUMP!THUMP!THUMP! Thump-thump, thump-thump..."* I woke up to the sound. *"Thump, thump, thump, Thump-Thump!, THUMP!THUMP! THUMP!THUMP!THUMP! Thump-thump, thump-thump."* I must have lain in my tent quite awhile that next morning before consciously becoming aware that I'd been gradually awakening to that same sound of the helicopters, over and over. Was it my own heartbeat that I heard in my eardrum? I couldn't tell what the sound was. I had never heard anything like it before. I learned later that it was the sound of a grouse beating its breast with its wings. It was an awesome, powerful sound. Those strange, deranged grouse intrigue you with oddball antics your entire summer. Now it was mating time and they were beating their breasts to attract mates.

We packed up and set out that morning knowing that we would finally reach Fontana Dam. This would be our day for mail, food, shopping, laundry, and showers. We relished a glorious morning hiking an easy six miles reciting Monty Python skits:

"None shall pass."

"Wha—?"

"NONE SHALL PASS!"

"I have no quarrel with thee, brave Knight. I am Arthur, king of the

Britons."

The teenage night-hikers had tented off the trail the night before. They had slept late and we'd gotten ahead. We knew that only because they flew by us now, passing us yet again, making their own push for town. They weren't through-hikers. This was their last day hiking. They were spread out all along the trail. One after the other surged past us every five minutes or so. We stopped and saluted the speedsters as they passed. I called out loudly: *"You are indeed brave 'O Sir Knight! We would like you to join us at Camelot!"* Then Ponder would start in again:

"Who are you?"

"I am Arthur, king of the Britons."

"Who are the Britons?"

"Why, you are, we all are, and I am your king."

"I didn't elect you."

"You don't elect a KING!"

"Well how did you get to be king then?"

I took a faraway look toward the clouds, chin lifted, hiking stick thrust toward the sky and said: *"The Lady of the Lake held aloft Excalibur from the shimmering waters—"*

"Look, some farcical aquatic ceremony including a woman lying in a pond dispensing of swords is hardly a viable system for electing a supreme ruler. Electing a government must come from a mandate from the People!"

And on and on. We laughed loudly but hiked slowly, at ease after three consecutive post-fifteen-mile days. The sky was dark all morning. With less than a quarter mile to get to our road, it began to rain. We pushed on in the rain and slipped down a slope to the road, Rte. 28, where a two-mile hitchhike left leads to Fontana Dam Village and the post office. Remarkably, we got a ride in the rain within twenty seconds of appearing from out of the woods. Trail Magic! We jumped in the back of a pickup and huddled together getting drenched by the rain until we arrived at Fontana Dam Village. We jumped out with our packs and ran for shelter up onto a long covered porch connecting a row of shops—Fontana Dam Village. This wasn't as I had expected. Fontana Dam Village is simply a cluster of vacation condominiums and a recreation center and restaurant on a hillside, with a row of tiny shops at the base of the hill below the complex. I stood on the long porch in front of the row of shops—post office, convenience store, ice cream parlor, Laundromat, souvenir shop.

Night at the Hilton.

Hiking 163 miles from Springer Mountain in fifteen days brought me to my first post office drop box. It was very exciting. Everyone gets a PO drop box at Fontana Dam. There were a dozen people about. Other through-hikers milled about up and down the porch outside the shops, eating, talking, lounging, washing laundry, reading mail. Ponder Yonder and I entered the post office. We gave our names to the postmaster. We got our mail and brought our packages out onto the porch. "Awesome!" Ponder Yonder shouted. He had gotten a box of cookies from his sister. I had gotten my drop box, a letter from my parents, and a letter from my girlfriend—ten *pages long!* An excellent haul. My girlfriend—the Y—had sent me a ten-page letter. I read half, and saved half for later. But it isn't just the letters you look forward to at your PO drop sites. The entire process of arriving at your post office drop box site is one of rebirth, rejuvenation. You empty your trash here, throw out candy bar wrappers, empty food packages, empty peanut butter jars. You inspect your equipment. You clean, dry, air out your dirty things. You organize. You wash your clothes. And you load up with your things, clean things, dry things. New life. Rebirth. You start fresh with each PO stop.

Ponder Yonder and I spent a couple of fine hours on the porch drying out and relaxing while eating junk food, reading our mail and washing our laundry. I sorted spiral noodles into ziplock lunch bags. I threw out all my trash. One measure of how much I'd learned already was the way I could sort through my drop box and recognize all that I would and wouldn't need. I sent back home almost half my box's contents including canned tomatoes, matches, string and about half my powdered drinks. In the Laundromat, I met my first southbounder, *London Bridge.* He was a recent Bowdoin College graduate, thus somewhat of a fellow Mainer. He talked endlessly about the glories of his hike, lording over us all he had seen and how green we were: *"You'll get a rush at Mahoosac Notch—if you make it that far."* His hiking partner, *Raven's Wind,* was a day behind. They had been out on the trail for seven months. They were taking their time. They called themselves *The Wandering Taoists.* Suddenly, two of the Portland-Four pulled up in a taxi, *sans packs,* looking dry and as clean as could be. They said they'd found trail names. This young man was now *Twig,* and the woman was *Moleskin Lynn.* They asked if we'd seen their partners. They told a strange story of lacking cash and splitting up to see which of them could first reach a bank. Now they couldn't find each other. Ponder Yonder and I climbed the hill to the restaurant for dinner. I called home on a pay phone and learned that my grandmother had suffered a stroke. She was still in the hospital, in Nashville, Tennessee. She would be fine.

Through-hikers don't sleep in the village. There is no place for us there. Instead, we sleep at the *Fontana Dam Hilton,* a large shelter on the trail just beyond the spot we'd hitchhiked from. After dinner, Ponder Yonder and I called for a taxi ride back to the trailhead so that we could get to the Hilton and spend the night. Our packs were in perfect order. We set out. But as we stepped into our taxi, an older man, fifty-one years old, sidled up and climbed into the back with his hiking stick. He asked if we minded his sharing our ride. That was how I met *Hydro* (how could I have guessed at the time that I would hike the next eight hundred miles with this old man?). It is possible to skip a tiny portion of the trail by getting a ride straight to the shelter, but I had our driver let us out at the road we'd left off on, so that we could hike the 1.1 miles through the woods to get there. It had stopped raining, but the woods were still wet. Hydro walked behind me.

"I want to thank you for bringing us back to pick up the mile," Hydro said. "The last time I hiked I didn't take any shortcuts. That was years ago. Back then I was careful not to miss an inch, but this time it isn't as important."

"Did you hike through here before? "

"Yes."

"Did you hike the whole trail before?"

"Yes."

"You mean you've already through-hiked? You're doing it again?"

What a concept.

The trail emerges from the woods at the dam. Fontana Dam (480 ft.) is the highest dam east of the Mississippi River. The trail follows a sidewalk across the dam, but we turned off the trail and walked a hundred yards down a paved road to get to our shelter, the Fontana Dam Hilton. This gigantic lean-to has two huge open barn-hole doors, a high vaulted ceiling, and a view overlooking Fontana Lake and the Smoky Mountains beyond. Inside were four large sleeping platforms—two on the left, two on the right—and each platform could sleep a platoon of ten. Outside the shelter are picnic tables, barbecue grills and a drinking fountain. I settled in and finished reading the Y's letter. I had hiked 165 miles through the woods for that letter. Now I couldn't wait to hike 105 miles more for my next one.

Bear arrived carrying beer, and he proceeded to jabber away all night with an overweight female hiker who somehow proved a superior yakker than even he. The woman announced that she and her husband were writing a book. She'd had business cards printed and she passed them around. Her husband was just then out hiking the Continental Divide and she couldn't keep still about it—the glories of fourteen-thousand-ft. peaks, the glories of the Colorado Rockies. She talked up a storm, but she never once made the slightest attempt to engage a single person in conversation. With us was a strange old through-hiker called *The Preacher.* He and Bear lit cigarettes and sat smoking. Another solo hiker off in a corner was *The Pessimist.* He piped up occasionally: *"Only good thing about hiking the trail is escaping the government. They'd follow you in here if they could."* Smoky Mountain National Park rangers dropped in and confiscated Bear's beer. *"See what I mean about the government?"* said The Pessimist. Hydro lay silent in a corner through it all. Later that night, I escaped the bedlam in the darkness by walking up the sidewalk onto the dam to the showers and pay phone there at the visitor center. Lake water lapped to my right against the side of the

61

dam, while over the left was a vertical drop of five hundred feet to a trickling creek in the darkness far below. I took a hot shower. Hydro was there at the visitor center on the dam using the pay phone. I asked why he hadn't spoken up when Bear and the other braggart had blabbed away about hiking feats. He admitted that the chatter had bothered him, too—but he said that it wasn't worth mixing it. He told me the woman was wrong about some of the information she had claimed. She had prattled on about the Pacific Crest Trail (a twenty-six-hundred-mile trail from Mexico to Canada), and about the Continental Divide. He knew, he said, as he had through-hiked the PCT in 1990, and in 1992 he had hiked two-thirds of the Continental Divide before quitting because he'd had a Grizzly Bear scare.

Late that night at the Hilton, I sat and looked out at the mountains which rose up across the dammed lake. The park border begins at the dam, so those were the Smoky Mountains. And that was where we were headed, up into those mountains. I had heard of the Smoky Mountains before. I had been in them once as a child. Returning from our annual summer vacation of visiting relatives in Nashville, we'd driven east to the coast one trip before turning north for home (stopping at every Civil War battle site along the way). I was young then, and the name of the Smoky Mountains filled my imagination: Were they really smoky? My father had parked the car at an overlook. We had seen a bear. I remembered that now. I felt connected. Here now, these Smoky Mountains contained the first patch of trail where I had been before, the first patch that I had a connection with. But this time there was no car by the side of the road. This time I would walk into the park on my feet and walk out its other end. The Smoky Mountains. I slept soundly that night in the Fontana Dam Hilton. My pack was filled with food. I only had 105 miles to hike to my next PO stop and my next letter from the Y.

7

Smoky Mountain Big Miles to Elmer's Inn

I like to hike.

—Hydro, GA-ME '93

A Neighbor To Birds.

I had yet to experience a trail town. You reach some form of civilization at least once a week all summer—a gas station, a store near the trail, a restaurant, a town some miles away. But there are only three great trail towns on the AT (Hot Springs and Damascus in the south, Hanover in the north). Two of them were just ahead now, growing closer with every step. To qualify as a great trail town, the AT must run directly through the town, and the town must offer every conceivable amenity in a small area—shower, bed, pay phone, restaurant, grocery store, outfitter store, Laundromat. Early in the trail's history, back in the '40s, '50s and '60s, just a tiny number of hikers passed through these towns per year. As the numbers increased in the '70s, '80s and '90s, these towns learned to accept, enjoy and finally celebrate through-hikers (and sell them ice cream).

I had stopped along the way my first two weeks on the trail, but Franklin didn't qualify as a trail town because the trail didn't pass remotely close, and Fontana Dam Village didn't qualify because it was two miles off the trail and it wasn't even a town to begin with but just a row of shops. Upcoming, however, are Hot Springs, North Carolina (105 miles away), and then

Damascus, Virginia (180 miles beyond that). It is mentally a very easy time on the trail not only because you are approaching these two trail towns, but also because your hike is still new and exciting. You are filled with confidence now, and the beautiful Smoky Mountains rise before you. It would take me just five days to walk 105 miles from Fontana Dam through the Smokies to Hot Springs.

Hydro was first up and out of the Fontana Dam Hilton. In all the time I would hike with Hydro—in eight hundred miles—I would never witness another hiker rise and set out on the trail before him in the morning. Not once. Ponder Yonder slept in. I left knowing that I would never see him again. We had planned for the split. Now we would hike our own paces (I would be speeding up while he would slow down). A new phase of my trip had begun. I filled out a National Park tag from a box near the Hilton and fastened it to my pack. I crossed the dam, entered the Smoky Mountain National Park. *Raven's Wind* approached me walking south, on his way to rejoin his partner, London Bridge. He grunted hello. I gave him a message. The postal clerk had asked me to tell him that he had a package there (I'm sure he knew). He grunted again. *Thanks for grunting—have a nice day!* I guessed that perhaps he'd already had his fill of peppy northbounders. He must have been bumping into about twenty a day. So much for the dynamic duo, London Bridge and Raven's Wind—*the Wandering Taoists*. The trail leads steeply uphill, finally gaining a high ridge which it follows all the way through the Smokies. People are allowed to ride horses in the park, so the trail here is torn, gored and mashed with melting snow into a disgusting, slippery mud festival.

You never lack shelter in the Smokies. Shelter options north of Fontana Dam lie at 5, 9, 12, 15.6, 21 and 27 miles. At noon, I caught up with Hydro. He sat bare chested in the cold by the trail, his trademark green T-shirt spread out over a bush to dry. He ate from an enormous bag of GORP candy—M&M's, Cheerios, peanuts, pretzels, raisins, and sesame seed sticks all mixed together. He said that he has a physiological problem with sweating. He said that he sweats so much, he has to drink water constantly to stay hydrated: *"That's how I got my trail name, Hydro—because I'm water-powered."* I gained the high ridge and at 15.6 miles reached Spence Field shelter at five thousand ft.

Shelters in the Smokies are different from all other lean-tos on the trail; they are larger, made of brick or stone, and each one has a chain-link fence covering its front face to keep bears out. Hunting is forbidden in the Smokies, so black bears will supposedly approach shelters for food. I never experienced this myself. People do die on the AT, but they aren't killed by bears; they are killed by other people. No, east coast Black Bears are nothing to fear. Bears, wild boars, poisonous snakes: they aren't what you fear. The only animal that a hiker must fear is a human. Every several years or so, some hiker gets murdered. Still, statistically, it is safer to live on the trail than to live off it. I found the Jersey Coalminer at the shelter when I arrived. He was surprised to see me. He was a fast mover and proud of it. I had caught up with him before, but he had considered that merely a fluke as I'd subsequently left the trail to rest *("See what trying to keep up with me will do to you?")*. But here I had caught him a second time so he had to rethink things. Hydro made it in. We ate dinner and we asked Hydro questions all night.

"So the PCT is longer than the AT?"

"Yeah. It's a few hundred miles longer. It runs Mexico to Canada, on the west coast—up through California, Oregon, and Washington."

"What's that like?"

"It's very different. It's far less traveled, has fewer towns, no lean-tos. More dramatic terrain. It leads through the Mojave Desert and then up over thirteen thousand feet in the High Sierras. And the Pacific Northwest has extraordinary volcanoes."

"So what's the Continental Divide Trail?"

"That's the longest and most rugged of all U.S. trails. It also runs Mexico to Canada, but it leads through the Rocky Mountains, up through Montana and Grizzly Bear territory, and it is often trailless wilderness."

"Parts of it are trailless?"

"The Continental Divide still has long stretches of unmarked land where you follow herd paths and use your compass."

Hydro was the first repeat through-hiker I had met. At first you find it hard to grasp that there are repeaters. But in fact there are people who have through-hiked as many as a dozen and more times. There are those who don't even return home when they've finished, but they just turn around and hike the other way. It's called *"yo-yoing."* For many the trail is their life, the trail is reality. The trail's greatest legend, Ward Leonard, supposedly has peanut butter jars buried the length of the trail so that he's never far from food. Nobody knows how many times Ward Leonard has through-hiked—twenty or thirty times. Trail lore tells that his family is wealthy and perfectly happy to subsidize his modest hiking costs to keep him in the woods and out of their hair. It's rare to see Ward, as he doesn't like people. You are more likely to be awakened in the middle of the night by the sound of him tossing stones at the roof of your lean-to, or to see his drawings in the shelter registers—drawings of a long-haired hiker holding bars from inside a jail cell, while mountains and trees are inside the cell with the prisoner.

Through-hikers are ambitious. They have set a goal and they strive to achieve it. Still, AT hikers have varying styles. There are fast-moving athletes, slow-moving contemplative types, and partying youngsters who hit every town for a bar and a beer. Retired crew cut military soldiers hike past Dead-Heads (and vice versa). I myself liked to hike fast and far. Each hiker has their own way. No one can ever truly know what the hike means to anyone else. What can be said of old hikers who perhaps can't see so well, can't hear so well? Are they missing *the experience* because their senses aren't as keen as a youngster's? Or what of the young with keen senses who are limited in years so they can't as easily put their hike in perspective? Or what of the young partying hiker who walks through the woods feeling nauseous while nursing a terrible hangover? What of the scientific-type who charts the great variety of flora and fauna, always reading, studying, writing, without enjoying the unique social fabric of the trail? Or what of the very social who always hike with partners, who are always talking to someone, always planning something, so they never know the solitary silence needed for introspection? In the end, it is all the same—you hike and hike and hike. You cross a high mountain range through thick clouds on an overcast day when you can't see a thing. You have good days and bad days. You focus on a grand view one instant, while the next instant you focus on any of the billions of incidental tiny particulars at your feet.

There is no single right way to hike the trail. There is no one correct way to experience the woods. No one can judge the worth of your hike. You alone know what you gain from it. No one else will ever know the degree to which you appreciate the trail. But through-hikers do have one common bond—we enjoy the woods—we value our time in the woods. We have arranged our lives to be here. Here we are! We physically brought ourselves to the woods. Thoreau: *"I made myself a neighbor to the birds, not by having imprisoned one, but having caged myself near them."* Various ages, backgrounds, looks, philosophies, temperaments—yet we all feel good walking in the woods. We feel something elemental in the woods. The woods are alive. Trees and grass are alive. The feel of wood, dirt, stone. Freedom. Birds are free; chipmunks are free. We enjoy this surrounding life—the sounds, the smells, the feel. We enjoy walking in the woods. That is our bond. I do like challenging myself, setting goals, testing my body, moving fast and far. That didn't mean I was wishing time away or missing *the experience.* Fast or slow, my hike meant more to me than anyone could know.

The Hiker's Prayer.

It is cold in the Smokies in April up at five thousand ft. I rose and left the Jersey Coalminer sleeping in his bag. I would never see him again. My shelter options were at 6, 11, 13, 19.8, and 27 miles. I spent a fine day walking the ridge. I stopped and chatted with a photographer from Poland. I caught up with Hydro as he sat by a stream purifying water. Water is the greatest need on the trail. I didn't carry a purifying water filter (about half of all hikers do). I only carried iodine pills, popping two pills into my water bottle every time that I filled it. Hydro took gulp after gulp of water. I asked him why he was drinking so much. He said it is called *"cameling."* He said that *cameling up* is when you drink more than you're thirsty for at a water source just to stay hydrated longer in case there is no water ahead. He said that while this isn't so necessary on the AT, he still does it now simply through habit. Knowing what water to drink is essential. Fast-moving water is safer than slow-moving water. Freezing cold water is safer than tepid water. Swift, cold streams of melting snow high up in the mountains in springtime are safer than lumbering, murky tepid rivers in low valleys that are downstream from factories and animal fields. The remedy is easy. With any questionable water, you pop two iodine pills in your water bottle and drink—or you strain the water through your water filter and drink. Just don't ever run out of water.

At fifteen miles, I came to the summit turnoff up high on Clingman's Dome Mountain—and this is the highest spot on the AT. The summit itself is just a hundred yards off the trail, and I set out on the quick detour, not wanting to miss this for the world. I climbed through snow on a side trail that immediately joined a paved road leading up to the summit. I walked up the road past two old women emerging from their car. You can drive a car to the top of the mountain, just like you can on Mt. Washington in New Hampshire. Trees cover Clingman's Dome's mountaintop, and a cement tower stands directly on the summit with a gargantuan, winding wheelchair ramp leading up to an observation deck above tree level. So the summit of the mountain is covered with concrete. I walked up the wheelchair ramp to the observation deck. The deck is above the tree line, but the sky was overcast hiding the view. I returned to the trail and continued on, having stood on the trail's highest point. Hydro had joked: *"Clingman's Dome is the highest point on the AT, so once you cross it the rest of your hike is downhill all the way to Maine."* I walked over packed snow in my sneakers down the north side of Clingman's Dome. I reached Mt. Collins shelter (5,680 ft.) at 19.8 miles on the day. It was the farthest distance I had hiked yet, and further proof of my growing strength as I had hiked my greatest distance on the same day I had climbed over the highest point on the trail. But I still hadn't broken the twenty-miles-in-one-day mark. This shelter overlooks a field. Hydro made it in, making eight of us in the shelter that night (Hydro and I were the only two through-hikers). A woman out hiking alone for the weekend offered us fresh asparagus. Trail Magic. Hydro told me:

"You are very fast on the uphills, but slow on the downhills. I think your running shoes prevent you from crashing down fearlessly on the rocks on the downhills. Did you ever try K10-ies? They might be a great hiking boot for you."

I asked Hydro who was the strongest hiker he had ever seen (imagining that he would one day be naming me).

"There are a great many strong hikers," he said.

"Yeah, but name one. Name the single strongest hiker you have ever met."

I expected Hydro to hedge again, but instead he answered: "I think that would have to be *The Traveler.*"

Hydro said he'd been present once when The Traveler had put in a fifty-mile day, then bragged at a campfire that evening that he would walk into town several miles away to buy beer if anyone wanted. The group sent him out to get rid of him and he reappeared in the dark two hours later with beer. Hydro said that the Traveler was a bore and a terrific bragger, but he was also the strongest hiker he'd seen. Hydro said that hiking long distances is called doing *"big miles."* He said that we'd be doing big miles in Virginia. He said that there is no secret to hiking big miles: *"You needn't hike fast, you just have to start early and hike all day."* Hydro said that he didn't like the shelter social scene anyway. He didn't like to sit in the shelters, gabbing. He thought for a moment and said, *"I like to hike."* Those four words came closer to Zen than anything those Wandering Taoists had mustered. I saw seven deer in the woods out behind our shelter that night. No bear approached. I never once hung my food from a tree my entire hike. I slept every night from Georgia to Maine with my food right beside me, and I never once had a problem with any animals except mice (is that cause to be happy or sad?). As we drifted off to sleep that night, Hydro whispered over:

"Have you ever heard of the Hiker's Prayer?"

"No. What's that?"

"It's the secret Hiker's Prayer—*"Dear Lord, if you pick 'em up, I'll put 'em down!'"*

Hydro's Tree Laundry.

My shelter options were at 8, 15, 20.1 and 28 miles. We remained high on the ridge at six thousand feet all day. Bright sunshine. Melting winter snow kept everything wet. We could hear the ice melting, cracking off the mountains. The mountains were bursting. Water practically flowed out their sides. I drank the high, icy mountain water untreated. We crossed U.S. Rte. 441 which leads fifteen miles off the trail into Gatlinburg, Tennessee, with its Elvis museum and Dollyland amusement park. Some hikers exit here and hitchhike in for the novelty of it, but they rarely return unscathed. Glitz loses its comic appeal to anyone who's spent time in the woods. At nine miles, I came to a rock ledge called Charley's Bunyon, where a boy had died the year before. He had run ahead of his family and the wind had blown him off the cliffs. I saw a baby bear far away down a slope. It looked like a dog, but it was black as coal. I glimpsed it for only an instant before it dashed behind some bushes on the run. It was the first wild bear I had seen on the trail. I would see only two more wild bears my entire hike, a couple together in Massachusetts.

I caught up with Hydro late afternoon on some rocks halfway up an endless climb on a curve around a mountain. To our right was the mountain while to our left was open air with a view out over the Smokies. We sat peering up at the long climb left ahead of us. I asked my usual thousands of questions. Hydro then told me his story. He had spent his young adult life refurbishing a home he had bought in inner-city Memphis, Tennessee. He had rebuilt the home block by block, brick by brick, board by board. He had rebuilt its three-story chimney by hand. His project was art and survival mixed into one. He had been a hippie back then. There was substance abuse, a fiancée, bad luck, bank loans, anxious times. Bittersweet memories of his time in that house. A magazine featured his home in an article calling it *"Gentrification."* Finally, in the end, after twenty years, he sold the home for enough money to live on the rest of his life. He married a younger woman, a teacher who lived in Florida. They bought a small place there and Hydro cleaned up his life. He began walking; then he began to run. He increased his running to six miles a day. Then he bought a backpack. Then he set out. He hiked from Georgia to Maine. Then he went home to his wife. Then he hiked from Mexico to Canada. Then he went home to his wife again. Then he hiked up the Continental Divide, from Mexico up through the Rocky Mountains where he had come face-to-face with a grizzly bear in northern Wyoming. Now he was back on the trail again.

Fifty-one, quiet, thin, statuesque, Hydro had a handsome face, sincere and small modest smile, glasses, razor stubble, short dark hair, and thinner legs than you would expect after all that hiking. He was unconfrontational, nonthreatening. He was friendly to everyone, able to talk about any topic. Just like my friend Tinling, he seemed to have at least some little knowledge of everything. He always seemed more natural speaking with locals who lived near the trail than with the rest of us gear-conscious, mile-conscious, summer-vacationing through-hikers. Hydro kept a rubber stopper over the bottom of his hiking stick, otherwise the point of his wood stick would wear away and grow shorter and shorter. His backpack was an old-fashioned external frame. He hiked with his rain cover always over it, even on the sunniest days. During odd moments he would coach me: *"Lean on your hiking stick when you're tired. Or lean against a tree."* Hydro said that he had never told his story to any other hiker before. We remained on the rocks, silent. We sat quietly at the turn of the trail halfway up that monstrous climb, looking out over the Smokies. Just then a young hiker came panting, sweating, huffing around the turn. He had long hair in dreadlocks, and a long beard, both of which reeked of cigarette smoke. He seemed to be sweating droplets of beer.

"How's it going?" he asked.

"It's going," Hydro said. "It's going great. How are you?"

"Excellent, excellent," this hairy thing said, walking forward to shake our hands. "I'm Stone."

"Stone? I'm Hydro."

"Hydro." He nodded, shaking hands. Then he turned to me.

"Sneakers," I said, lifting one foot and pointing at it.

"Cool, cool," he said. Here was *Stone,* back on the trail after two days' partying hard in Gatlinburg, now aiming to rejoin his group of friends who were all up ahead following *Low Rider.* "So what's going on—are you guys taking a rest or what? Say, have you guys seen Low Rider?"

"He's at least a day ahead," we said, judging from his register entries of poems, songs, crossword puzzles, and drawings.

"Well, I'll catch up. Good luck, you guys. I'm pushing on."

Stone hiked on. He must have considered us two old farts dumped down by the trail, but little did he know. Finally we rose and put on our backpacks. I laughed to myself as we breezed by Stone not ten minutes later on that long uphill stretch. We reached Tri-Corner Knob shelter after 20.1 miles, making it the farthest distance I had hiked, and my first twenty-mile day. It had come on the eighteenth day of my hike. This shelter lies in the woods at fifty-nine hundred ft. It has no view, but faces a trickling brook. There was a clearing across the brook to the left and a ravine ahead and across the brook to the right. At the far edge of the clearing stood the exposed roots of a toppled tree blown down in the one-hundred-year snowstorm. The roots stood ten feet tall. Hydro hung his wet sweaty clothes on the roots of that tree—colorful socks, shorts, shirts hanging about it: Hydro's tree laundry! Stone arrived and played solo hackey sack in the clearing, kicking that little sack, bouncing it in the air off his knees, ankles, feet with perfect control. In the shelter with us was a father with his teenage daughter and son. They seemed unfamiliar with each other, as if he had custody just for the weekend. The daughter sat removed, whittling a spoon. The father spoke to us instead of her. He grew taken by the concept of through-hiking and proceeded to badger us with questions without the slightest trace of humility in his actions or words. He thought he was still in a board meeting which he could control, but we weren't on the board. He assumed we were wizards with magic and answers to all possible questions. That seemed funny to me. I wanted to tell him: *"There is no magic. This is new to me, too. We are all making this up as we go along."* He was taken aback by my Abdominizer. He couldn't get over the sight of it.

"What is that blue plastic sled on your pack?"

"This? This is an Abdomonizer. It's for sit-ups."

"Yeah? Well what do you use it for?"

"I use it for sit-ups."

"No, I mean, what do you use it for *on the trail?* What's the hiker secret? It looks like a sled. What is it, a fire fanner, a wood hauler, a pillow holder? Why did you bring it?"

"I brought it for sit-ups, so that I could do sit-ups at night."

"Ha, ha, ha," he laughed briefly, but somehow he still didn't get it. He wondered: Was I playing him for a fool? He swallowed hard, composed himself, and then, incredibly, he repeated his question a fourth time: *"Really.* What do you *really* use it for?"

"For sit-ups."

Businessman couldn't muster the gumption to ask the question a fifth time, so he turned away and I ate my dinner. The family tried to build a fire but were unsuccessful as all the wood was wet. I collected some tinder and built a fire for them. That is one thing I have always been able to do—build a fire. In starting my hike I couldn't use a stove, couldn't hang food, and couldn't pack well, but I could build a fire. It is not a skill that a through-hiker has any use for on the trail (we use stoves), but it was one skill I'd always had since I was a kid back at camp in the Adirondacks. After dinner I rinsed out my pot; then I walked to the edge of the ravine in front of the shelter and stood shaking the water out of my pot to dry it. I snapped my pot back and forth with my wrist, to shake out the water, when all of a sudden it slipped out of my hand and it flew through the air sailing fifty feet down into the ravine. Had anyone seen? Strange thoughts filled my mind. I thought I might fetch my Abdominizer and ride it like a sled down into the ravine to retrieve the pot. That way at night I could lean over and whisper to the dumbfounded Businessman:

"Look, I couldn't tell you this earlier because there were too many listening ears, but what I really use the Abdominizer for is that each night after dinner I like to throw my cooking pot way down into a ravine, and then I take my Abdominizer and I ride down to get it!"

Food, Food, Food.

My fourth and final day in the Smokies was my first twenty-five-mile day. The day began in the dark of morning with a familiar rustling sound. It was Hydro carrying his things outside to pack. I knew the sound by now. That was his system. He never packed in a shelter in the morning because the noise would wake the others. Instead, he carried his belongings outside and he packed in the cold and dark where he wouldn't bother anyone. Shelter options were at 8, 15, 25 and 36 miles. At fifteen miles I reached Davenport Gap, Tennessee, the AT's northern exit of the Smokies. There, a short hitchhike leads to *Mountain Mama's Kuntry Store* (people spell poorly in the hiker shelters deliberately—*"Ate a lite lunch last nite on my thru-hike"*). I didn't detour because I was moving well and I didn't wish to alter my flow. Besides, the "huge cheeseburgers" advertised didn't appeal to this vegetarian. At eighteen miles I reached I-40, one of the largest interstates that the trail crosses (you can't walk northward from Georgia to Maine without crossing a few chunks of perpendicular asphalt). The trail follows a road which dips beneath an underpass. Three men stood under the bridge beside a pickup truck. I was alone. They asked me a question. I couldn't understand their accent. They asked again. I still couldn't understand. They asked a third time:

71

"Have you seen any snakes?"

No, I hadn't. Strange thoughts flashed through my mind: *Say, you ain't from around these parts, are ya?*

Darkness fell at 22.7 miles on the day for me as I crossed over Snowbird Mountain with its radar tower, humming generator, and satellite dish (part of the national aviation network). I put on my headlamp flashlight so that I could hike in the dark, but it kept falling off so I carried it by hand instead. I trudged through the darkness knowing that my shelter was just three miles beyond Snowbird. My flashlight battery faded until it gave off just a dim ray of light, so I turned it off and walked in the dark, which was actually easy enough as the trail here was as wide as a street through the trees. I heard a dog (or a coyote) baying in the distance. I shuffled on, sticks cracking beneath my feet. Then suddenly I realized that the dog was barking at me! That dog knew I was there. The bark came from the shelter far ahead, down in a valley. I imagined the dog breaking from its chain, tearing off through the woods to get at me. I continued forward. I was afraid of the dog, but the dog was afraid of me, or anxious to get me. Alone in the dark and tired at the end of the day, your imagination runs wild. I grew close enough to hear distant voices and laughter from the shelter. At that moment the street-wide path opened into a large clearing where I lost the trail. I couldn't find it. I came very near to plopping down right there for the night, but the still-audible distant laughter pulled me on like a magnet. I finally found the trail and hiked down to the shelter. I stepped out of the darkness into the campfire light. The dog wailed. I had made it. A woman inside the shelter muttered: *"Unbelievable!"*

A large crowd filled the shelter and overflowed into two tents outside. Hydro was there. He introduced me. We had hiked through the Smokies and were down off the ridge now. This shelter lay low at 2,950 feet. I warmed myself by the fire. *Sawman,* an old man, muscle-packed, was the life of the shelter. He carried a saw with him and he sawed wood at every shelter on the trail. He was ten years older than Hydro and in the process of changing his trail name to *Bear* (another Bear). He had white hair and the most muscular arms of any hiker on the trail. He had been a parachute photographer. He told a story of how he'd once taken photos while flapping around tied to a rope outside an airplane, not even wearing a parachute. Sawman had held a large party earlier on in his hike, and now he was planning a major party in Hot Springs, but he had to meet up with Low Rider to plan the details. The conversation around that fire was all about food. *FOOD, FOOD, FOOD.* Through-hikers talk incessantly about food. The talk is greatest upon approaching a town after having spent several days in the woods. It is always the same:

"I heard there's a Western Sizzler in town."

"Western Sizzler? Not me. I'm heading straight for that meat-lover's pizza!"

"I could eat a whole chicken myself."

"Pork chops."

"T-bone steaks."

"Steak Tar-Tare."

"Beef Wellington."

"Clams Casino."

"Lobster Thermidor."

"Grilled Ahi on a bed of Belgian Endive."

It had greatly surprised me to find so many carnivores on the AT. I had been expecting to meet many more vegetarians. It is the greatest irony of the trail. At its core, through-hiking is a celebration of freedom, movement, mobility. Through-hikers understand how beautiful, essential, fulfilling this freedom is, yet they sustain themselves on factory-farmed animals that are denied freedom, that are confined in small cages. A carnivorous through-hiker either is not aware of this fact, or does not care. Or perhaps they believe that factory farming is somehow a part of the natural order of things. On the trail there exists the extreme—*Buckskin,* out in the woods proclaiming his meat-based diet with a source of pride. Buckskin, the frontiersman, leather-wearing, Bowie-knife-wielding, hunter-adventurer. Eating meat is a part of his credo. Here on vacation on this trimmed, orderly sidewalk through the woods, devoid of its native large animals, comes wild, rugged, untamed (untamable!), leather-clad, old-school Buckskin (hunter-man!) bravely stepping off the trail into town and plopping down at the local McDonald's. Whatever. Thankfully, at least no one eats meat in the shelters at night. In the woods all hikers are vegetarian. No one carries meat because it spoils. Through-hikers simply talk about eating animals while in the woods, and then they eat animals in town. I set up my tent and lay down to sleep, vowing never to hike in the dark again. I had hiked 25.3 miles in a day. It was my first twenty-five-mile day, and it had directly followed my first twenty-mile day. These were big miles. The next mileage milestone was at 26.2, the distance of a marathon. Next milestone after that would come breaking the thirty-mile mark.

Elmer's Inn.

Day twenty for me, and it was to be a town day. Hot Springs was 25.8 miles away, and I would make it there! I woke up late, alone, disoriented. Exhausted, I had heard no one leaving. It was eerie looking out my tent to find no evidence that anyone else had even been there are all. I got up hurriedly and packed. My shelter options were at 11, 13 and 22 miles; and at 25.8 miles there was Hot Springs, North Carolina, if I could make it that far. That town pulled like gravity, reeling me in. Shower, bed, laundry, mail, telephone, post office box, junk food—*SHOWER, BED, LAUNDRY, MAIL, TELEPHONE, POST OFFICE BOX, JUNK FOOD!* I hiked quickly all day, barely stopping at all. At six miles I hiked over Max Patch mountain, a grassy bald mountain with not so much as a tree

73

or bush upon it. Later I came upon Sawman sitting in a thin, airy wood, lying back against a birch tree reading a book (the only time I ever saw a through-hiker reading a novel on the trail). He said:

"Hey man. I'm looking forward to Elmer's."

"Elmer's? What's that?"

"Elmer's Inn, man. In Hot Springs. Look in the hiker's handbook."

I looked and read that the inn embraces an ethical philosophy of vegetarianism. Elmer, the caretaker, is a gourmet vegetarian cook. Incredible. I was shocked to think that I hadn't picked up on this sooner. How had this fact escaped me? Now it was right in front of me. It couldn't have come at a better time. I needed it badly. Suddenly, I was no longer heading for Hot Springs; now I was heading for Elmer's! At thirteen miles, I reached Walnut Mountain shelter where inside were parked a few of the through-hikers I'd only briefly met in the dark the night before. At 22.6 miles on the day I reached Deer Park Mountain shelter, just three miles short of Hot Springs. There, I made a mistake. I was very tired, lonely, hungry, and I stopped and talked with an old man who was sitting there alone. I had been alone for many hours myself, and I valued company. The old man was a retired minister, off for a night in the woods. Our conversation turned to religion. Of course we couldn't make viewpoints meet, and by the time I bid good-bye and rose to leave it was dark. It had been a mistake to stop, but nothing would stop me from getting to town. I set out in the darkness, my flashlight dead. Not twenty yards from the shelter, I stumbled into a dense bramble. It tested my will. I fought through the bramble and stumbled on. Moonlight helped briefly, but then clouds rolled in and hid the moon. I tripped on a root and fell forward onto my face. I got up and hiked on without lifting my feet very far from the ground. Then I stubbed my toe on a rock so hard that I wanted to cry. I told myself I would never, never, NEVER hike in the darkness again. *This time I MEAN it!* After three dark miles, I finally found myself on a bluff looking down over a valley lit up by hundreds of lights—Hot Springs. A beautiful sight. If I hadn't walked in the darkness I never would have seen that sight. But I was so tired, I didn't pause long to reflect. The trail drops down from the bluff, zigging and zagging to the valley of Hot Springs. It was too late this night for Elmer's, but I knew from the handbook that a Jesuit hostel with bunk beds stood at the spot where the trail exits the woods.

I emerged from the woods and found the hostel. I had hiked 25.8 miles in a day—the longest distance I had ever hiked. On each day for the last four days in a row, I had made my longest hike. It was 10:30 PM. The hostel was open as hiker hostels are always kept open. There were several hikers inside. A few were up, but most were asleep. Inside were four rooms with bunk beds. I signed my name in the register and set my pack by a bunk. I found a bathroom and brushed my teeth. I met *Buckskin,* who was younger than I was and much taller.

74

"Hey. You Sneakers? Enjoy that night hike? Hydro said to expect you tonight."

I realized then that Hydro had gotten to know me pretty well.

Hydro and I left the hostel early next morning, headed for Elmer's Inn. We followed the trail half a mile down a hill along Highway 209 into the very small town. Most of the few shops and homes in town face main street. We found Elmer's Victorian Inn, and we knocked on the back-porch door at 7:30 AM. Elmer appeared. Usually Hydro spoke for us, but this was my scene. I blurted out: *"We're looking for rooms. I'm Sneakers. I'm vegetarian and I've been looking forward to this for a long time."* Elmer is very reserved. At first he didn't understand. Lodgers from the previous night were in at breakfast, and they would need time to eat and pack before leaving. Elmer thought we were asking to enter right then, at that moment, but we weren't. We had just gone early to reserve space for later, as we didn't want to miss out. Finally this clicked. Elmer requested that we return hours later. He said he would give us rooms then. I was ecstatic. Perhaps Elmer realized that I wouldn't have taken no for an answer. We hid our packs on the front porch (risky), and set out to get breakfast. We ate at a diner, waiting for the post office to open. It was Thursday, April 15, my twenty-first day on the trail, my three-week anniversary. We collected our mail and carried our drop boxes and letters back to the inn where we sat on the sidewalk by the street, sorting, reading, hanging. Several through-hikers milled about, including the Portland-Four whom we'd left far behind many days back. They had already been in town two full days. Having not made good time in the woods (while on a strict deadline), they had hitchhiked around the Smokies. A passing hiker told us how a piece had broken off her pack. She had called the pack company, and the company had sent her a replacement piece which arrived in the mail the very next day, in twenty-four hours. Hiking companies take care of through-hikers. They know you are out walking in the woods, walking and talking. A great deal of talking: *"I bought brand-X, and it broke!"* They didn't want that.

We entered the inn at 11 AM. Built in 1840, the inn is listed on the National Register of Historic Places. Elmer bought it in 1978 and has run it ever since. Inside are antiques, sofas and chairs, guitars and sheet music, and most noticeably there were walls and walls stacked with books. Upstairs are three bedrooms and two bathrooms with large antique sunken bathtubs. Elmer led me downstairs and gave me a room of my own in the carpeted basement. The ceiling was low with a support beam in the middle of the room. There was one other room down there with a through-hiker in it. I had a large bed, an antique desk, a chair and one window high on the wall which had just enough room to look out above ground. I dropped my things, went upstairs and bathed in an antique tub with two scoops of green, pine-scented bathing salt. Hot Springs is famous for its baths. This enormous tub was so large that only my head stuck out. The evergreen smell filled my lungs. Intoxicating. My first bath on the trail. After my bath, I shaved and then weighed myself on a scale to make sure that I was not losing weight. I checked myself in a full-length mirror to make sure that I looked okay. I paused on the stairwell after my bath and leafed through a Mark Twain book from a stack that was topped by Frances Lappe's 1971 best seller, *Diet for a Small Planet.* Twain's book was creased open to a chapter called *"Judging the Animals,"* and I read a long passage that parodied humans judging the horse, the rabbit, the pig. The human court condemned some to death, others to slavery, others were granted companionship. Here was *Walden,* too, creased open to chapter eleven: *"On Higher Laws"*—nine pages that Thoreau had devoted to vegetarianism: *"He will be regarded as a benefactor of his race who shall teach man to confine himself to a more innocent and wholesome diet. I have no doubt that it is a part of the destiny of the human race, in its gradual improvement, to leave off eating animals."*

In the living room, I found Rodale's 1975, *Hiking the Appalachian Trail, Volumes I and II.* The volumes are rare, out of print. Each of the two enormous volumes is over one thousand pages long. I glanced through them, glad to have met Elmer. Someone whispered that Elmer had studied cooking in Paris. Someone else mentioned that he knew the martial arts. A third listener knew for a fact that Elmer had lived in Nepal for six years (I thought to myself that certainly Elmer had partied in Nepal with Eddie-B just before the two of them circumnavigated the globe in a hot-air balloon!). Elmer Hall publishes an Inn at Hot Springs newsletter, with a piece that reads:

> We will continue to offer the hospitality of the Inn based on the fundamental vision we have followed here since 1978. These goals are simple: create a warm environment that is sane, safe, and supportive; serve the best and healthiest vegetarian food as graciously as we can; charge as little as we can while still being able to cover our bills; invite the best guests, musicians, and teachers we can find; know that leisurely meals with animated, engaging conversation are a saving grace; be aware and care about what is happening in the larger world; be an active part of an ongoing personal, social, and spiritual transformation.

I passed the afternoon in peaceful comfort downstairs in my cool basement room. I lay on my bed with my sleeping bag covering me, reading my second letter from the Y. This time she had mailed me five life-sized footprints cut out from colored construction paper. She'd written her letter all over those feet. Those feet caught me up with her life. I sat at the desk and wrote her back, sharing some jokes to give her a taste of my life on the trail:

Through-hikers are like Godzilla: we have enormous legs, as thick as trees and as big as buildings, but our upper bodies have shriveled and shrunk into tiny, insignificant little arms which flap about ineffectively and serve hardly any purpose at all!

A woman in town sat on a bench and spied a through-hiker emerging from a store opening a bag of M&M's. The bag popped open and M&M's spilled all over the ground. The through-hiker stooped and started picking them up. The appalled woman cried out, "DON'T EAT THOSE!" The hiker sheepishly retreated and went back inside the store to buy a new package. Just then three more through-hikers walked up, spied the spilled M&M's and dropped down and started picking them up and eating them! (true story).

How can you tell the difference between a day-hiker and a through-hiker? The through-hiker will stop to pick up the spilled M&M's off the ground.

What do heartsick through-hikers write home to their lovers: "The SECOND thing I'm going to do when I get home to see you is take off my backpack!"

Whoops and shrieks from outside suddenly invaded our peace and quiet. It was Sawman meeting Low Rider outside the inn near the porch. They yelled and screamed, gleeful, boisterous. Crazy kids. Now they could plan their party. But the screeching sounded unnatural near the inn. Elmer had no rooms free for them, so they went down the street and grabbed a hotel at the far edge of town. A bell rang us for dinner. We had been asked not to be late. I hurried upstairs where I bumped into a tall, quiet young man sweeping the floor in smooth, gentle strokes like David Caradine—it was Coyote! I had thought I would never see him again. I had thought he had left me far behind in his dust. He had been staying at the inn for several days. Not only that, but he was remaining there indefinitely. People occasionally did that at Elmer's. Hikers would occasionally stop here and never leave. One of the cooks was a young woman who had stopped here two years earlier, while an aspiring through-hiker, and had remained here ever since. There were fourteen of us in the dining room, seated at three tables. There were many vegetarians including Coyote and a young through-hiking couple, *Bad Boy Bean* and *Katydid*. Before we ate, we were asked to stand, introduce ourselves and relate something about ourselves. I said: *"I'm Sneakers. I'm vegetarian. This stop means a very great deal to me, and I will never forget it for the rest of my hike. I've needed it so badly.*" I also added that I was considering changing my trail name, so that I didn't have to exist as a plural noun. It is indeed a strange concept that you can name yourself anything you want, and that this name will be your identity for many months. All along we'd had fun dreaming up deliberately dreadful trail names: *Squirrel Turd, Asswipe, Can't Hike Worth A Damn.* I'd been struggling with my trail name and I was even contemplating changing it. There was still time. I considered some possible choices: *Steppin' Wolf, Mountain Do, In Tents, Seymour Glass.*

Dinner was a five-course vegetarian meal of soup, vegetables, homemade bread, a rice dish with beans, a rice dish with onions and cashews, a pasta dish with tomato sauce, and apple pie for dessert. Elmer served the meal himself. It was part of his philosophy to be a quiet server who exists peripherally, silently helping, giving, serving others. On my entire hike from Georgia to Maine, just three meals would stand out: one was the frozen pizza at Rainbow Springs; a second was a bowl of ginger carrot soup with sesame crackers in a café in Delaware Water Gap, Pennsylvania; and the third was every speck of Elmer's five-course meal. A woman described fasting. Bad Boy Bean said:

"I hope in my life to be able to enjoy my leisure time. So few people are really able to learn to enjoy their leisure time."

"*Yeah?*" said Hydro, who had been quiet all evening. He looked up from his plate and spoke his first words: "*We used to have a name for that. It's called class distinction.*"

I retired to my basement room with the Rodale AT book, volume I. I sought solitude. I cared only to be alone with the book and my thoughts. I read about the history of the trail. One man alone had conceived the idea of the AT, back in 1921, Benton MacKaye, a forester, author, and philosopher from Massachusetts. Back then Vermont's Long Trail rose the height of that state through the Green Mountains from Massachusetts to Canada. Benton MacKaye devised his idea for the Appalachian Trail while seated on Killington Mountain on the already-existing Long Trail. He published his idea in the October 1921 issue of the Journal of the American Institute of Architects in an article entitled: "*An Appalachian Trail, a Project in Regional Planning.*" MacKaye was a regional planner who had valued his time in the woods as a child. He was focused on preserving nature. He designed cityless highways, and highwayless cities. He dearly felt the urgency of preserving green spaces. MacKaye saw the Appalachian Trail as "*a levee, the barrier of barriers, to control the deluge of the metropolitan invasion.*"

The first field work on the Appalachian Trail began in 1922, first in New York and then in New Jersey. The trail took fifteen years to complete (finished in 1937). Myron Avery, of Maine, became, in 1936, the first person to hike the entire AT, but it took him a decade to do it as he hiked it in sections (the first *section-hiker*). Avery was a Bowdoin College graduate with a Harvard Law degree. He is credited as one of those who brought the trail into being, having shown leadership during a time in the twenties when interest in Benton MacKaye's idea was waning. The first true through-hiker (and yes, in the early years they spelled out *through-hiker*), came eleven years after the trail's completion when, in 1948, Earl Shaffer, at age twenty-eight, through-hiked the AT in four months and one day. The first woman to through-hike was Grandma Gatewood. Grandma Gatewood through-hiked in 1955, at age sixty-eight. Grandma Gatewood later became the first person, male or female, to repeat through-hike when she did it again in 1957 at age seventy. Grandma Gatewood was one of the trail's original personalities. At the time of her first hike she had eleven children, stood 5' 2", weighed 155 lbs, carried no pack, no map, and wore sneakers (the original Sneakers!). Gatewood had grown up on a farm in Ohio as one of fifteen children. Answering why she wanted to repeat, she said: *"To see some of the things I missed the first time."* Gatewood always hiked by herself. She never carried a tent, sleeping bag, or frame backpack. Instead, she carried a blanket, rain cape, plastic curtain and her homemade shoulder bag. She went through six pairs of Keds on her second through-hike. She once tried hiking in leather boots but they gave her the only blister of her career and she went back to sneakers. Grandma Gatewood died in 1973 at age eighty-five, having added a third AT hike to her list (this one, a section hike), as well as a through-hike of the Colorado Trail out West.

I relished these random facts. The Rodale volumes include this passage: *"In 1890 the Census Bureau proclaimed that America was completely settled and no longer had a frontier. In 1960 conservation was occasionally being spelled with a capitol C. By 1965 it was one of the thoughts of the thinking man."* The trail passes through fourteen states, two national parks, eight national forests. A 1938 agreement still stands today between the National Park Service and the U.S. Forest Service providing for the "Appalachian Trailway," a mile-wide zone on either side of the AT stretching along the entire AT from Georgia to Maine wherein it is forbidden to build new parallel roads or any other development incompatible with footpath use. The Appalachian Trail is listed in the Federal Register as an entity under government protection. It took great effort to progress this far. Benton MacKaye, devisor of the Appalachian Trail, wrote this in 1921:

> The old pioneer opened through a forest a path for the spread
> of civilization. His work was nobly done and the life of
> the town and city is in consequence well upon the way
> throughout the country. Now comes the great task of
> holding this life in check, for it is just as bad to have too
> much urbanization as too little. America needs her forests
> and the wild spaces quite as much as her cities and her
> settled places.

8
The Place

*We ask two fundamental questions: What and Why? The
answers often enough have to do with a sense of
destination: the conviction that we are on a journey
that matters, the sense that we have something ahead
of us, a place waiting.*

—Robert Coles

Escaping Gravity.

After Hot Springs comes Damascus, Virginia—*"The friendliest town
on the trail."* Damascus is the second and last great trail town in the south.
Damascus lies just across the Virginia border, so you know that when you
reach Damascus you will have reached a new state as well. With twenty-four
hundred people, Damascus is twice the size of Hot Springs. The trail runs
through town, and through-hikers sleep for free in a three-story hiker home
called *The Place*. The Place has a grassy lawn where you sunbathe and air
out your tent. The town holds an annual through-hiker carnival called *Trail
Days*. Best of all, once there you can stop and reflect that you've then covered
one-quarter of the trail. One-quarter of the trail! To reach Damascus from Hot
Springs it's 182 miles (nine days?), snaking back and forth along the North
CarolinañTennessee border.

I overslept at Elmer's. This happens in town. You have grown accustomed
to sleeping outdoors, waking up with sun and birds, so then when you

suddenly sleep indoors, the morning sun tries to reach you, but it tires fighting its way through some small window off in the corner. I was up and out at twelve noon, walking north out of tiny Hot Springs. I passed a Dairy Queen, crossed a bridge, followed another section of the Nolichucky River, walked back into the woods and climbed straight uphill. The going was slow as I felt the tug of *"gravity"* from town. Gravity sucks you from both ends of town. When you approach a town, gravity pulls you out of the woods speeding you toward your destination, which helps. Yet later, gravity unfortunately also sucks at your back making it hard to leave the town and reenter the woods. It is difficult exiting a town while remembering that last shower, that last bed, or walking past that last pay phone. It is also difficult exiting a town while wearing a heavy pack. You enter a town with a light pack because you have eaten all your food in getting there. Next you spend a zero day in town walking around without wearing your pack. But then suddenly you must put on your backpack again to leave town, and your pack is now at its heaviest as you have just picked up your post office drop box and filled your pack with water and seven day's worth of food. In moving through the woods you have momentum; but once plopped down motionless and comfortable in a town, you must overcome inertia. And most trail stops lie not on mountaintops but in valleys, so approaching a town invariably means descending down from the hills, while leaving a town means climbing steep hills to get back into the mountains. Leaving behind comfort, convenience, and weightlessness to carry a heavy load straight uphill into the woods? No, you never bolt out of town; gravity sucks at your back.

The nearest shelter is eleven miles out, but I didn't make it there. I walked just eight miles and crashed. I found a level spot near a water spring, and I set up my tent for a quiet night alone. I was glad for that. I was sad to leave Elmer's, and after that wonderful stop, I didn't feel ready yet to get back into the shelter swing with strangers. Also, I decided to use my tent, as Hydro had persuaded me not to mail it home. Increasingly, I was growing to consider it nothing more than seven needless pounds in my pack. It was a bitterly cold night and I awoke with a thin shield of ice frozen over my tent and frost on the ground. I ate my morning PowerBar breakfast. Hydro had taught me to sleep with it inside my sleeping bag to keep it from freezing overnight, and then in the morning to put it between my legs to warm it. He also taught me to wear the same clothes day after day, no matter how bad they smelled, no matter how dirty, wet or cold they got, and to spread my damp clothes out under my mattress at night (after first hanging them up on nails in the shelters in the evening) to warm and dry them.

I set out as quickly as I could in the cold. My shelter options were at 4, 12, 19 and 25.1 miles. I had an early start, I felt strong, and I planned to catch up with Hydro who had blazed out of Hot Springs. Late afternoon, I walked up behind *Buck Naked, Tinman,* and *Bear* (yet another Bear). Buck Naked

81

was a seventy-four-year-old bowlegged three-time through-hiker with white hair and a pure white beard. He wore a blue Gortex rain suit. We reached Jerry Cabin where at four thousand ft. in the mountains was a mailbox (no delivery), a telephone (no connection), and a light (no electricity). I posed for pictures standing beside the fake amenities. Buck Naked scoffed: *"Hey, here's a broom. Why don't you come over and take a picture standing next to this broom?"* I left that group behind and continued on to Flint Mountain shelter, 25.1 miles on the day. Hydro was there with two strangers, *Macon Tracks* and his sidekick Chris (no trail name yet). They were both Georgians with Southern drawls. They were heading away from home; I was heading toward home. Macon Tracks had through-hiked once before. Chris was his satellite as I was a satellite orbiting Hydro, learning whatever there was to learn. I asked Macon Tracks what he did. Unemployed. He asked me the same, and I offered my job title, which he didn't seem to appreciate. I asked how he'd gotten his trail name.

"Are you from Macon?" I asked.

"No shit," he sneered. *"They really don't make 'em much smarter than that up north, do they?"* He proceeded in the next few minutes to insult all northerners, homosexuals, and everyone with a formal education. I decided that I wouldn't spend a second longer around him than I had to. If it meant that I'd have to hike thirty miles a day to get by him, I would do it.

I disliked Macon Tracks, but his skills and efficiency were impressive. He got out his stove in the morning and cooked a hot breakfast of oatmeal and coffee; then he cleaned up and packed all without moving an inch, and, incredibly, all in the same time it took me just to open my eyes, pack, and leave. Shelter options were at 8, 18, and 28 miles. At 9.9 miles, I crossed U.S. 23 at Sams Gap where the road was dug up, detoured, and littered with cones and heavy machinery (a road widening in all its glory). I climbed a barren hill beyond the road which had been transformed into just tree stumps and sawdust. At 16.9 miles I reached Big Bald mountain where I overtook *Sidetracker* and her sheep dog. Sidetracker was fifty. Her husband, *Chuck Wagon*, wasn't hiking himself but was following along in their camper, meeting her at road crossings, cooking her meals, and having her in to sleep whenever she needed. Chuck Wagon had a bum knee and a beer gut. He pulled a barbecue grill behind their camper. He cruised the back roads, helping hikers, drinking beer, listening to Chopin, having the time of his life. Everyone knew the Chuck Wagon. He cooked for you if you needed a meal. All stories were passed on to him, so he could provide whatever information you needed to know about who was where, when and why. Big Bald mountain is a grassy bald mountain with no trees or bushes of any kind on top. The light was clear. Sidetracker struck a sharp figure with her red bandanna, hiking stick, and powerful dog. I snapped a photograph of her hiking along. Then I ran on ahead and snapped another. She thought I was crazy. I had been meaning to take far more pictures, but I had no system for carrying my camera. My camera was too big to fit in my chest strap pocket where it would have been handy. Instead I had to take off my pack to dig out my camera. If a bear or a deer crossed my path I would never be able to capture the moment. At eighteen miles that day I reached forty-nine hundred ft. Bald Mountain shelter, sharing that double-decker chicken coup with Hydro, Macon Tracks, and Chris. It was another night of cynicism. Macon asked if we'd seen the Shelton graves from the Civil War that lay beside the trail a day back. The Sheltons were three brothers from Tennessee, Union soldiers who were returning home to their families at war's end when they got ambushed and killed by a group of Confederates. Macon Tracks joked about the glory of that Confederate ambush: *"The South shall rise again!"* Hydro eased the tension by telling Chris his *Just Bruce* story:

"We had a through-hiker in eight-nine named Bruce," Hydro said. "He didn't have a trail name. Whenever anyone asked his trail name, he'd say that he didn't have one; he'd say that his name was *'just Bruce.' 'It's just Bruce,'* he used to say. *'What's your trail name?' 'It's just Bruce.'* Well, it went on like that for a few weeks until finally he had his trail name. He was *Just Bruce* for the next five months."

Dead Elephant.

We were shooting for Nolichucky, with its hiker bunkhouse. I hadn't been long out of Hot Springs, but already a hot shower and a bed beckoned me. Shelter options were at 10, 17.1 (Nolichucky Expeditions), 20, and 32 miles. At sixteen miles, I ran into a backlog of hikers on the high ridge over the Chestoa Bridge. From a bluff we looked straight down at the bridge and river so far below that the cars and people looked like toys and ants. We all moved quickly. We ran, slid, and fell down the bluff's steep drop. It became a race to the bunkhouse. I reached the valley floor and the river ahead of the others. I crossed the bridge and hiked into Nolichucky. Nolichucky Expeditions has a remote, spacious, comfortable riverside spread. Hikers mill about. Some sleep in the cool screened bunkhouse, others sleep in tents on the grass by the river's edge. The office sells Coleman fuel and has a pay phone on the porch. Workers shuttle hikers and rafters into town. I entered the bunkhouse and set down my pack on a metal bunk bed. Over the fireplace mantel is a framed newspaper article with a photograph of a dead hung elephant, the elephant dangling over a gorge suspended by a crane. In 1947 the people of nearby Erwin, Tennessee, had held a trial for a circus elephant that had stepped on and killed both a child and a worker. At the trial, the town convicted the elephant of murder. A mob from town walked the elephant to the top of a gorge, tied a steel chain around its neck, and pushed it over the edge hanging it by a crane. This boggles the mind. I had to turn the photograph to the wall so that I wouldn't have to look at it.

Hydro arrived and arranged us a ride into Erwin to a Laundromat. Inside was television footage of a fire destroying a large building in the countryside. There were helicopters, tanks, ambulances. The caption on the screen read: WACO, TEXAS. It was Monday, April 19, 1993, and David Koresh and his Branch Davidians were burning. It was the end of a standoff that had begun long before I had left on my hike. What had happened? Why the fire? World news reaches you infrequently on the trail, and usually it seems either meaningless or unreal. Nineteen sixty-eight through-hikers Everett and Nell Skinner learned on Blood Mountain the news that Martin Luther King, Jr. had been assassinated; then later that summer, in a post office in Pearisburg, Virginia, they learned that Robert Kennedy had suffered the same fate (they must have been scared to arrive at any more towns). Nineteen sixty-nine through-hiker Andrew Giger had sat huddled with friends around a transistor radio in a shelter in Vermont, listening to commentary of Neil Armstrong's first step on the moon.

We ate dinner in a Pizza Hut at the mall. Hydro phoned home and had difficulty with his wife. Their neighbors at their Florida villa were causing her to question her wisdom for having allowed him to leave again. He blamed their petty jealousies for infecting her with doubt. The Nolichucky worker picked us up and drove us back, telling us about a course he had taken at the University of Alaska for climbing Mt. McKinley. Back at the bunkhouse, a large group had gathered: *Buckskin, Buck Naked, Buck-eye, Monkey Butt, Sun Dog, Walkabout, Kooky Moose, Macon' Tracks, Just Chris, Yellow Cab, Purple Peach, Pilgrim.* I met a through-hiking lesbian couple. A pair of lesbian through-hikers had been shot and killed down South on the trail back in 1984 by a local who had discovered them together and didn't approve. The Portland-Four were there at Nolichucky, settled down by the river in their tents. They popped into the bathroom that evening to brush their teeth looking as clean and well-rested as ever. They had hitchhiked here straight from Hot Springs, having not even attempted to walk in the woods. They did have their deadline to keep, after all. Actually, it was reassuring to know that we would see them at every stop. It was something to count on. They had been behind me, had never passed, and had wound up waiting for me at Fontana Dam Village. They had also been waiting at Hot Springs when I'd arrived, and now here they were at Nolichucky. I soon expected to leave every town before them, never once see them or hear about them hiking in the woods, but somehow incredibly find them waiting at the next trail stop looking as clean and as fresh as could be. So far they were keeping quite a fast pace. I wrote in my journal and tried to get to sleep early. I felt sad. I was growing tired of things—hung elephants, shot lesbians, bullet holes in every trail sign by every road crossing we came to. I wanted to bolt, to get the hell out of there. I thought maybe things would be better in Virginia.

Bolting away from Nolichucky, I was up and out second, behind only Hydro. Shelter options were at 3, 15, and 23.8 miles. We were back up at four thousand ft. and the terrain was difficult. I passed Hydro early and I moved fast all day. I reached Clyde Smith Shelter at forty-four hundred ft., at 23.8 miles on the day. No one else from Nolichucky made it this far. I had left an old group behind and had run into a new pocket of hikers. This was the first time I had moved past Hydro, although I knew for certain that I would see him again. The shelter was crowded. *Droopy, Snowflake, Hippie Dad,* and three others had spread their belongings out liberally, having not expected anyone else to arrive. I had once asked Hydro if he had ever seen a shelter too full for a hiker in need. I wondered what would happen if you got to a packed shelter during a rainstorm and you didn't have a tent. Hydro had told me: *"I once saw a shelter so full on a rainy night that two hikers had to sleep sitting up. Then another hiker arrived an hour later in the dark but there wasn't even any more sitting room. All those lying down had been lying on their backs. It was a small shelter and there was only one way to make room for the new hike—someone yelled, 'SUCK IT IN!' and everyone rolled onto their side."* This shelter wasn't as crowded as that, but I was bothered still by the memory of the hung elephant, so I sat alone outside on the ground behind the shelter and cooked my dinner. I discovered then that I had lost my spoon. One spoon was all I'd been using to cook and eat with; now it was gone. I improvised. I found a stick and I cleaned it as best I could. I cooked dinner and ate with that stick, diving into my pan, shoveling noodles into my mouth. Snowflake came around the shelter to tell me that they had made room inside.

"Hey, come inside. Hippie Dad cleared some spa—*are you eating with a stick?"*

Embarrassed, I looked down and discovered the stick in my hand. There was a noodle hanging off it. I had to think quickly. I said: "Yeah. I prefer to eat with a stick."

Fishhooks and Kidney Stones.

It takes time to catch your breath at the start of the day. In the early morning it feels good to go slow. Shelter options were at 5, 9, 11, 19.2, 19.7 (Roan Mountain motel), and 34 miles. It was bitterly cold. The trail led uphill immediately. I crossed Roan High Knob (sixty-three hundred ft.) at five miles, slipping twice down its far side on ice that covered a dirt road. I detoured off the trail to see dilapidated Overmountain shelter at 11.4 miles; then I staggered for two miles through a sudden, blinding snow blizzard while crossing the exposed, endless Hump Mountain treeless balds. The storm was fierce. Visibility nil. Legs aching. Wind-whipped thick snow in every direction, blowing me off my feet. At 19.2 miles, I passed the Apple House shelter *(MA From PA* were inside). At 19.7 miles I reached Rte. 19 and walked up the road to a grocery store bar. My legs were numb from that day's effort. Some locals sacked out in the bar looked me over, but I didn't feel bad as I knew there were hikers in there everyday. Besides, I was too sublimely tired to care. I called the Roan Mountain motel and Jersey John came immediately and picked me up. The hiker's handbook warns of disturbances here in past years. Locals angry at forest rangers had burnt down a shelter and had hung fish hooks from tree limbs on the trail at eye-level.

Hung elephants, murdered hikers, razed shelters, hanging fishhooks, bullet-riddled trail signs. And now a backwoods motel. I was expecting the worst at Jersey John's, but I was pleasantly surprised. I dropped my pack and entered a dining room where five through-hikers sat before a spaghetti dinner, tomato sauce only, which meant I could eat! At the table were *Garlic & Basil, Freedom Walker, Little TR,* and *Wrong-Way Peripidus.* This was a nice group. I'd known them all by their trail names as I had been reading their journal entries in the shelters for weeks. Garlic & Basil were vegetarians, a shy young couple. Freedom Walker, in his early twenties, was the poster boy for the AT with the archetypical ponytail, beard, chiseled features, American-flag bandanna. He was gregarious, articulate. I would learn later that he would never finish his through-hike. He would leave the trail in the middle of the summer to work at a kids' camp. Little TR was eighteen or nineteen, through-hiking with his father, *Big TR.* They'd been hiking together until four or five days ago when Big TR had gone on ahead. Now Little TR not only couldn't catch up, but he was chagrined and a little embarrassed and hurt to find that his father didn't appear to be showing any sign of slowing down to wait for him. Little TR asked me to get a message through to his father—to stop and wait! *Wrong- Way Peripidus* (a peripidus, apparently, is a slow-moving snail) was a forty-year-old high school biology teacher traveling alone. He knew everything about plant life. He would often stop to identify family, genus, and species of things along the way. Habitually, he supplemented his evening meals with roots and plants. This had nearly gotten him into trouble. One night in a shelter on the trail Peripidus ate some roots and mushrooms for dinner as was his custom. Then later, at midnight, he awoke in the shelter, clutching his stomach and screaming in pain in the darkness. He turned to the hikers beside him and said: *"I ate a poisonous mushroom. I think I'm dying."* Then he rolled to the front of the shelter and vomited. Alarmed, a through-hiker named *Unleashed* carried Peripidus four miles out of the woods in the middle of the night and got him a ride to a hospital. It turned out that Peripidus hadn't poisoned himself at all, he was merely passing a kidney stone.

Six of us slept in a single room. Morning options for a ride back to the trail were 7 AM or 10 AM. Only Wrong-Way Peripidus and I left early. Shelter options were at 13, 21.3 and 32 miles. Deep wet snow covered the ground. The snow had fallen fast and dry up high on Hump Mountain, but down here the snow had fallen thick and heavy and wet. This snow covered signs, weighed down leaves, snapped off tree branches. Wrong-Way Peripidus and I set out but got lost in a snow bowl. We couldn't find where the trail led up out of the valley. We trudged up and down the valley slopes until we finally found the trail. That was actually a great fear of mine, that after a full day's hike I would suddenly discover that I'd headed south. It had happened weeks earlier to Wrong-Way Peripidus. Back on the trail after passing the kidney stone, in one of that summer's most classic maneuvers, he had sat down at a shelter with two young through-hikers and they all ate lunch together. Peripidus finished first, and he rose, bid them good-bye and started off. They called out to him: *"Hey! You're walking south! You're going the WRONG WAY!"* Peripidus said no, he was sure that he was heading north, and off he went. He hiked south for two hours before he discovered his error. They called him *Wrong-Way Peripidus* after that.

I hiked on ahead of Wrong-Way Peripidus and struggled for hours fighting my way through soaking-wet river valleys of snow-covered rhododendron. Snow-laden rhododendron leaves hung low, barricading the trail. Pushing through them meant taking a shower, water spraying me from every direction. I got soaked to the bone. It was my wettest day on the trail. Then I slipped and fell in a freezing puddle of slush, landing on my hiking stick and breaking it in half. That is always traumatic. You get used to your hiking stick (its weight, its shape, its feel), and then when it breaks—when that relationship ends—you must leave the easy path and stomp about in the dense woods to find another. I passed Moreland Gap shelter at 13.6 miles where inside lay *The Janitor* still in his sleeping bag at 2 PM. He had fallen sick and had slept in. At 20.6 miles I followed the trail down to a riverbed and waterfall in Laurel Fork Gorge, then climbed back up again to Laurel Fork shelter. Section-hikers were settled there with a friend who was visiting from Germany. The German woman spoke broken English with a German and Southern drawl that was not pretty to hear. The Janitor arrived and made vanilla pudding for her. She was old enough to be his mother, yet they had developed some type of bond. They lay close together, face-to-face, side by side in their sleeping bags, whispering. Looking out, I saw one of my few sunsets of the trail. A tiny bat the size of a lifesaver roll hung above us inside the shelter from one of the ceiling beams. It hung so motionless with its wings wrapped around it that we couldn't tell if it was alive, dead, brave, stupid, sleeping, or frozen. We let it be.

I had 49.9 miles left to reach Damascus and my post office drop box #3. I calculated the day of my expected arrival in town. You pay attention to when you will arrive in town because you want your mail. We were fifty miles out on a Thursday night with a long, flat section of trail ahead. Hydro had told us that this was one of the easiest stretches on the entire trail. He said if there's anyone who hasn't yet hiked a twenty-mile day, they will get it here if they want. For me, two twenty-five-mile days would get me to town Saturday evening, too late for the post office and my mail (my M&M's, my letter from the Y). A situation like this meant that I could either slow down or speed up. I could slow down, relax, and collect my mail Monday morning, or I could speed up and race to beat the clock. I knew what to do. The post office hours were 8 AMñ11 AM Saturday morning, and I was determined to reach there by then. Night hike, no sleep, whatever it took I would have my mail. A fifty-mile dash. My food was nearly gone so my pack weight was low. And this fifty-mile stretch of trail heading north into Damascus was supposed to be easy. That night I wrote in the shelter register:

April 22, 1993—spent a wet day hiking through wet snow. Loved Jersey John's! Unfortunately got a fish hook caught in my eyeball upon reentering the woods. The hook had a line attached to it tied to a tree branch. The branch broke off and I wound up dragging the branch through the woods by my eyeball. It might not have been so bad except that I discovered later that a section-hiker had jumped on for the ride. I think I'll leave the fish hook in my eyeball and drag the branch and the section-hiker all the way to Katahdin.

Fifty-Mile Dash.

Up and out before 6 AM, I began my fifty-mile dash. At one mile I came to the base of Pond mountain. The AT turns right and climbs three thousand feet over Pond Mountain, but there is a blue-blazed shortcut which leads straight ahead and follows level ground knocking five miles off your hike. Blue-blazing around Pond Mountain is common. Pond Mountain is the AT's litmus test for blue-blazers. Hurry or no hurry, mail or no mail, I never considered taking the blue-blaze. The trail leads over Pond Mountain, so I turned right and climbed over Pond Mountain (searching for a new hiking stick all the way). I found a new hiking stick, but I had grown so accustomed to looking for them that I accidentally found another one, too. I double-fisted, hiking along with them both, trying to decide which one to keep and which to discard. I took an early lunch at Watauga Lake shelter at 10.7 miles at 10 AM. I passed Vandeventer shelter at seventeen miles, and later sat with *Beauty and the Beast* at Iron Mountain shelter at 23.7 miles at 3:45 PM. Beauty and the Beast were a couple, but they weren't getting along. Their trail joke was that he was *Beauty* while she was *The Beast.* It was a good joke, except that later they would separate on the trail and he would walk up alone to a shelter of men none of whom he had met before.

"Who are you?" they would ask.

"I'm Beauty."

Farther on, I got the worst scare of my hike. Twilight had fallen and under a dark sky I suddenly spied someone up ahead standing beside the trail on a deserted jeep road. Creepy! I stopped to observe. Who was this, and what was he doing here? The man didn't move, so I didn't move. Why was he standing out here in the dark? How could this man be up to anything good? His just standing there unnerved me. Minutes passed. I had to decide. I couldn't wait forever. I wondered if I should hike a wide circle through the woods around this stranger, or if I should walk straight up, greet hello, and walk by. My heart raced. I finally inched forward. I crept cautiously closer, as I had to continue my hike. The night was black now. I inched closer and closer. Closer and closer. Then finally I saw—a scarecrow! Someone had fitted a rubber wet suit over a cross, complete with rubber gloves, boots and a ski hat. The fright had drained me. It quelled my enthusiasm for miles. I continued in the dark just one mile farther, stopping at Double Springs shelter at 31.7 miles on the day—the longest day I had hiked (longer than the length of a marathon, and so far the farthest distance I had ever traveled on my feet in one day in my life). This shelter was empty so I was alone on my quest, without comfort or companionship. Eighteen point two miles shy of town, I had until 11 AM the next morning to make my mail. I would make it. I lay down. No stove, no dinner. I barely unpacked. I munched on snacks in the dark and set my alarm for 4 AM.

At 3:45 AM, I sprang bolt upright in a sweat in the utter darkness. My heart pounding. I gasped. Something had awakened me. I had heard something. An animal? What? I was primed, wired, adrenaline surging. I reached out and gathered my things in the dark with a wave of my arm, pulling things toward me, blindly, stuffing things in my pack. I set out with my new pen flashlight (had bought in Hot Springs) and walked north fifty yards up a slope to a clearing, but there I lost the trail. I followed a wide dirt road to the left, but there were no blazes on it. After thirty yards, the dirt road narrowed to a path and then the path narrowed and stopped dead. No blazes anywhere along the way—a bad sign. My pen light was dim. I fumbled in the dark for forty minutes, walking up and down the path, up and down the dirt road and all around the clearing trying to find the trail. At 4:30 AM, I finally gave up. I'd had enough. My search was futile. I had run out of time. I wouldn't make it. My mail would have to wait. My letter from the Y would have to wait. I was tired, frustrated. Now I only wanted to sleep. I started walking back to the shelter, but I hadn't taken ten steps before I saw lights bumping around from out of the woods down near the shelter coming toward me. It was frightful. Another frightful sight. Was it hard-core through-hikers who had risen early and were hiking along at 4:30 AM? Who else would be up this early? I called out loudly:

"Hey! Who is that?"

An answer came through the woods: *"Turkey hunters."*

Two men with shotguns walked up the trail and shone their flashlights on me. They discovered me standing there in the darkness on the trail wearing my backpack. They shined their lights around the clearing and found a white blaze to the right where the trail led into thick bushes. I hadn't seen that. New hope. I gave thanks and set out. The sun soon rose; the going was easy; the ground was flat. For eighteen miles I shuffled, danced, ran, and flew, constantly calculating and recalculating my time to determine whether or not I would make the post office. I passed a little snowman in a patch of snow by the trail. It was the last snow I would see on my hike. My last sight of snow came on my last day before entering Virginia. At 14.7 miles I reached the state border and stepped out of Tennessee and into Virginia. Three states down, eleven to go. It was 9:45 AM. With just 3.5 miles to go, I picked up my pace, jerking, jogging down the trail. I knew that it would be close. I shuffled down a hill, practically bowling over a pack of incredulous day hikers, and I popped out of the woods into a residential neighborhood at 10:45 AM. The post office closed at 11 AM. The trail led straight ahead into town, but I didn't care about the trail now. I had made it to the center of town, so I no longer cared about the trail. I only cared about the post office. I had come too far. But how far away was I still? I stopped an old woman who was just at that moment backing her car out of her driveway beside me. I asked for the post office—I only had fifteen minutes before it closed. One false move and my fifty-mile push was for nothing. The woman said: *"Take your first left, then go straight three blocks and—no...go straight ahead two blocks to Holy Angels, then when you see the bridge by the—no..."* I couldn't stand it, so I cut her off. I asked if she would take me there. She wasn't afraid; she knew through-hikers. She could see I was frantic. I threw my pack into her car and she drove me six blocks through town depositing me in the post office parking lot at 10:50 AM. Ten minutes to spare. I had made it! I had made my fifty-mile dash by ten minutes. I entered the post office and picked up my drop box #3 and two extra letters (what if my package and mail hadn't been there?). I carried my mail one block to the center of town, picked up the trail's white blazes and followed the AT three brief blocks to *The Place*. I recognized the house from a photo I'd seen.

A Hug from the Y.

Damascus, Virginia. There were hikers inside The Place, but all were busy. The entire house was just for through-hikers. No one took much notice of me. I plopped down on the bottom mattress of a bunk bed in a side room on the ground floor, my sleeping bag covering me as a blanket. I broke open a package of M&M's and I read the first page of my letter from the Y. Then I closed my eyes in happiness. I had made it. I had my mail. I was happy. I relaxed. Napped. Dreamt of the woods.

"Who's this guy?"

"I don't know. He showed up this morning and crashed."

"He's been sleeping all day."

I awoke from my nap—activity in the house, voices in the room, some hikers about, backpacks, a lawnmower whirling far off, the smell of mown grass wafting in with a breeze through an open window—spring breeze! Sunshine. Laughter. I had slept several hours. Still, I remained in bed. There was no place I needed to go, nothing I needed to do. My legs tingled. They twitched. It felt good just to lie in bed. *Jersey* came and said hello. She knelt beside my bed. She was a young through-hiker from New Jersey with short dark hair. I told her my story of the turkey hunters in the dark and how I'd raced for my mail. Next I met *Mozyin'*. He was also twenty-nine, like me, and almost entirely bald. We could have been brothers except that he had twenty more pounds of muscle on him. I told Mozyin' how the old woman at the edge of town had carted me to the PO so I'd missed my first little bit of trail. Mozyin' hadn't missed a centimeter of trail (nor would he all summer). Of all the Purists on the trail, he was the most pure. Of the hundreds of hikers of various styles, temperaments and personalities on the trail that summer, here was the one hiker that many admired the most. A Penn State grad, frat boy, sub-3:10 marathon runner, he had quit his job for the hike. The two of us agreed that Jersey was the goddess-ideal of female through-hikers and we both fell in love with her. She was friendly and strong, gracious, graceful, and beautiful. Beauty enjoys a natural look in the woods, where makeup and hairstyles don't belong. The essence of beauty is pure in the woods. Sun warms your face; wind blows your hair; a cold chill reddens your cheek; your body grows lean and strong climbing hills and mountains. The search for the sight of a secret pond makes your eyes sparkle, grace develops tiptoeing over stones in crossing a creek. The sun, the moon, the wind, the stars, the grass, the leaves, the noises, sights and smells of the forest are the most natural makeup of all. Hikers feel alive in the woods. Alive and aware. You appreciate a simple meal in a pot in the dark in the deep woods at night in a shelter. You enjoy easy talk there with friends.

I rose from bed that afternoon and walked to the outfitter store. Inside was a rack of shelves devoted to hunting video tapes—a man with his arm lovingly around a boy, the boy sighting a gun, both of them wearing camouflage clothes, a dead deer slumped by a tree in the background. I walked through the store. I bought a new spoon and a hiking stick. It was my first store-bought hiking stick. I needed one that would last because I couldn't stand the heartache of breaking another one. A newspaper reporter was in the store interviewing hikers for the annual *Trail Days* insert for the town paper. Each spring Damascus holds a festival called Trail Days, but the festival wouldn't begin for another couple weeks. The reporter took my photograph and he took down my trail name. I met *The Family Circus* in the store. It was this couple with their two dogs who had almost been squooshed in the A. Rufus Morgan shelter by the fallen tree. Outside the store were *Food Dude* and *Easy Stryder*—two athletes, strong hikers. They snubbed me. Food Dude was big, tall, arrogant. *A walking arrogance machine.* One year out of UNH, he had been captain of his college rowing team. He'd gotten his trail name in a restaurant by eating four ham sandwiches, french fries, coffee, a Coke, and a pizza and then when his friends came in to eat, he sat with them and ordered dinner. Someone who saw him later that night had stopped and pointed at him from across the street, yelling out: *"Hey, I know you—you're that FOOD DUDE!"*

The Place is owned by an adjacent Methodist church. It is only for through-hikers. It has a kitchen, bedrooms, bathrooms, and showers. You do what you want, but you are asked to stay no longer than two days. Hikers lounge about. I showered upstairs. I signed the register. Hikers stay in a variety of places in other towns, but here in Damascus this is the one and only place to stay. I met *Big TR, Blazer, Heel and Toe, Tea Bag, Jive Mama, Towanda, Llama Mama, Chaos,* and *Kilgore Trout.* Big TR promised that he would stop there and wait for Little TR. Blazer was a tough old military man from the Adirondacks. A decorated Vietnam War veteran, he was retired from the army and also retired from work at a saw mill. He was hiking partners with Easy Stryder who was much younger but also out of the military. *Heel and Toe* were an older couple from Michigan. They were high school science teachers who lived on a self-sufficient farm. They bought all their food from stores along the trail and they kept scientific journals. She was Toe because she always hiked in front. They had begun early and had gotten hit by the snowstorm; then weeks later Toe had broken her right forearm from a slip on the ice coming down Roan mountain (exactly where I had slipped and fallen twice myself). She had just gotten her cast off and she now carried her X-ray negatives in her pack from town to town for checkups. Tea Bag had come over to hike from England. He was the tallest hiker on the trail. His pack was tall, too, reaching so high over the back of his head that he constantly ducked, bobbing and weaving as he hiked along so as not to hit tree branches. We tried calling him *London Tower* but he wouldn't accept the name change. He was hiking partners with Jersey. That faked us out as we'd thought that they were a couple. Towanda and Jive Mama were both eighteen, vegans and intrepid environmentalists. They left nothing in the woods. They swallowed their toothpaste when brushing instead of spitting it out, and they bagged and toted out even their used toilet paper. They never even bathed in creeks. Jive Mama had red hair and freckles. She was tough, a former gymnast. But Towanda wasn't as strong. She had never played sports, and she now found herself in foreign territory. Her feet were blisters, her legs were tired, and she was unsure of herself. Her knees had hurt so much that she had spent two days walking through the woods crying in pain. She lacked an athlete's knowledge. An athlete knows how to read their body. An athlete might have pulled up short to rest, if they felt that such terrible knee pain was something that should be listened to. Towanda didn't understand how to listen to her pain. Llama Mama was lanky and tall, full of enthusiasm. He was a good, cheerful kid, although having read his trail name I really had been expecting him to be a woman. Chaos was a journalist out hiking with her dog. And last but not least, there was Kilgore Trout, from Boston. He had been in business. Kilgore smoked a pipe and wore a straw hat. He was terrifically eccentric at age twenty-six. He wore red gaiters and hiked with two ski poles, one in each hand, skiing his way up the trail. He sat grinning from ear to ear.

"Kilgore Trout? How do I know that?" I asked.

"Do you read Kurt Vonnegut?"

"Kurt Vonnegut? Yeah."

"Kilgore Trout is the bad science-fiction writer—"

"Oh yeah!"

"Yeah. You know. He's the science-fiction writer in all the Kurt Vonnegut novels who is so bad he can only get his stories published in the airport paperbacks—"

"—that get illustrated with the pornographic drawings!" I say.

I lay back in bed and I finished reading my letter from the Y. This time she had mailed me a hug—a torso made from construction paper with life-sized arms that folded out in a five-foot wingspan to wrap around me. Her tiny practically microscopic writing covered the body, the arms, the hands. Beauty and the Beast made it in. I walked outside and The Beast took a photo of me standing in front of The Place with my hug. Dinner was pizza in a restaurant. I had my first beer on the trail. A shirtless, tan Hawaiian man with an enormous beer belly spent the day lying outside on the front lawn. It was day #30 for me, my one-month anniversary on the trail. I slept.

I awoke refreshed. It was Sunday, April 25, day thirty-one, and this would be a zero day in town. I walked to the town library and read stories out of the rare and hard-to-find Rodale AT books, volumes I and II. Jersey's ex-boyfriend showed up at The Place on a BMW motorcycle with a built-in CD player and a headset in his helmet. He let teenaged Llama Mama ride his motorcycle up and down the street. Kilgore also had friends who showed up in a car, and four of us drove to a mall in the next town where we all bought lightweight, fake Teeva sandals to wear around the shelters at night. Here was my first chance to get rid of my gimmick trail-running sneakers, which I never had grown to like. The tiny shoe store here had only two pairs of running shoes—Discount Running Shoes. I asked the worker why they were so cheap. She answered that they had the cheapest prices around (she never mentioned anything about their being factory rejects, but I would find that out for myself later). I never returned to pick up my missing .4 miles of trail at the south edge of town. If I had missed forest miles, I would have gone back, but this was just town yardage I'd missed and I figured that the amount of town miles I'd walked in those two past days more than made up for it. Dinner was french fries and a cheeseless veggie sub at a Dairy King. Back at The Place, I sorted through my pack. I decided then to mail home my Abdominizer from the PO Monday morning before leaving town. Everyone said I should keep it, just for a joke. But it never had been a novelty gag for me. I had carried it in earnest; I had just never used it. I finally realized, however, that it was a crutch subconsciously linking me to my life off the trail. I had to let it go. I couldn't be afraid any longer. I couldn't be afraid to *just* hike the trail.

At first you just hoped to hike at least one hundred miles so that if you had to go home you could still save face. But now, having reached Damascus, it is no longer a question of saving face. You have hiked 449 miles to get here. Now you know you can do it. By now you actually have already done it all. You haven't seen all the sights yet, but you have experienced every logistical circumstance. You have done everything. You know how to pack and how to purify water. You know how to greet fellow hikers, how to read the data book and the hiker's handbook. You know how to follow the blazes, how to pick up mail, how to find Coleman fuel, how to hang out in town, how to find cash machines. You have learned that you will probably survive if you run out of food, but that you certainly won't if you run out of water. You have done everything, and yet three-quarters of the trail remains. You wonder, what will that be like? I had thought Hydro would show up, but he never did. Would I see him again? I read ahead in the hiker's handbook to learn what lay in store. I was in Virginia now. Damascus had been a fine stop. I had made it into Virginia having hiked 449 miles thus far, and the next morning I would set out up the state. I read the Y's hug all over again and drifted off to sleep.

9
Virginia

*My days were not days of the week, bearing the stamp
of any heathen deity, nor were they minced into
hours and fretted by the ticking of a clock; for I lived
like the Puri Indians, of whom it is said that "for
yesterday, today, and tomorrow they have only one
word."*

— Henry David Thoreau, *Walden*

T railzilla.

They say that Trailzilla hits northbounders in Virginia. Trailzilla is the trail monster of boredom. It strikes once your hike is no longer new and exciting, once single-minded purpose slips into routine. You have hiked a prodigious 450 miles, yet you still have 1,697 miles to go. Virginia itself can seem endless. It alone holds one-quarter of the trail. Five hundred and forty-five trail miles in Virginia give it the most AT turf of any state (Maine is a distant second with 275 miles, while Pennsylvania is third with 231 miles). Fortunately, Virginia is beautiful. And gentle. The personality of your hike changes here. With the approaching summer, temperatures rise making it easier to get out of your sleeping bag in the morning. You no longer start the day wearing long underwear only to change into shorts once you've worked up a sweat—now you can put on shorts immediately and hike in them all day. Also the days have grown longer so you have more daylight hours for hiking. The terrain becomes easier in Virginia, and your physical condition has improved. Your pack weight is down because you've mailed home useless

95

junk, and your daily routine is established so there's no more fumbling around. Big miles come easily. With your lighter pack, the longer days, and your improved condition you can hike about as fast and as far as you want. What's more, the trail straightens out. The southern quarter of the AT zigzags from mountain to mountain to such an extent that with random glances at your compass through the course of the day down there you will see the dial pointing in every possible direction: west, northwest, north, northeast, east, southeast, south and, most disturbing of all, *even southwest*! You head every direction early on, meandering and winding along; but suddenly in Virginia the trail straightens and makes a beeline straight up the coast. You can see your daily progress on the map.

You get out of the woods in Virginia. You cross fields and open hills. Northbounders value these changes. Hiker bottlenecks dissolve here as everyone has spread out, so the shelters breathe more. In the southern quarter of the AT everyone rests and resupplies at the same spots—Neels Gap, Fontana Dam, Hot Springs, Damascus. But in Virginia the trail towns are gone and you stop for mail and to rest in a wide variety of places. No two through-hikers move through Virginia the same way. Spring breaks have ended and summer vacations are a month away yet, so you get a respite from hordes of weekend warriors. Through-hiker friendships solidify. You now know everyone hiking at your pace so you can hike with anyone around you. You hike with confidence now. You do strange things in Virginia like mail home your stove, hike naked, eat wild onions, hide rocks in each other's backpacks. Me, I never felt Trailzilla. I never got bored. I had a vacation waiting for me at the end of the state which kept me motivated. I enjoyed the warmer weather, the open spaces, the cow fields, and progressing north. Reaching the end of Virginia means reaching Harpers Ferry, West Virginia—the spiritual halfway point of the trail (already you have thoughts of halfway!). My PO stops in Virginia were at Pearisburg, Troutville, and Tyro. I would spend twenty-six days in the state. I would feed wild ponies. I would hide from a rainstorm in a portable toilet. I would see a man die in Virginia.

My trek through Virginia began inauspiciously. I was climbing a hill just four miles out of town when a piece of metal from my running shoe broke through its seal, jabbing into my foot, drawing blood. I took off the shoe and tried hammering back the protrusion with a rock, but that didn't help. I would hike the next 163 miles with the metal chunk sticking into my foot. Now I knew that the shoe store saleswoman back had lied about the "discount" running shoes. I limped to Saunders shelter 9.4 miles out of Damascus, sharing it with an all-marathon group: Mozyin', Easy Stryder, Blazer, Food Dude, and Chaos. Easy Stryder was the only one of the six of us who had never raced a full marathon (he had merely run a half-marathon). It was a pure coincidence. You don't need marathon conditioning to through-hike, but having trained in sports does give you valuable knowledge of your body; it gives you experience listening to your body with an acute ear. Chaos was vegetarian. I asked her why.

"For me it isn't for bleeding-heart reasons," she said.

"For me it is," I answered. *"Ow, Oh! My heart is bleeding! Stop the bleeding!"*

My foot pain worsened. That next morning I exited early and caught up with Kilgore Trout who had left town a day earlier and was moving slowly. He picked up his pace and we gabbed together nonstop. He talked me through Earth First, and Edward Abbey's *The Monkey Wrench Gang.* I talked him through Kerouac's *The Dharma Bums,* Bukowski's *Post Office,* Kotzwinkle's *The Fan Man,* and *Dr. Rat.* As with Ponder Yonder, we continually reverted to Monty Python skits: *"There's a penguin on the television!"* Kilgore said I would have liked his friend *Scotty* who was on up ahead and hiking fast (Scotty would later quit his hike in Harpers Ferry). Scotty was dedicating his through-hike to his friend who had died of AIDS. Scotty set the trend that summer of hiking with two ski poles. Now Kilgore hiked with two ski poles and the style was catching on. As I walked along a patch of grass, suddenly one of my legs didn't lift when I tried to step forward, and I fell forward flat on my face. Kilgore couldn't stop laughing. We came out of the woods near Hurricane Campground where we sat by a parked van and discussed *Yogiing* (Yogi the Bear). Yogiing is when you beg a non-through-hiker on or near the trail for food without your victim's even knowing it. Through-hikers have turned Yogiing into an art form, into a science. The classic style is to wait until your victim is eating or has food spread out; then you drop the bomb:

"Yeah, everything's fine. I'm enjoying the hike very much... except that I haven't been eating that well for the past few days." Or:

"The trail is really the greatest place...but it is true that you get hungry a lot."

Or if you spy a weekend warrior with homemade cookies you say:

"Wow, cookies! You know that's one thing I really miss on the trail, you just don't get any of Grandma's cookies...What? Oh yeah sure, I'd love to try one. Thanks!" (and proceed to eat six).

When done right, champion Yogiers can deliver seemingly innocuous phrases with weighty suggestion:

"Hey, that smells good..."

Yogiing isn't quite considered an embarrassment to the ranks because you know that weekend warriors deserve it; they enter the woods with food enough to feed an army. In a way you are doing them a favor by lightening their load. Plus, day hikers and weekend warriors become fair game when they sit and ask you endless questions. You Yogi them in return; that's part of the bargain. Still Yogiers find it hard to retain dignity. It is begging after all. Just then an older couple in street clothes emerged from the woods and walked toward their van carrying pails of blueberries and raspberries. We sat up and Kilgore approached them with the poorest attempt at Yogiing I ever saw in 147 days. He said something so bad it was like:

"What do you have? Oh, berries? Wow. You know, I'm really hungry."

I bent over double laughing so hard. Kilgore knew that he'd failed miserably, so he mocked himself holding out cupped hands like a beggar toward the old couple after they had driven off, staggering after their departing van like a stiff TV zombie. We continued on, giddy with laughter. In high spirits at 18.8 miles we reached Thomas Knob shelter on the high plateau beside Mt. Rogers, which is Virginia's highest mountain at 5,729 ft. The mountain's summit is a mere two hundred yards off the trail to the left of the shelter, but trees covered its top and my foot hurt bad so we didn't detour. Into the shelter just moments behind us came Blazer, Easy Stryder, Mozyin', Food Dude, and Chaos. The land drops away behind the shelter down the rocky hillside of Grayson Highlands State Park, home to feral ponies. There were ponies grazing just then behind the shelter, and Kilgore and I walked out back with our cameras. We tiptoed down the hillside over holes, around boulders, through briars and tall grass, gently attempting to approach close, but the ponies calmly retreated. Late that night in the utter darkness we were all awakened by Chaos' dog and Food Dude's dog who howled demonically. We grabbed flashlights and pointed them out the shelter to discover that a large pony had wandered up to the front of the shelter and was sniffing around in the darkness. The pony had scared the dogs silly, and now vice versa.

Hydro had fallen behind me. He had taught me well. Without him around I was always first up and out in the morning. Early risers see morning mist, morning dew, sunrise, wild animals. You know you are first on the trail in the morning when you spend your day peeling spiderwebs off your face. Spiders climb high at night and then drop down and swing across the trail with the wind and connect the bushes and branches on either side with their webs; and if you are the first hiker through the woods in the morning you will clear away many freshly woven spider webs with your face. But here, up so high on the open rocky expanse of Wilburn Ridge in Grayson Highlands we were up out of the forest, up out of the woods, so there were no spiderwebs to break through. Crossing the high rocky ridge that dew-wet misty morning, alone before the others, I saw five deer grazing amidst a dozen wild ponies on a grassy patch of trail ahead. I continued walking. The deer fled, but the ponies remained. I fed dried fruit to the feral ponies. The sun rose slowly and I spied a second herd of ponies on a far hill. They seemed to lead a charmed life, yet the herds are culled annually, meaning that somebody grabs at least half the ponies every year and sells them to petting zoos, riding farms, and fairs for people to poke, pinch, prod and spill ice cream on. Ah, nature.

That misty morning with the deer and the ponies, the open view, and the jumble of jutting rocks was one of the highlights of my hike. A twenty-five-mile limp brought me to Trimpi Shelter. For a while it was just me and

Mozyin' there until all the others showed up (minus Kilgore, who hiked at a mellower pace). Two fighter jets buzzed by overhead with supersonic pops. We were moving as slow as humans can move while the pilots were moving as fast. Next day at noon, Mozyin', Easy Stryder, and I followed the trail out of the woods and up beside the Mt. Rogers Recreation Center headquarters with its museum, visitor center, and soda machine. We sat on the stone patio in the sun and drank three sodas apiece. I removed my mutant sneaker and put seven Band-Aids on my wounded foot. The pain had grown worse. My feet hurt in five places, including my left pinkie toe which had somehow freakishly managed to lodge itself sideways underneath its neighbor toes. I had developed an underarm rash that hurt so bad I had to wad gobs of Vaseline on it to keep from crying. I was falling apart. Finishing that 21.9 mile day was an arduous task. Mozyin', Food Dude, and Chaos had gone on ahead to our day's destination, the Atkins Truck Stop Motel beside the trail on I-81. Blazer and Easy Stryder and I dragged in all together, bringing up the rear. The end of that day was pain, pain, pain, pain, pain. Blazer cried his continual daily refrain:

"My knees are burning me! They're burning!"

"I have a blister on my left heel," said Easy Stryder.

"Yeah?"

"And it has a blister on it."

"What?"

"My blister has a blister on it."

"That's nothing," I said. "I have a blister that has a compound fracture."

It was funny to me. For two tough army guys, they sure cried a lot. The pair of them were becoming legendary blue-blazers, looking for shortcuts constantly. We crested the final hill and looked down at the interstate and our truck stop hotel destination below. The trail looped far around to the right, but these two left the trail and began bushwhacking straight down the hillside through thick bushes and tall weeds (and who knew what else). I limped in last. Our group ate dinner together in the diner and we shared three rooms in the little ranch hotel connected to the truck stop. I bought Gatorade and doughnuts at the truck stop gas station, and I bought salt and soaked my foot.

Never Vent.

Our group scattered in the morning. Mozyin' and Food Dude continued hiking north. The hotel owner drove Blazer, Easy Stryder, and me to the post office in the nearest town where I mailed home my tent—seven pounds gone, just like that! This time Hydro wasn't around to talk me out of it. In thirty-six days, I had used my tent only once out of necessity. I only wished I had mailed it home sooner. It took some weight off my sore foot. The novice doesn't realize the difference a few pounds can make. *("Ounces make pounds.")* Not only was my pack now an entire universe lighter, but I no longer had to deal with the bulk of the tent with its poles and flaps and storage bags. It was gone! I felt light and free. No tent—just me, my stove, my food and my clothes. NO ABDOMINIZER, NO TENT, NO SAW, NO NOVELS, NO CHESS SET, NO SNOWSHOES. NO BLUE BUTANE STOVE, NO HEAVY POTS AND PANS, NO CANNED TOMATOES, NO HEADLAMP FLASHLIGHT, NO SOAP OR SHAMPOO, NO NEEDLESS CLOTHES, NO HURRICANE MATCHES. Now I carried only essentials. While I would have preferred a smaller and lighter camera, and while I was the only hiker on the trail with a foam mattress pad instead of a Therm-a-rest air pad, I knew that my pack was materially set; I knew then that I would no longer change it much for the rest of my hike. I called home to have my parents mail sneakers to me in the next town, Pearisburg. Blazer and Easy Stryder picked up packages and then hit the trail, but my foot hadn't healed, so I returned to the truck stop oasis to soak it in salt water for a second straight night.

Walking back toward my hotel room, I spied a familiar hiking stick leaning against the wall outside my door. I could have recognized that hiking stick anywhere—store-bought, slim, dark wood, little rubber stopper on the bottom—it was Hydro's! I searched and found Hydro in the diner drinking a milkshake. I told him my story of the turkey hunters in the dark at 4 AM and racing for Damascus. He said he had been just a day behind me, arriving in Damascus on the day I had left. It was good to see Hydro again. The pause at Atkins truck stop helped invigorate me, but I still had foot pain and I had to go slow the next morning. It was ninety miles farther to Pearisburg for my next PO drop box #4 and new sneakers. Hydro went on ahead. I did my best to stay on his tail. I passed Chaos who was tenting out with *Eggman* by a pond on a hillside. I continued on to Chestnut Knob shelter, a stone shelter on the exposed summit of Chestnut Knob mountain, 22.8 miles on the day. I shared the shelter with a frizzled bearded weekend warrior from a nearby town who told me he frequently climbs up and sleeps there.

"Do you want some *Polish Kilbassa?"* he asked.

I said: "It's funny to me how we breed pigs, raise them in darkness in cages in warehouses, then slice them open to drain their blood and cook them, and then we mix their ground bodies with herbs and spices and call this something exotic."

He could tell that I didn't want any.

We walked outside and he showed me how to identify wild onions, called *ramps* in the south. We found some ramps. I pulled up a few bulbs and threw them in my pasta dinner. Throughout the rest of Virginia we all looked for ramps and we cooked them in our meals. Some towns down South have ramp festivals. Several times I saw locals out digging ramps in the hills.

Hiking big miles means passing many lean-tos through the course of the day. You pause at the shelters you pass near the trail to eat lunch, read, rest, sign the register, or write some notes in your journal. Noon that next day, I reached Jenkins shelter to find it full of Christian religious pamphlets. It is like that all through the South—a continual bombardment of Christian leaflets in all the shelters. Zealots know that you are literally wandering in the wilderness, and so they believe that you are figuratively wandering through the wilderness, too—that you are a lost soul that needs saving. I had finally had enough. Blame it on my foot pain, the daily bombardment of religious pamphlets, or on *Polish Kilbassa* cooking in the woods, but my annoyance peaked and I broke the cardinal sin of the trail, which is that you never vent. I wrote: *"It is our great conceit to believe we are special, to believe we are chosen. It is not a humble attitude. It is not a humble belief."* I spelled out my objections toward religion (a gentler, more creative response was an entry I would read in a later register: *"Jesus saves sinners—and redeems them for valuable cash prizes!"*). I might not have vented had Hydro or Mozyin' been behind me to read my missive, but I knew that they were both on up ahead and would never see it. The hiker's handbook warns you never to write anything bad about anyone else in the registers and never to air your grievances. It says if you write something bad, it will always come back to haunt you.

Late afternoon I caught up with Family Circus, Jersey, and T-bag, who had all left Damascus before me. They were just now all returning from an evening at Levi Long's, two miles off the trail, in Bastian. Every summer Sunday the best fiddlers in the Appalachian Mountains gather at Levi Long's home to play. It was Sunday. Mozyin', Blazer, and Easy Stryder had also spent the evening at Levi Long's, but they had gotten earlier rides back to the trail. Hydro, of course, had hiked past this large group while they were off dancing. Hydro does not like dancing off the trail. Hydro does not like the social scene in the shelters. Hydro likes to hike. That's what he does. Most in this crew weren't even aware that Hydro existed. Hydro is a stealth hiker who chugs along with perfect consistency. If you step off the trail, he's by you, and then when he's on up in front you won't even know it because he virtually never signs the shelter registers. Meandering hikers like those in this large group get off the trail for a single evening and they never even know he went by. Most hikers need to take breaks; they need to recoup; they need a diversion, a little R&R in a town. They need a fiddling festival, a beach day at a swimming hole. Something. Anything. But not Hydro. He didn't need that. *"I like to hike."* That was the truth. Hydro was the most consistent hiker on the trail. He never had bad days. He never required anything more than a path through the woods.

I approached Helvy's Mill shelter when suddenly Mozyin' came bolting down a hill hiking south. He wore his backpack and was motoring faster than I'd ever seen him hike before. He yelled hello and said he would explain later. The shelter made it 25.1 miles on the day for me. Easy Stryder was there. He suddenly discovered that he'd lost his wallet. It had been in his jacket which he had left by mistake back at Levi Long's. He wasn't worried. He wouldn't go back. He would continue on. Two days later *Brick Boy* would hike up behind him and hand him his jacket and wallet. It was nice to see Jersey again. She was having foot problems (a bad thing to have) and motivation problems (worse). We would later hear that she left the trail and spent the remainder of her summer on a beach in the Florida Keys with a girlfriend. Mozyin' returned an hour later and explained his story. His ride back from Levy Long's had driven him too far, past the spot he'd gotten off at. He was accepting a favor, so by the time he realized the mistake, he was too embarrassed to say anything, and he got out of the car and hiked up to the shelter knowing that he had missed a section of trail (albeit an extraordinarily *small* section). But later, sitting in the shelter thinking about the meaning of his hike, he knew that he wanted to be able to look back someday and know that he had hiked *every inch* of the AT, so he had decided that he had to go back, but instead of going back without his pack, he went back wearing his full pack because he wanted to hike the whole trail *with his pack on.* I admired him greatly, even if this game of inches seemed anal. Later that summer, while hiking together in Maryland, we would come to a grooved dirt path that veered left fifteen feet off the trail to a public restroom and shower in a park. After showering, upon leaving, I would follow a second worn path that led fifteen feet ahead to the trail, but Mozyin' would walk back fifteen feet along the original path and *then* forward. Fifteen feet! In Maine, where the trail crosses the Kennebec River, a hiker once got swept away and died fording the river, so they established a canoe service to ferry hikers across. Mozyin' wouldn't accept the canoe ride across the Kennebec. He wouldn't even let the canoes take his pack while he walked across. Instead, he would hold his pack over his head and ford the swift river on foot. Mozyin' took his hike nice and easy, true to his trail name; but he hiked with a code. Family Circus set up their tent in a clearing and hung their food high between two trees. They showed us a trick they had taught their dogs. They said: *"Hey! Southbounder! Where's the Southbounder?"* and the dogs sprung to their feet, barking and snarling.

Just two more days to Pearisburg—a town with hotels (hot shower!), restaurants, my PO drop box #4, and the end of my mutant metal-spiked "discount" sneakers. I hiked with Mozyin' 22.8 miles to Wapiti shelter past a little pond. The day after that we hiked together 16.2 miles into town in a torrential downpour. Those final miles into Pearisburg were the most painful I would have on the trail. I kept my hood down leaving my head exposed to the downpour, allowing the pelting rain to crash down and explode on my head in a vain attempt to distract my mind from my foot pain. We took the last downhill mudslide into town very slowly. We stepped out of the woods off the trail into a car dealership parking lot. We turned right toward the town center and walked a quarter mile along a major road until we came to the

Pearisburg Hotel.

Death in Pearisburg.

I had hiked 162 miles from Damascus to Pearisburg in medieval-torture-chamber discount running shoes, a metal piece of one sticking into the side of my foot the entire way. Hydro was already there at the hotel. By now it feels strange to sleep in a room with four walls and a closed door, but you do relish the escape from wind and dirt. That first night was glorious. I shared a room with Hydro and Mozyin'. I bought a bivy sack from Mozyin' for $100, but I had no cash so he said I should pay him later. My sleeping bag fit into the bivy sack, and the bivy sack was supposedly waterproof, so I would be safe outdoors in an emergency as I no longer had my tent. Hydro left early morning and Mozyin' left at 10 AM, but I would stay put for a zero day. I lay napping all morning with the hotel room door wide open, a breeze blowing in. I walked to the PO and collected my mail, but my sneakers hadn't arrived. I washed my laundry down the street.

Walking back through town at twelve noon, I looked up and saw a fragile old man with a cane crossing the town's empty road diagonally. This ninety-year-old man wasn't halfway across when a truck crested the hill driving toward him. The truck drove slowly at thirty miles-per-hour, but it appeared right away as if these two objects would have a close shave. The old jaywalker never looked up, never turned his head, never spied the truck. *("This is my town!")* I stood anxiously at a distance. Calling out would have frozen the old man in his tracks in the middle of the road. Didn't the truck driver see the old man? The jerk driving the truck wasn't giving much room. I thought that the driver was trying to make a point—*("It may be your town, but it's my road!")* I assumed these objects would miss, but then on came the truck. Then, *"THUNK!"* The truck's front corner just clipped the teetering old man. Just clipped him. It looked like it never should have happened. Two more feet and that old man would have been out of the way. The old man spun twisting off the truck.

I knew that instant that the old man was dead. It wasn't a solid hit, just a graze off the front corner. But it was the sound. It was the high thunk sound and the way that the old man's body twisted. It had all happened in an instant. It had all happened before my eyes. Several people ran out to the old man lying on his back in the road—some blood in the road—legs, noise, pain, dizzy, and everything brown. I hadn't yet moved an inch from my spot. Then I turned and ran back to an open doorway I had passed on the street where I had seen paramedics resting beside an ambulance in an open garage. The crew jumped into their ambulance and arrived on the scene not sixty seconds after the hit. The truck driver sat stunned by his truck with a rescue worker. The truck driver was another old man who hadn't seen a thing; he'd just had

103

the sun in his eyes. I stayed and gave a police report—the pedestrian had jaywalked, crossing the road diagonally, at a snail's pace.

All day I heard the sound, saw the old man twist through the air. It kept making me flash back to the photograph of the hung elephant, too. Disturbing images that I couldn't shake out of my mind. I wanted to get back to the woods, but I couldn't leave town without my new sneakers. I checked out of the hotel and walked the terrifically long walk through town to the hiker hostel barn far from the AT beside a cow field beyond a residential neighborhood. Hiker-helper Bill Gautien gave me a ride into the neighboring town, which back then had the nearest automatic money machine. I had to get cash to pay Mozyin' his $100. Bill had heard about the accident and he stopped by later that evening to inform us that the old man had died at the hospital that afternoon. I phoned home and discovered that my parents had mailed my sneakers Federal Express. The sneakers had already been delivered there to the hostel. Had I remained at the hotel, I never would have known. Two young female section-hikers from my native hometown were there. One of their aunts had been my third grade teacher. The women hiked with their two muscular black Labs and with a ski instructor from New Hampshire named *Sky King*, who carried a small ukulele. Buckskin had hitchhiked forward into town to grab a PO box. Food Dude was there with his dog, stranded in town waiting for his friends to mail him special gourmet dog food. An old, happy through-hiker named *Barkeater* was there. He was bowlegged and low-tech with an Ace bandage wrapped around one knee. He was from the Adirondack mountains, like Blazer. Barkeater had worked for the telephone company for forty years, putting his two daughters through college and graduate school. Now, after forty years, he was treating himself to a break, a vacation. I showered and slept on a mattress on the floor in the loft upstairs. Slept while still seeing that old man crossing the road, slowly, so slowly, over and over and over, never reaching the other side.

Flaming Stove.

I left Pearisburg with new sneakers and a new foot system: Food Dude had taught me to wear plastic bags over my socks (with a hole in the front for my toes), and I hiked the entire rest of the trail with rubbing alcohol (available at any trail stop) for nightly drying and healing foot massages, à la Ponder Yonder. My new sneakers were comfortable New Balance 520s. I'd had a poor choice of sneakers up until now, but just two pairs of the New Balance would take me 1,526 miles from Pearisburg to Katahdin, and neither one would wear out from the effort (I would still use both pairs for hiking years after the AT). From Pearisburg, I hiked forty-nine miles in two days and caught up with Mozyin' at Niday shelter, handing him $100 cash. Mozyin' sat in the shelter reading a map, surrounded by a pile of Fig Newton cookies, Tootsie Rolls, and raisin bread. He had mailed home his stove from Pearisburg. In this feeble attempt at lessening his pack weight he had kept his tent which he wasn't using, but he had mailed home his stove which he was.

"What are you doing?" I asked him.

"I'm just munching."

"What's for dinner?"

"This is it," he answered, waving his arm over the spread, munching away.

Iona from Iowa shared the shelter with us. Her husband had died a year earlier in a snowplow accident. She was on the trail grieving. Each night she set up a shrine beside her sleeping bag with a burning candle and a photograph of her dead husband propped up beside it. It was a little creepy. I motored on that next day trying to catch Hydro. I saw a wild turkey fly through the woods. It was sleek, powerful, graceful. I found a beheaded turkey beside the trail. Its body was there but the head was gone. I came to a putrid-smelling roadside clearing thick with swarming flies and found three buckets of deer parts—mostly legs, hoofs and skulls. The smell made me gag. I passed two camouflaged men carrying guns in the woods.

"Seen any turkey?" one of them asked.

Hours later I passed a woman who asked if I'd spoken to the hunter back at the last stream. She said he had stepped out from behind a tree to speak to her. I hadn't seen any hunter. Did that mean some camouflaged man with a loaded weapon was hiding in the woods watching the trail, creeping out to chat with women who walked by? Graffiti in one of the shelters read:

"Kill Deer."

Someone else wrote:

"When the snow flies, Bambi dies."

I caught up with Blazer and Easy Stryder at Catawba shelter at twenty-four miles on the day. They were my friends, but the next shelter was only two miles farther and Hydro was still up ahead, so I left them and pressed on. But no luck, no Hydro there at Campbell shelter either. Instead there were five men, all weekend warriors. It was a party of three (including a male nurse), and a party of two (a college professor and a doctor). I knew how I appeared to them. Upon arriving at dusk after a twenty-six-mile day, I filled my water carrier at the nearby stream and hung it on a shelter nail within reach, hung my food bag inside the shelter on a nail within reach, spread down my nylon tarp on the shelter floor, set down my mattress pad and sleeping bag, changed into dry clothes, and took out my stove to cook dinner all within five minutes of arriving at the shelter. I fielded endless questions about through-hiking. They poked fun at me. One of them said: *"Hey let's watch him and learn—he's a through-hiker!"* My stove had been acting up recently, spouting a high flame no matter how I adjusted the valve. I wondered if this night it would cooperate. I sat inside my sleeping bag; then I reached out and lit my stove (the moment of truth). There was a great whoosh; then a flaming geyser leapt fifteen inches to the height of my chin and remained there. I calmly waited, hoping that the flame would die down, as it threatened to set my sleeping bag and indeed the entire shelter on fire. This was clearly an aberration, yet incredibly none of the other men so much as batted an eyelash. Finally, one of them asked:

"Is there something wrong with your stove?"

"What do you think, Al? He is a through-hiker. He must have at least some idea of what he is doing."

I laughed to myself. I thought: *If that flame doesn't drop in the next five seconds I'm going to scream and hurl the stove out the shelter to save our lives!* The flame finally subsided. A funny night. The male nurse had green tubes which he broke open after dark creating glowing florescent green lights, so we felt like space aliens. That next day I hiked 15.2 miles for a hotel room and a bath at Best Western, trailside, off Rte. 220. Another of Nabokov's "Functional Motels"—comfort oasis—ice machine, vending machine, telephone. The following day I hiked thirteen miles into the Blue Ridge Parkway, after first pausing midday, one mile off the trail, in Troutville for my PO drop box #5.

Amongst The Trillium.

The Blue Ridge Parkway was one of only two places that had stuck in my child's mind on that family trip decades earlier driving home to New York from Tennessee on summer vacation: *Were the Smoky Mountains really smoky? Was the Blue Ridge Parkway really blue?* Northbounders enter the Blue Ridge Parkway at a spot where a marker counts down from 97.7 miles to 0, as you head north. The trail follows alongside the road, sometimes parallel, sometimes zigzagging across it. I watched a bicycle race fly past. Colorful Jerseys. I inspected a painted, custom-converted VW van parked at an overlook whose owners said that inside was a bed and a kitchen. I peeked inside through a parted window curtain and saw two shelves stacked with books. Through-hikers occasionally blue-blaze this stretch by walking the Blue Ridge Parkway, by actually walking down the road instead of hiking the trail in the woods beside it. For Blazer and Easy Stryder it wasn't the Blue Ridge Parkway at all, but the *"Blue-Blaze Parkway."* They walked the road arguing that the views were nicer from there (which was true). I hiked 19.6-, 21.8-, 22.4-, and 21.9-mile days here, sleeping in shelters all the way because my tent was now gone. Shelter graffiti and register entries in Virginia are glorious:

"Very important—someone called for somebody. I can't remember."
"May your miles be full of smiles."
"Build a little birdhouse in your soul."
"If baby birds can't fly, where do they use the bathroom?"
"A friend with weed is a friend indeed."
"Do bongs."
"Keep your feet dry and your spirits high."
*"WEATHER FORECAST: we will have light showers in the morning,
    followed by drizzles at lunch and deluges in the afternoon."*
"This is indeed a footbath in the wilderness."
"That which does not kill me makes me stronger."
*"Sometimes what you think you can't do limits that which you
    actually can."*
"Conservatives worship dead radicals."
"Evolve or die! —Charles Darwin."
"Okay, you may use the urinal, but don't eat the big white mint!"
"Is an incongruous paradox really illogically insensible?"
"It is cold right now and I'm not getting my pancakes."
"It got cold so I burned my underwear."
"We went down to the spring. It is not worth it."
*"I have two doctors. My left leg and my right leg.
—Trevelyan."*
*"Not what we give, but what we share, for the gift without the giver
    is bare."*
*"From things that go bump in the night, Good Lord, deliver us. —a
    Scottish Prayer."*
*"There is a race of man that don't fit in. A race that can't stand still.
    So they break the hearts of kith and kin and roam the earth at
    will.—Race of Man, Robert Service."*
*"Hi. My name is Sara. I live in Middletown, PA. I'm freezing. I stayed
    up until 1:30. We told jokes. PS: Got to go!"*

Someone carved a pie chart into the Matts Creek shelter wall with three equal portions labeling them: SEX, DRUGS and ROCK 'N ROLL. Someone else had then come along at a later date to add with a pen a tiny sliver-slice in one of the three portions labeling it: SYNCHRONIZED SWIMMING. Truly those are the four things in life that matter. On the outhouse wall near Brown Mountain Creek shelter, someone wrote: FREE BURRITOS! and drew an arrow pointing down toward the toilet seat and the scary, surprise-filled, burrito-brown darkness below. I met a young southbounder called *The Wanderer.* He carried a little bag of stones and a small homemade bow and arrow. He had been hiking south for nine months already. He had gotten off the trail for forty-five days at *Rusty's,* which is a potato farm where hikers crash. I asked where he'd camped at the night before. He said he had waked late and had hiked one mile when a storm threatened, so he'd stopped and had set up his tent in the trail—one mile! I met another southbounder, *Elvis,* in a torrential downpour. I said:

"Nice rain, huh?"

He stopped and looked at me quizzically.

"What do you mean?" he answered.

"It's raining," I said, lifting my arms, rain cascading down in great sheets all around us, making a river out of the trail, deafening our ears. "Can't you tell?"

"Oh this?" he said. "This is dew. This isn't rain. I actually haven't had a single day of rain yet."

Dragons Tooth and McAfee Knob hold great views. The Jim and Molly Denton shelter has a solar-heated outdoor shower. There are road walks in Virginia. A hermit who lives near the trail was seen walking around naked carrying an axe. There is the eighteen-ft. circumference, three-hundred-year-old Keffer Oak (we don't even realize that trees grow this old). I guarded against *trail mirage.* That's when you are tired at the end of the day and you start imagining that you see your shelter destination on the trail ahead. After a long day hiking, every boulder, every tree starts to look like the roof or the walls of a shelter. Blazer and Easy Stryder took a short break off the trail in a town called Buena Vista. I met *Cyclops* who said that Hydro was two days ahead but was getting off in Waynesboro to spend a day at the fire station. For a week it rained like clockwork at 4 PM everyday. You could set your watch to it. I met a minister who was out walking his regular loop in the woods. He asked if I had read *Blind Courage* by Bill Irwin, the blind man who had through-hiked the trail with his seeing-eye dog Orient in 1991 and gave full credit for his hike to his faith in Christ. *"Hike with that book,"* the minister said, *"and when you hit a rut, when you get down, pull out that book and read a chapter."* I told him that I hadn't felt down.

Northbounders and southbounders experience the trail differently. All the southbounders you see warn you about The Priest mountain. They tell you how difficult it is. But heading north, you are already high on a ridge of which the Priest's summit is but a pimple, and then all you must do is descend the steep north side that had hurt them so. Continuing down The Priest, I hiked into Tyro that afternoon for my post office drop box #6, my last PO stop in Virginia. A man in a tiny store beside the PO let me use his rotary telephone to call long distance. I had been calling the Y from every trail town, sometimes reaching her, sometimes leaving messages; but I had a bad feeling about this call. She was due to travel to Germany for seven weeks to play for a tennis team in a small village in Bavaria, but I couldn't remember on which day she was due to leave. I knew that this would be close. Her answering machine told me that she was gone. I had missed her. The Y was gone. I wondered what it would do to my mail. I had come to depend upon her letters. They fueled me through the woods; they powered me on to the next and the next and the next letter, to the next and the next and the next PO. I couldn't imagine arriving in town at a post office without a letter from her. Here in Tyro was a letter which began: *"As you read this I'll probably already be in Germany."* The Y was taking great care of me.

Back to the trail, it was on to Maupin Field Shelter for fifteen miles on the day to find Blazer and Easy Stryder sitting comfortably, studying their maps. From here people exit the trail to Rusty's Hard Time Hollow, a potato-farm hiker hangout, but we wouldn't be going there. I had passed these two earlier in the day, but then they had taken a shortcut hiking a blue-blaze side trail called Mau Har which avoids a tough trail climb over Three Ridges. So now here they were in front of me again.

"How do you get behind us?" Easy Stryder asked.

"I hiked the trail," I said.

Blazer and Easy Stryder studied their contour maps with military precision. Truly, they psyched themselves out over what they would have to climb each new day. Studying their maps, they bemoaned, begrudged, resented every steep climb that they noticed ahead. They scoured their maps, constantly searching for shortcuts. I was glad that I didn't carry maps. You know that you will have to climb hills and mountains every day (*on the trail what comes down must go back up), s*o you might as well take the trail as it comes. But this pair blue-blazed so often that whenever they actually had to hike on the trail it was like a chore. They were indeed a strange pair—two tough guys who kept blue-blazing. They spoke of how treacherous the Mau Har blue-blaze shortcut had been, to justify their actions: *"Harder than the AT,"* they said. Then Easy Stryder announced:

"I'm going to write in my journal."

He took out his journal. It looked like it hadn't been used in a while. He fought open the crease, eagerly anticipating reading back over the good times of earlier days on the trail. He sadly discovered, though, that he had logged only one previous entry. Still, overcome by nostalgia, he read it out loud:

"Day number two: Hiked a lot today. Really tired."

Then he took out his pen and he added a subsequent, follow-up entry:

"Day number forty-five: Hiked all day. Exhausted!"

Blazer had served on active duty in the Vietnam War and earned a Purple Heart. He wouldn't talk about all the friends he had seen get blown to smithereens, or about all the people he had killed himself. In the army he had eaten iodine pills daily for years on end. In Vietnam he had drunk polluted water out of muddy puddles. Once he'd scooped black water from a river, popped five iodine pills into his mouth, swished it around and drank it down. He did 150 push-ups every day, as he had done for the past thirty years, and he'd once run a sub-3-hour marathon, faster even than Mozyin's sub-3:10. Blazer was from the north, while Easy Stryder was from the south.

Easy Stryder was short, had a crew cut and wore glasses. Trail gossip held that his family owned land. His girlfriend was an Atlanta Hawks cheerleader. He carried a photograph of her, and he also carried a little newspaper clipping about himself from his local paper which had previewed his hike. These two had never met before the trail, but their common military bond made them inseparable. Young Easy Stryder had been an officer, while army-lifer Blazer had spent his military career as an enlisted man. They hiked together like father and son.

Just then a woman walked past our shelter carrying a burlap bag. She returned a half hour later and greeted us cordially:

"Did you notice the white pine back there amongst the trillium? It's certainly odd. The white pine is not indigenous to this area. There must have been a homestead."

We were three dumb jocks seated in a row at the edge of our shelter with our feet dangling down. We tried to smile. We grunted responses and then she left. Alone again, we laughed at ourselves. Blazer spoke up as if the woman still stood before us. He said:

"Lady, we wouldn't know a white pine if it fell on our heads!"

We were living in the woods yet we knew virtually nothing about its flora and fauna. We had glazed-over looks in our eyes. We were pathetic zombies, motoring through the woods. We were crazy, insane, hiking day after day, still in Virginia. We laughed at ourselves. We laughed at our strange habits, at all the silly things we did on this ridiculous trek. We laughed at our single-minded purpose, our narrow vision, our obsession with backpack weight loss, our corny jokes *("Does anyone have a Swiss Army sofa?")*. Everything seemed funny.

"I'm cutting arm holes and leg holes in my sleeping bag," said Easy Stryder.

"Why are you doing that?" I asked.

"It will save me some time in the morning. I won't have to get out of my sleeping bag anymore. Instead, now I can just stand up, pop out my arms and legs, and start hiking."

"Cool," I said.

"Yeah. Why not? This way I can hike in my sleeping bag with my arms and legs out all day, and then at the end of the day when I'm tired, I'll already be in my sleeping bag, so I can just lie down in the trail and sleep!"

"Excellent."

"That's right," said Easy Stryder; "there are lots of things that we don't take advantage of. Did you know that the average person eats one hundred spiders in his lifetime while he sleeps at night? It's true. We should use that. From now on I'm sleeping with my mouth open and I'm eating every spider that crawls inside. I need the protein. That's called Efficiency. I'm fine-tuning my hike now. Whatever it takes."

"That's so right," I agreed. "It's time to become perfectly efficient."

"Exactly," said Easy Stryder. "We have thousands of changes to make. For one thing, sure we've reduced our pack weight, but there are still ways to hike lighter. We're carrying extra weight everywhere. Look at ourselves. Anything at all that is extra weight, it has to come off."

"What, like body hair?"

"Yeah. Right. Body hair, liposuction, fingernails."

"Fingernails?"

"Yeah, fingernails. I'm pulling out all my fingernails. And you'd be wise to do the same if you want to hike light. They're nothing but needless extra weight."

"You know, you're right," I said.

"I know," said Easy Stryder. "The point is that it just doesn't matter what happens to us after the hike. Completing the hike now is the only thing that matters. Whatever it takes."

"You know what?" I said. "I wasn't going to say anything, but that's really why I'm heading into DC—I'm heading straight for a plastic surgeon. I've already got an appointment. I'm getting the outer rims of my ears removed. They don't serve any purpose at all."

"They really don't."

"I know, they don't."

"And you don't need your left arm, either."

"Yeah, I really don't."

"You only need one nut," said Blazer.

"And one lung."

"And one kidney…"

"I'm sleeping with my pack on tonight," said Easy Stryder. "That way I'll get an earlier start in the morning."

"Excellent," I said. "Excellent idea. I'm doing that, too. I'm sleeping with my backpack on over my special sleeping bag with the arm holes and leg holes, and I'm sleeping kneeling in the sprinter's position at the edge of the shelter, so all I have to do tomorrow is open my eyes and leap forward."

"Still in your sleeping bag!"

"Still in my sleeping bag," I said. "Then I'll hike all day without stopping, and flop down onto the ground to sleep at night when I can't go on any longer."

Easy Stryder had horrible bug bites all over his body. He rubbed pink Calamine lotion all over his face and body and he slept inside his tent in the shelter. Pink boy. Something was always going wrong for these two. We had just eighteen miles left to reach the northern end of the Blue Ridge Parkway at Rockfish Gap.

Slippery Logs.

The Blue Ridge Parkway's northern tip touches the southern tip of Skyline Drive at a place called Rockfish Gap. At Rockfish Gap the trail leaves the Blue Ridge Parkway behind and picks up Skyline Drive which runs 107.7 miles up through the Shenandoah National Park. I left Blazer and Easy Stryder behind at Maupin Field shelter that next morning, never to see either one of them again. I reached Rockfish Gap after eighteen miles for an afternoon meal at a restaurant, gas station, souvenir store. I ate with a southbound section-hiker who had rigged up a thermal cooling water carrier flat on top of his backpack with a tube leading down to his mouth; then I walked to the Skyline Drive entrance booth at Shenandoah National Park, and I filled out a tag attaching it to my backpack for permission to enter the park (just like we'd done in the Smokies). A car full of through-hikers pulled over. It was *Water, Salamander* and *Z* returning from a trip they had made down south back to Damascus for the Trail Days Festival. Water was the lead hiker that summer (not including Eddie-B). Water had begun his hike extremely early. He had left off far up ahead on the trail, but here I had met him already. He pulled over.

"Hey, you want a ride? I'm dropping these guys at Calf Mountain shelter."

I turned down the Yellow Blaze. I wanted to hike the trail, not drive it.

"Another Purist."

Up on little Bear Den mountain with its funny deserted junkyard of rusted carousel seats and spray-painted warnings of rattlesnakes, I got caught in a sudden violent rainstorm with thunder and lightning. I hurried on down the mountain off the exposed summit and came to a portable toilet at the edge of a parking lot. I'd had no time to put on my pack's rain cover, so I ducked into the Port-O-Let to stay dry. The space was too small to sit down in, so I stood in that Port-O-Let for thirty minutes listening to the violent storm, eating Snickers bars and waiting for the storm to pass. Finally, I continued on. Up at Calf Mountain shelter, 25.4 miles on the day, I met a new pocket of hikers: Salamander (from out of the car), *Mighty Mike,* and *Mercury Mark.* Also inside was *Z,* a thirty-five-year-old through-hiker who had given his backpack the name *Crash Diet.* I was getting water at a spring when I heard Mercury Mark issue a blood-curdling scream. He had left Rusty's that morning, and he only just now discovered that his friends had hidden eight pounds of rocks in the bottom of his backpack which he had been carrying through the mountains all day.

This group (excluding Z) was young and wild. They had just returned to the trail from *Rusty's Hard Time Hollow,* a potato farm near the trail. It is a barn with bunk beds where hikers can stay indefinitely. There is no electricity there, but there is a wood-powered hot tub, horseshoe pegs, and games of checkers, chess, Frisbee and hackey sack. Rusty drives his guests to the grocery store for supplies, and he drives them to and from the trail so that they can slackpack (hike without a backpack!) different sections of trail by day but then still sleep back at Rusty's by night. Rusty's is not listed in either the data book or the hiker's handbook. You have to hear of it word-of-mouth. You are cool if you stay there. Rusty's is the Litmus test for cool on the trail. If Pond Mountain was the Litmus test for blue-blazing, then Rusty's is the Litmus test for cool. The longer you stay at Rusty's, the cooler you are. No one describes how relaxing their stay was, they just say how long it lasted.

"I stayed at Rusty's three days."

Cool.

"Three days? Man, I stayed there for eight."

Much cooler!

Next day I met *Mosby,* a through-hiker from the previous summer who was out for two days reliving his hike, thinking things over. We ate lunch at a picnic table. Mosby told me how he'd gotten a wisdom tooth taken out while on his through-hike, and how he'd carried the pulled tooth the rest of the way to Katahdin. He said that he had hiked very slowly with a group that covered just eight miles a day. They had formed into a group on the trail, and they had hiked together the entire way. After the trail, they had all moved out to California and shared an apartment together in San Diego. Mosby was back east now on vacation. He said that his trademark had been taking frequent diggers (falls). He said he had fallen down so often that his friends began calling it "taking a Mosby."

"Man, I took a bad Mosby back there."

"I took four Mosby's today."

A swarm of bottleneck flies descended upon us that was so dense and relentless we couldn't talk long. I hiked 26.3 miles to Pinefield Hut. That next day, southbound slackpackers approached me down a mountainside, down a graded series of zigzag switchbacks. They didn't have backpacks, but I could tell that they were through-hikers. It was their beards, the dirt, the hair, the energy, the confident strides, the gaiters on their legs. They were hiking south, but in fact these were northbounders. Here was *Amblin' Aggie, Chinook, Going Home, Caveman* and *Oz.* They were *slackpacking*—hiking without backpacks. This entire group was staying at Rusty's, and Rusty was now driving them north to different sections of trail, and picking them up again after they slackpacked each section south. This was the first time I had ever witnessed slackpacking, and I knew right away that it was something I wanted to do. I ate lunch with the slackpackers.

"You didn't stop at Rusty's?" they asked me.

Uncool.

Chinook, in this group, was a young and powerful hiker (trail name means a breeze over a mountain pass). At lunch someone asked him:

"Hey Chinook, I saw what you did at the stream; how can you run across slippery logs like that?"

"My son," Chinook answered, clasping his hands together in praying posture like Kung Fu. "How is it that you *cannot* run across slippery logs?"

Reaching Harpers Ferry.

That night I caught Hydro at Bearface Mountain hut after thirteen days apart (20.8 miles on the day for me), and we hiked together the final one hundred miles in Virginia all the way into Harpers Ferry. We hit the patch of Skyline Drive that is lined with restaurants. There is no other stretch like it. We passed three restaurants in a single day. I declined breakfast with Hydro, but I stopped alone for lunch at Big Meadows with its all-you-can-eat salad bar. I sat alone at a table, shivering, chilled in its enormous air-conditioned dining center, potted plants all around, glass walls with a view over the mountains. A tour bus pulled up and out filed senior citizens, teetering in to fill up the tables.

I pushed on. I passed a compound marked: CLOSED FOR THE SEASON. We were passing through the park too early. Summer hours hadn't yet begun. On Wednesday, May 19, I came to a french fry, soda stand that said: *CLOSED WEDNESDAY, MAY 19, ONLY.* If we'd had a name for the opposite of Trail Magic, then certainly it would have applied here: *"Trail Non-Magic,"* or *"Trail Curse!"* I saw a deer standing in a deserted open amphitheater in the woods. Hydro and I had been following the writings of *The Wildflowers,* two young women hiking together whom we had heard delicious rumors about. On this day, just when we believed we would finally reach them, they had left the trail and had gotten rides ahead into Washington. I reached Gravel Spring Hut after 28.2 miles, expecting to meet them.

I was an hour ahead of Hydro. Inside were *Caveman, Oz, Chinook,* and another of the former slackpackers from Rusty's. Two of the young men had long hair in ponytails. I pulled a joke on Hydro. When he arrived I introduced the two ponytailed men to him: *"These are the Wildflowers."* Hydro was sick that night with chills and a fever. He spent the night coughing and shivering. He barely slept. Still, he was up and out first that next morning. Hydro was a machine. We reached the end of the Shenandoah National Park together and we hitchhiked into the town of Front Royal for pizza. From there I called Toot in DC, leaving a message on his machine, telling him roughly when I would arrive. We got a ride back to the trail in busy traffic from a young female school teacher to finish a 24.3-mile day to Manassas Gap shelter. Only forty-five miles left to the Shenandoah River, the end of Virginia, and the town of Harpers Ferry, West Virginia—THE SPIRITUAL HALFWAY POINT OF THE TRAIL.

It was a roller-coaster ride, hiking the final stretch of Virginia into Harpers Ferry. Up and down, up and down, up and down. Treacherous! It was here that I realized with certainty that I was insane, because, while motoring up a hill shoveling handfuls of dried fruit into my mouth, I choked and snorted dried fruit chunks out my nose while gasping for breath. I choked, gasped, and snorted dried fruit out my nose—all the while surging ahead, uphill, without stopping, *without even breaking my stride!* After 23.3 miles we hit Bear's Den Youth Hostel, a charming quartzite castle, one of my favorite spots of the trail. An orienteering guy out on a training run came in to return a bandanna I'd dropped. That next morning, the last nineteen miles in Virginia brought us to the end of the state. We reached a bluff called Loudoun Heights and looked down upon the merger of the Shenandoah and Potomac rivers. Two great rivers flowing east toward the ocean here become one mighty river flowing east toward the ocean. And tiny Harpers Ferry rests wedged inside the fork of these rivers with Maryland state lying northeast, beyond. We had reached the end of Virginia after hiking 541 miles in that state. I had spent twenty-six days there. We bid Virginia good-bye. Four states down, ten to go. We descended the bluff, crossed the Shenandoah River bridge, turned right, and climbed over a guardrail following the trail fifty feet to a turnoff where stone steps climbed left off the trail up a hill to the high part of town. Harpers Ferry. We walked two blocks down a street to the Appalachian Trail Conference headquarters. This building was the nerve center of the trail. From here they had mailed me my hiker books and the catalogue months ago. It felt thrilling to enter the building. Inside was a 3-D contour model of the trail on a long table showing all its mountains, hills, and ridges. We signed the halfway register and they took our photographs to add to their album. We checked out the photos of the few through-hikers who were on up ahead of us: *Eddie-B, Water, J-Zero, Peaked in High School, Griff, Strider and Eowin, Unleashed and Homeward Bound, Lancer, Battitude* and *Padre with Pooches.*

It was late afternoon. Hydro continued north pushing on out of town, but I remained behind. I would be leaving the trail here for my vacation. I would ultimately reach Katahdin before Hydro, but I would never see him again. He had been a good friend, a good mentor. Now, alone, I needed a place to crash in town as that next morning I would ride the train from Harpers Ferry into Washington to visit Toot. Sadly, the historic town of Harpers Ferry with its John Brown monument, its Civil War military arsenal museum, and the home of the ATC trail headquarters, has no hiker hostel. Alone in Harpers Ferry with nowhere to stay, and stubbornly unwilling to buy a hotel room as I knew I'd be spending money in DC, I walked back toward the trail and laid out my sleeping bag on a concrete landing behind a building (National Park Service Training Center). I sat alone behind the building at dusk in my sleeping bag cooking my dinner when a woman walked by pushing a baby stroller. I felt vulnerable. Exposed. I slept fitfully on the concrete. It was May 23, a Sunday, and my fifty-ninth day on the trail. Nine hundred and ninety miles behind me. That next morning I would ride the train into Washington, DC. I felt I had earned my vacation.

10

The Thrill of Halfway

I am going through Central Park, man, with no phone,
no trash pad, no cockroaches, and I feel disoriented,
man. I'd better lean against this litter basket and get
an energy transfer.

—William Kotzwinkle, *The Fan Man*

Dead Doors.

You feel odd stepping out of the wilderness into a city of one million people. On the trail you greet everyone. When you meet a hiker you pull up, lean on your hiking stick and prattle on about whatever hills, bumps, mountains, and molehills you've just crossed, what's ahead and what's behind. You wish each other luck. You laugh at yourselves, you laugh at each other. You smile. You make a little joke. It is different in the city, where people walk past each other on the street—or else they would never have time to get through the day (ignoring each other is a function of time, it is done through necessity!). Almost a million people live here in this area. At my pace on the trail it would have taken me just two days to walk past them. Yet I was not bypassing them now but entering into their midst. Walking downtown, wearing my backpack, smelling like pine needles, I followed Constitution to Pennsylvania to meet Toot at his office. Toot was a lawyer working for two years as a prosecutor in the civil division of the Justice Department. By

116

chance I spied him standing outside on the street at the branch building at 901-E talking to one of his colleagues. He was just at that instant returning from a brief trip on a case out of town. We greeted hello.

"Oh you reek!" he said, staggering backward, waving his hand in front of his nose. "You need a shower. Are you going back to my place? The key is still under the mat. If you go in take your shoes off. But don't get anything dirty. And take a shower, please. Right away."

It was Monday, May 24, my sixtieth day on the trail. Now, four days' rest in the city. I hadn't been anchored in one place so long since I'd started my trip. These days proved restful. I relaxed while Toot worked. I made phone calls, napped, wrote letters, and listened to CDs in Toot's apartment on Macomb Street, Northwest. I walked up and down the street to the grocery store. I sat with Toot's yoga-teaching landlord in her backyard on a bench by her goldfish pond, watching her frogs and goldfish, surrounded by an ivy jungle all around (a little slice of the jungle right there in the city). I walked down the block to a movie theater and watched a matinee in the air-conditioned darkness—*Benny and Joon.* I met Toot at his office one day for lunch down in the basement cafeteria at Main Justice. Again, we hit tennis balls at Georgetown; but this time I couldn't run very well, as after 992 miles my legs were accustomed now only to smooth and straight and sure and slow. I walked to the post office with a box, waited in line, and then reached the counter where I asked for tape. On the trail you are always the sole customer in the small POs, and they take out tape and they seal your box. You talk about hiking, discuss the weather, whatever. Here the worker said: *"You seal it, over there, and get back in line."* My post office drop box #7 got sent to Toot's apartment where I also got mail from home and mail from the Y who had sent her letter the day before she had left for Germany. She wrote that her letters would continue as she had my PO destinations with her, and that she had already mailed to my next stop. I drove Toot's Acura Integra to Chevy Chase, Maryland, at night, to the REI camping store where I'd stopped two months earlier. It was a thrill to drive again. *"Riders on the Storm"* came on the radio. It was a magical feeling flying down the highway listening to the Doors. Song rain fell and song thunder cracked, reaching me in perfect quadrasound from the speakers in the four corners of the car. I could see that it wasn't actually raining, still I rolled down my window to feel with my hand just the same. On the trail you have learned to trust your senses, but your senses can be fooled in the city where movie theaters create night in the middle of the day, where electric lights create day in the middle of the night. Radios bring rain in the dryness, the dead Doors back to life. All things are possible in the city. There are comforts in the city. I developed pain in my stomach. I was anxious about returning to the trail. I felt that if I stayed off the trail any longer it would get harder and harder to return to a little bag and a little pot in the woods. Then suddenly all that I wanted was to return to the trail, to get back to the woods where day is day, night is night, hot is hot, cold is cold, rain is rain, dry is dry. In the woods all is as it is, and you see what it is and you hear what it is and you smell what it is and you feel what it is and you taste what it is. In the city all is as you arrange it to be. What does it mean to live in the woods? What does it mean to live in the city? What will become of the woods as the cities keep growing—and won't the cities keep growing?

Tunnel Vision.

Leaving DC. Buildings, asphalt receding behind me out the train window. Bushes, trees, hillsides, grassy fields, forests appearing ahead (Stephen Crane: *"The great Pullman was whirling onward with such dignity of motion that a glance from the window seemed simply to prove that the plains of Texas were pouring eastward")*. Back in little Harpers Ferry, I climbed the steep street from the station by the river up to the ATC headquarters on the hill. I retrieved my hiking stick from under a bush behind the ATC where I'd hidden it four days earlier. I peeked inside the ATC register to see who had passed by— Mozyin', Blazer, Easy Stryder, Cyclops, Chinook, Mighty Mike, Mercury Mark, Going Home, and Heel and Toe had all since made it in and gone on ahead. Then I picked up the trail where I'd left off and followed it down old stone steps, back down to the lower village at riverside. The town itself, with its old brick buildings, is preserved as a National Historical Park. Momentous events had occurred here, yet on the trail you don't care about that. Through-hikers have TUNNEL vision. A town interests you only if it has conveniences. And Harpers Ferry is no trail town. It has no hiker hostel, no drug store, no camping store, no convenience store, no Laundromat, no fast food restaurant or greasy diner. It merely offers a place where trod the footsteps of George Washington, Thomas Jefferson, Meriwether Lewis, Abraham Lincoln, Frederick Douglas, W.E.B. Du Bois, John Brown, and Robert E. Lee.

Harpers Ferry—ideal for harnessing power from the Shenandoah and Potomac Rivers—first housed mills, and later housed the nation's armory. Goods leaving town traveled north, south, east, and eventually west on the Chesapeake & Ohio Canal, and on the Baltimore & Ohio and the Winchester & Potomac railroads. Here in 1859, John Brown and twenty-one men raided the nation's armory with pikes and spears, hoping to seize one hundred thousand muskets and rifles to use to end slavery by force. The raid failed and the U.S. Government hung John Brown, but the event fueled the nation's debate over the issue of slavery, and the nation headed into Civil War. During the war, Harpers Ferry was a border zone between north and south, and it changed hands repeatedly, once with the Confederate Army sending all the town's weapons down south and then burning down the armory, another time with President Abraham Lincoln coming here himself to review the Union troops in 1862. After the Civil War, in 1867, Baptist ministers founded Storer

118

College in Harpers Ferry to educate former slaves. Frederick Douglass, one of Storer's trustees, spoke at the college about freedom and workers' rights (Storer College closed its doors in 1954 with the end of legal segregation). Further back in the past, long before the Civil War, Meriwether Lewis stopped here in 1806 in the heyday of the armory, holding an unlimited credit slip from President Thomas Jefferson to gather whatever guns, boats, and supplies he would need for what was to be his three-and-a-half-year trek across the uncharted country from St. Louis, Missouri, to the Pacific Ocean and back—the expedition of Lewis and Clark. Heading into uncharted land, Lewis and Clark believed that they might encounter Wooly Mammoths and erupting volcanoes. They were searching for a water route west to the ocean, and they never imagined that they would bump into the Rocky Mountains. Of their group of twenty-seven men (and one woman, and a dog) who trekked for three and a half years to the Pacific Ocean (where they saw a beached whale), and back—crossing the Rockies twice, encountering grizzly bears and numerous Native American Indian tribes, as strangers—only one man died on the trip. Back further still, before Lewis and Clark, Thomas Jefferson in his youth stopped here on his way to serve at the Continental Congress in Philadelphia. He called this area: *"Perhaps one of the most stupendous scenes in nature"* (a bit of a reach). Back further still, before Jefferson, a young man named George Washington surveyed this area and mapped its future canal. Impressed by the spot, later, as president, Washington worked with Congress to establish the armory here. The first permanent settler in Harpers Ferry was Peter Stephens who opened a ferry service across the rivers in 1733. Robert Harper bought Stephens' ferry service in 1747 and the town took his name.

Exactly Halfway.

I walked over the Potomac River on the Byron Memorial Pedestrian footbridge and stepped into Maryland leaving West Virginia behind. Five states down, nine to go. At just two miles total on the day, I reached the Sandy Hook youth hostel. It was dinnertime, Friday, May 28. I entered the hostel and read that Mozyin' was there, but before I could search him out, I heard my name called by a frizzy-haired crazy man who at that moment was scurrying toward me, calling out: *"Sneakers!"* Who was this old man? I couldn't place the face. But then suddenly I realized—it was *Maddog!* Maddog, from my first night in the woods, from Black Gap shelter on the Springer Mountain access trail. In a million years I would never have thought I'd see Maddog again. Judging from that night two months earlier, I guessed that he hadn't hiked here, and I was right. Maddog joked that he had logged five thousand miles by train but only fifteen miles by foot. He laughed and laughed. He said that he'd quit his hike after a week of back pain, and that he'd then ridden back home to California by train. But once home he had missed the trail so

119

much that he rode back again to the AT. He now had a part-time job at the ATC headquarters and was living in his tent out in back of the Shady Hook hostel, walking across the Potomac River to work every day. He had read my ATC headquarters entry a few day's earlier in the ATC register, so he knew to keep an eye out for me.

Maddog knew so few hikers from his time in the woods that he was excited to see me and share some memories. It was very nice, but even as we talked I was anxious to break away to find Mozyin'. I finally found Mozyin' out back in the yard with two teenage girls. He had emptied their backpacks on the ground and was reviewing the content as Wayne had done for me at Neels Gap: *"Keep that, keep that, get rid of that."* It made me realize that we could now do that for any hiker. We had become Neels Gap. We *were* Neels Gap. We could help plan anyone's trip. We could lecture at hiking stores. We had learned all the practical hiking knowledge we would ever need to know, and our trip was only half over. I had been nervous about returning to the trail, but now I was back, and happy. My best night of sleep anywhere on the entire Appalachian Trail that summer was my first night back in the woods after leaving DC. I could relax once again.

All through these next dozens of miles, you live in halfway-euphoria mode. You have passed the ATC headquarters, but you still have yet to reach the actual halfway marker, which is seventy-eight miles north of Harpers Ferry. After having hiked so long in one state, here you have a stretch of forty-four miles that occupies four separate states—Virginia, West Virginia, Maryland, and Pennsylvania (you can hit all four states in one day if you try). Mozyin' and I left the Shady Hook hostel early morning and followed alongside the Potomac River canal path. We climbed up Weverton Cliffs with its view looking back at Harpers Ferry. After eight miles that day, we crossed our one thousandth mile on the trail. At a park we met hiking legend *Tom Horn* (his trail name) and his thirteen-year-old Beagle. That dog had logged fifteen thousand lifetime trail miles and was still going strong.

Mozyin' and I took hot showers in the park with Mozyin' anally walking fifteen feet south upon leaving the shower (and then walking north) so as not to miss any trail. We caught up with Heel and Toe, and *Strider and Eowyn* that night after 21.3 miles, at Pine Knob shelter. It was Memorial Day weekend. Forty weekend warriors had settled into the clearing around our shelter. Most of them didn't use stoves. Instead they scooped up every fallen branch, stick and twig within two hundred yards for their fires, raping a huge circle around the clearing to create a barren, unnatural wasteland. One man walked back and forth in front of our lean-to carrying armload after armload of wood back to his tent. Another came over and asked us for help with his stove. We showed him how to light it. Then he picked up his lit stove and he carried it back to his tent (good thing he didn't trip).

My second day out of Harpers Ferry, I left Mozyin' behind never to see him again that summer. I had enjoyed his company in the shelters, but I valued the freedom of hiking alone. Mozyin' was perhaps the strongest hiker on the trail, but he was content to progress at a casual pace while I liked to make miles. The trail led me out of the woods, into the Pen-Mar (Pennsylvania-Maryland) Park where thousands of people were gathered for a Memorial Day weekend festival. There were food booths, bands, clowns, and people of all ages engaged in every form of celebration. An extended family adopted me, grabbing me, pulling me over, and plopping me down at their picnic table. My rotund host asked:

"Why do they call you Sneakers?"

I pointed down.

"What? A snake will bite right through those! Hey, you seen any copperheads? No? Good. Listen—around here we have a saying about copperheads: *If you get bit by a copperhead, find a comfortable spot and lie down. Because that's where you're going to stay!"*

The man's brother laughed in little snorts, and he told a snake story of his own:

> *Two men were out camping in the woods, when one got bit on his ass by a Copperhead. Right on the ass. Well the second man, he didn't know what to do, so he ran into town. He found a doctor and he told him what had happened. "What should I do?" he asked the doctor. The doctor replied: "Well, you have to rush back right away and suck the poison out or else your friend will die." The hiker ran back into the woods to his bitten friend. "What did the doctor say?" asked the sick man. The friend replied: "He said you're gonna die."*

Talk in the park was news of a woman found burned to death in the woods by the AT the day before. She was not a through-hiker; she was a local woman with a history of mental problems and attempted suicides. Continuing on beyond the park, I reached a sign which marked the Mason-Dixon line. Here in the woods was the Pennsylvania-Maryland border, the border between North and South. *"Now I am in the South,"* I said out loud. I stepped over the line. *"And now I am in the North."* I considered this long and hard. I thought to myself: *I am a Northerner and now I am in the North. I am home.* Six states down, eight to go. I spent that night in the Tumbling Run double-shelters, twenty-five miles on the day, having caught up with Cyclops. Cyclops slept in one shelter and I in the other as we hadn't become friends. There was a note tacked onto one of the shelters instructing Easy Stryder to call the police. Apparently Easy Stryder had seen the woman's burned body

121

in the woods. Cyclops told me that Easy Stryder had just left the trail for a few days with Blazer. I would pass by without seeing either one of them ever again. Flyers inside these shelters advertised the existence of a Jacuzzi at the Ironmaster Hostel, 29.3 miles ahead. Succumbing to the gravitational pull of the Jacuzzi, I hiked the full 29.3 miles that next day, arriving at the gigantic old Ironmaster Youth Hostel mansion only to find that the manager had just that day emptied the water out of the Jacuzzi to clean it. *Trail Curse!* I was shattered. I had worked so hard to reach it. You constantly dangle carrots in front of your head for incentive. That Jacuzzi had been one big carrot that was now ripped away just at the moment I was ready to grab it. *Going Home* was here. That next morning I walked with Going Home two hundred yards up the trail to a lake where stands the halfway sign. Halfway. We took off our backpacks. We snapped photographs. We considered the moment. It was June 1, my sixtieth day on the trail. The sign was a tall totem pole with one arrow pointing south and another arrow pointing north. Each arrow had a mileage marker.

1,068 MILES TO SPRINGER

1,068 MILES TO KATAHDIN.

The distances marked were the same. One step past the marker meant that you were now more than halfway done. No more halfway-euphoria mode. You are beyond that now. You are now on the homestretch. You aren't counting the miles up anymore—now you are counting them down.

11
Hitting a Thin Spread

And, as in uffish thought he stood,
The Jabberwock, with eyes of flame
Came whiffling through the tulgey wood,
And burbled as it came!

—Lewis Carroll, *Jabberwocky*

Bodily Oddities.

Only Pennsylvania, New Jersey, and New York are left now before you reach New England. Here, you remember the scaled, three-dimensional model of the trail that you saw back in Harpers Ferry at the ATC headquarters. That scaled replica sat on a long table in a back room. You remember staring at it, visibly taken by the sight of the whole trail laid out before you, tactile, with mountains at both ends and low ground in the middle. Now here you are, low in the middle states. There are hills and there is rugged wilderness here in these middle states, but it won't be until New England when you move past Connecticut, up through Massachusetts and into Vermont that you will hit real mountains again. Here in the middle states you plod along through stretches of low open ground under the heat of the sun.

Pennsylvania, New Jersey, New York (ten days, one day, five days). Tiny, sharp rocks cover the trail in Pennsylvania. You have been listening to warnings about them for weeks, but you had to wait and find out for yourself if it was true because you've learned by now that on every inch of the trail you get misinformation. There is always someone approaching from the opposite direction who will offer bizarre advice or tell you how difficult the *next* section is: "Oh sure you've been fine so far, but you'll never make it through *Boozly Hill Gap.*" Southbound weekend warriors meeting you from the opposite direction will swear that what they've just staggered through, what you are heading toward, is simply too difficult for any human to bear. Hydro had once joked that we could be standing at Rainbow Spring campground with 2,140 miles behind us and some southbound day hiker coming down off Katahdin will say: *"You'll never make it up there—it's too tough!"* But now you see for yourself that these infamous Pennsylvania rocks do live up to their billing. No exaggeration. These rocks demand your attention and earn your respect. They are small and pointy and they litter every inch of the trail in Pennsylvania so that you can't step around them, you can't avoid them. So small are they that when you step on one your foot is never wholly supported. So sharp are they that people swear they've seen Boy Scout troops up in the hills sharpening them. Shelter register entries in Pennsylvania mirror those at the start of the trail; they are filled with confessions of pain: *"Razor blades would feel better than this."* People enjoyed predicting that my running shoes would fail me in Pennsylvania—sure, they had served well so far, but I couldn't possibly continue with them through these rocks. But my running shoes would serve fine. I would cover Pennsylvania's 230 trail miles in my running shoes in ten days.

I had hit a thin spread so far out in front of the big waves of hikers. I was caught alone in a gap with my old friends now behind me. Only Chinook, Mercury Mark, Mighty Mike, and Hydro were those that I knew who were up ahead. I knew I would soon catch the youngsters ahead, but Hydro's mileage was so consistent that I wasn't sure I would ever catch him. It was a spooky area to move through alone. In Pennsylvania a young through-hiking couple had been murdered on the trail just a few years earlier. Another concern in Pennsylvania is the summer heat. Spring is over. Now in June, summertime, down low on the trail, gone are the cool mountain breezes. Bodily oddities continue to surprise you here, as they have all along. *Restless Leg Syndrome* hits you at night. Your body has grown accustomed to hiking now, and so your legs continue hiking at night (why stop moving?). Now they twitch and snap and twist all night like the legs of a sleeping dog that dreams it is running. You find this unbearable. I had to sleep with my sleeping bag unzipped so that my legs could twitch, or else I might have been driven insane.

A second night visitor is *Automatic Sprinkler System.* Your sweat glands turn on and off like a faucet all day as you hike up and down mountains—on and off, on and off. After so many weeks on the trail now, and with nights so hot, your internal faucet hits automatic pilot. Your personal sprinkler system turns on and off at night with no regard for the relative angle of the sun to earth. Your sprinkler system achieves independence, deciding for itself: *"I haven't been on in a while, I think I'll turn on now!"* I often woke up in the dark completely drenched, sweat pouring off me. Now you are hot in the day, and night brings new twitching, sweating adventure. You wonder what is happening. Finally you realize that your body has taken on a mind of its own.

Killer Stones.

Despite the rocks, I turned up my mileage in the middle states. Three slackpacks helped me motor. I wasn't racing, I wasn't trying to conquer the trail, I was merely enjoying big miles, and I was anxious to reach New England. Stepping beyond the halfway post at Ironmasters, I hiked 19.2 miles into Boiling Springs where inside an Appalachian Trail Conference regional building I met two workers who were just heading home. They drove me back to their house—ten miles to the north and also directly on the trail— for a beer, shower and a night in a bed (*Things You Never Knew Existed* magazine in the bathroom; FREE CORKY THE WHALE flier on the coffee table). Here was my perfect chance to have my first *slackpack,* and so that next morning I left my pack at their house and they drove me back to the regional office where I'd left off; then with only my hiking stick, water bottle and a smile, I jogged from the regional office to their house, ten miles through fields in the Cumberland Valley lowlands. It was the fastest I had moved on the trail all summer. I skipped, jumped, jogged, turned, and twisted effortlessly. Freedom! *Running Deer* at last. That ten-mile slackpack went by too quickly. I wanted more. I vowed to somehow do it again. At the house, I reclaimed my backpack and continued on, hiking nine miles farther into the small, peeling-paint, crumbling mountain town of Duncannon, Pennsylvania, and my PO drop box #8.

Duncannon is where the '90 murderer met his two through-hiker victims. I spent the night on main street, downtown, trailside in the Doyle Hotel. The Doyle is a trail institution. Through-hikers have always stayed at the Doyle. I bathed in a community bathroom on the fourth floor with broken floor tiles and plaster hanging off the ceiling, and I slept with my bureau blockading my door as both its bolt and lock were broken. The young murdered hiking couple had been southbounders moving alone through here in the fall of '90. A drifter from Florida with a history of mental disease had befriended them in the bar at the Doyle and then hiked with them into the woods. The three settled into a shelter to sleep and he killed them that night. The double murder occurred south of town and was an isolated incident, still I didn't feel safe. At 10 AM the next morning, I found the Doyle's bar already filled with smoke as several locals were bellied up to the counter, empty beer bottles stockpiled before them. I bolted out, grabbed my drop box at the post office (and my next letter from the Y), and followed the trail out the north end of that small town. Hiker-friendly to a person, some kids in a car drove by and yelled at me out the window.

You exit Duncannon by crossing the Susquehanna River on the Clark's Ferry bridge, with Peter's Mountain ridge rising high across the far side of the river like a wall. North of the Susquehanna, I crossed railroad tracks and climbed uphill into the woods. My shelter options were at 5, 12.3, and 19 miles. With my late start, I stopped after 12.3 miles on the day for a night alone in the spooky hills above town in the Peter's Mountain shelter. All I could think of as I drifted to sleep was the savage attack on that couple three years earlier. Twenty-one miles that next day brought me to the Blue Blaze hostel, which is a private house in the woods with owners who have turned their two-car garage into a hiker hostel. Inside the hiker hostel garage were two beds, a sleeper sofa, chairs, a shower, and a refrigerator stocked with Cokes. There was a bookshelf: Mark Twain's *Ascent of the Riffelberg;* Washington Irving's *Rip Van Winkle;* Richard Bachman's (Stephen King's) hiking story called *The Long Walk;* the Rodale AT stories (Volume II only); and a June 3, 1991 *People Magazine* saved there with the article *"Murder in the Mountains,"* detailing the Duncannon murder story of the two young hikers. Here at the Blue Blaze hostel you have reached a milestone, for here northbounders now have fewer than one thousand miles left to hike. A three-digit mileage countdown is all you have left. The garage door remained open, night air blowing in. The home owners came down to visit.

"Who are you hiking with?"

"I was hiking with some people. They're all behind me now."

"You didn't want to stay together?"

"No, I'm just hiking my own pace. I got off in DC, and when I got back on, some of them had gotten off."

"Yeah. There haven't been many come through here this early."

You grow to depend upon sleeping with company beside you at night. Like a pack animal, you feel the need to sleep in a group. Privacy is fine, and you never thought you would feel this way, but by now you have come to rely on sleeping with other humans in the lean-to beside you, be it old friends or perfect strangers, northbounders or southbounders, through-hikers, section-hikers or weekend warriors. Caught in my empty gap, I'd meet company by day, but this Blue Blaze hostel marked my third straight night sleeping alone. And it came at a spooky time. I needed company. So when I reached the 501 shelter in a heavy downpour after thirteen miles that next day, I pulled up short and went in. The 501 shelter is an enclosed box house with beds beside the trail. I would have gone on but I needed the company.

Inside was *Virginia Slim* and two section-hikers. I had met Virginia Slim a day south of Harpers Ferry. He had passed me while I was vacationing in DC, but now he was stranded here because he had mailed home his sleeping bag during a bout of warm weather only to have the temperature drop on him the next day. Now he was too scared to continue until he got his sleeping bag back in the mail. A group that I'd passed in the rain an hour earlier came inside—*Elfman, Mountain Goat* and *Mouth Gravy.* Two were young and experienced section-hikers who had just gotten on the trail in Pennsylvania, while Mountain Goat, in his thirties, had befriended them. He sneered and swore through the afternoon; then that evening he scared us by telling a strange story of his expulsion from an organized group-hike across America, and of his subsequent arrest for selling pot in New Orleans where he had gone to kill time. He'd been tried, convicted, and sentenced, but he'd jumped bail and was still wanted by the police. He wore a black sweatshirt that had a bust of Albert Einstein on the front wearing a headband and smoking a pipe (Albert Einstein with his wild hair, looking very much like a through-hiker). The hostel caretakers lent Mountain Goat their car that night, and he drove into town to a bar with his young friends and returned hours later, drunk, loud, knocking things over, fumbling around. I bolted away once again in the morning, mad at myself, disappointed over my weakness for having stopped short on the day just to have company. To escape this group (and to purge my sloth), I shot away from 501, hiking ninety miles in three days—28.2 miles to Windsor Furnace shelter, 28.1 miles to Bake Oven shelter, and 29 miles to Wind Gap near New Jersey. It was a mighty push over Pennsylvania's killer stones. My feet ached.

My last long day into Wind Gap brought me the sight of my first poisonous snake. Descending a mountain of rock ledges and loose stones down into Lehigh Gap, I suddenly stopped and looked back. Something had caught my eye. I discovered then that I had walked right beside a Copperhead that was sunning itself in the trail. Its body was thick, its head was massive. Its eyes were stubborn, deadly, defiant. It was a beautiful, dangerous creature. It was one very tough snake. A palpable menace. I reached back with my hiking stick to stir it and move it off the trail so that it couldn't hurt anyone and so that no one could hurt it, but then I stopped, remembering how someone had told me that snakes can leap the length of their bodies. This snake was as long as my stick, hence I shouldn't touch it *with* my stick. Still, I wasn't afraid because I could look down the hill and see traffic on a busy highway below. Had I been bitten at that moment I could have rolled down the hill to a car.

I crossed the roads down in Lehigh Gap, lost the trail and finally found it again climbing up a cliff out the other side for the first hands-and-feet rock climb of my trip. Next came a brief stretch of some of the most torturous terrains on the trail—an exposed two-mile ridge walk over hot rocks under the blazing mid-state summer sun through an area devoid of foliage (a nearby defunct zinc mine had killed all the plant life years earlier). Upon reaching Wind Gap after twenty-nine miles that day, I now had only fifteen trail miles left in Pennsylvania. I was soon to reach New Jersey. An old family friend lived in New Jersey close to the trail. I had called Moor once already from a trailside restaurant called Raccoons, and now I called again from my Wind

Gap hotel room to finalize plans. Moor worked at Blair Academy in New Jersey and was my older brother's best man and lifelong best friend. He would first help me slackpack and then he would take me off the trail for a brief escape for a day. Everything settled, on Tuesday, June 8, I lay on my bed in the Wind Gap motor lodge and I watched a movie on Home Box Office. It was a graphic bondage, rape, murder, butcher movie with some of the most disturbing footage I had ever seen. Anywhere. Ever. I wondered that children could watch that movie. I wondered that adults could watch that movie. I went to sleep sad and shaken.

Church Basement.

Just fifteen miles from Wind Gap to Delaware Water Gap would take me to the end of Pennsylvania. Moor met me that next morning at the Wind Gap post office and he drove away with my drop box #9 and my backpack. On this second slackpack, I ran through the woods in a thunder and lightning rainstorm. I passed a lean-to where seven hikers were waiting out the storm. Inside were Chinook, Mercury Mark, Mighty Mike, *Lightning Rod* (a 1990 through-hiker who was out for a week), and three senior citizens who wore ponchos and had umbrellas fixed to the tops of their packs.

"Is that *you,* Sneakers? Are you *slackpacking?* How did you manage that?"

This large group examined me standing outside in the rain with just my hiking stick and slackpacker's smile. I continued on, running, leaping over slippery boulders on a ridge, thunder clapping all around. The rain tapered off; then quite suddenly it stopped and the sun broke through the clouds as mist rose from the ground and off the trees in the woods. A deer crossed the trail in front of me. Then a rainbow emerged. And I was weightless, without a pack on my back. It was the single most potent, charming instant of my hike. A mile farther I stepped out of the woods onto the property of the Presbyterian Church of the Mountain in Delaware Water Gap, Pennsylvania. The church basement serves as a hiker hostel. The church holds the highest ground in that single traffic light, upscale town. A skateboarder descending the steep church driveway down to main street and then farther and faster down main street to the lower body of town shops would pick up speed to a dangerous degree and would never arrive in one piece. Hiking sticks stood propped against a shed beside the church. I descended into the church basement. A back room in the basement has bunk beds, a toilet, and a shower. The carpeted front room has a refrigerator, coffee table, sofa, and chairs. I read the hostel's trail register. Homeward Bound and Unleashed had arrived but had gotten off the trail to visit friends. Besides Eddie-B, this meant that now only Water, J-Zero, Peaked in High School, and Griff (and possibly Hydro?) were ahead of me (Padre with Pooches had left the trail). Only four northbounders remained up ahead of me. I signed in; then Moor arrived and took me away.

Moor and I spent the rest of that day playing squash at Blair Academy, lifting weights, and eating in the faculty cafeteria. I read my latest letter from the Y. It was the longest one yet and the first from Germany. It was fifteen pages detailing every event of her arrival in Germany—her plane ride, the airports, her arrival in town, the tennis club. That night I told Moor that I would marry the Y. She would be my wife. I was certain. Moor was the first one to know. You grow very sentimental like that on the trail. Small gestures, simple kindnesses become unbearably profound. No one had ever taken care of me like this. Every stop, a ten-page letter. I had come to depend on the Y's letters. I always knew I would have one waiting for me at my next PO stop, encouraging me, urging me on. That next morning Moor drove me back to the Delaware Water Gap church where I spent a zero day in town in the basement with Chinook, Mercury Mark, and Mighty Mike who had all made it in. We ate rhubarb, raspberry and cherry pies baked fresh from a pie shop in town. I ate ginger carrot soup with sesame crackers in a café across the street—delicious. It was Thursday, June 10. Thursday is barbecue night at the church. *"Kindness, compassion,"* they teach at the church: *"Too much violence, not enough kindness in the world today."* But come to our church and eat chickens, cows and pigs—innocent living beings, confined, subjected, butchered, consumed. Saddened again. To purge my thoughts once again, I planned a very long slackpack, my slackpack #3. In the outfitter store at the bottom of town I arranged with a man for $60 to shuttle my backpack forty-three trail miles away that next day from Delaware Water Gap, Pennsylvania, to High Point State Park, New Jersey. I was eager to try. I retired early, drifting to sleep listening to the three-umbrella senior-citizen weekend-hikers discuss an ocean kayaking trip that they planned to take that next summer. It was a joy in my head, listening to them.

4 5.7-Mile Day.

It was forty-three miles to my backpack (I would spend only one day in New Jersey). I awoke at 4 AM by my watch alarm. Wide awake, adrenaline surging, within five minutes I was outside in the darkness descending the street to the outfitter store at the bottom of town. In the parking lot at the outfitter store I tucked my pack into the backseat of a blue Nova and I locked the car doors behind, trusting that my pack would be waiting for me at the end of the day at the High Point State Park information center as arranged. I walked back up to the church with only my hiking stick and water bottle; then I walked north on the trail out of town on I-80, crossing the bridge over the Delaware River and stepping out of Pennsylvania into New Jersey. Seven states down, seven states to go. The sky lightened by 5 AM; then day broke. I had a good start and felt strong. I climbed up through a park on smooth, groomed paths. I passed Sunfish Pond, the first glacial pond on the AT moving north. I had plenty of water. I jogged some, walked some. I had far to go, so when I walked I walked fast. I jogged along a flat ridge and came up behind two hikers and their dog so quietly that I spooked the dog as I passed so it swung around snarling and frightened. This was a good stretch of flat trail. I passed five shelters that day, signing in at every one. I telephoned the park headquarters from Worthington's Bakery by the trail in the early afternoon and a woman told me that my pack had indeed been delivered (thus alleviating a small concern in the back of my mind).

I made my forty-three miles, reaching the High Point State Park information center just after 6 PM. My pack was there, but the workers had set it beside a leaky air conditioner so its bottom got drenched. The rangers asked to take my photograph for the woman I had spoken with on the phone. She had left for the day but she wanted to see what I looked like. I put my arm around her empty chair, and they snapped the shot with an instant camera. Then two rangers drove me to a pizzeria for dinner. I still had 1.2 miles to hike that night to reach the nearest shelter north of the visitor center, but I lingered at the restaurant. Finally, I began stiffening up, so we left.

Back at the visitor center at 7:30 PM, I grabbed my pack and set out. At .7 miles I reached an observation tower and the great white spire of the High Point monument. Then darkness fell. I walked at a snail's pace through the dark woods, expecting to bump into the High Point shelter on the trail .5 miles beyond the monument. Hydro had taught me to beware of perceptions at the end of the day. At day's end you are tired and anxious to reach your destination, so your perception of distance becomes warped. You believe that you should have already reached Whazzit-Called shelter. You grow impatient and disoriented, but you should not be deceived. You must remain calm and take your time. This was excellent Hydro advice.

I remained calm and I walked slowly through the darkness, but I never saw the shelter. I knew that I had walked too far when I came to U.S. 516, which according to the data book is 1.3 miles beyond the shelter that I'd never found (2.5 miles past the visitor center). I did not despair. I felt calm, sleepy, content. I had already eaten. My stomach was full. I had plenty of water. The sky was clear. What did I need the shelter for anyway? U.S. 516 is 45.7 miles from Delaware Water Gap. I had hiked 45.7 miles and there was nothing that I needed to do now except lie down and close my eyes.

I picked a spot on the trail at the edge of a field one hundred yards from the road. I felt that it was important to sleep directly on the trail because that way if I died in my sleep from exhaustion at least they could find my body. I lay down in my sleeping bag with it tucked inside my bivy sack. It was my first night sleeping outside on the ground under the stars. It was my first night in the bivy sack that I'd bought from Mozyin' back in Pearisburg. The ground felt soft compared to the hard wood lean-to floors. I fell asleep instantly.

Nose snorts from a very large animal woke me up in the middle of the night. I listened. They continued from a spot a short distance across the field. I knew that it was a black bear. The bear was sounding its presence, staking its territory, angered by this trespasser who was sacked out larvalike in a bag at the edge of its field. It sounded big and brave and mad. But I wasn't afraid. I was too tired to care. I drifted back to sleep. I awoke again later, needing to use the bathroom, but I was too tired to stand and walk away from my bag to urinate so instead I crawled about a yard through the weeds, naked, just far enough away to keep my things dry and I urinated; then I went back to sleep. How could I have known then that a little microscopically small jabberwocky-mite had crawled on me? How could I have known then what a great impact it would later have on my hike?

Fatigued—postñ45.7 miles—I awoke that next morning only when a passing hiker discovered me prone on the trail at 10:05 AM. I leapt up and hiked twenty-four miles to the Wawayanda shelter in glorious sunny weather, over 112 log bridges through New Jersey's *Vernie Swamp* and around *Wallkill River Valley Sod Farm,* which were gorgeous fields called *The Flats.* I felt proud for having followed my longest day with a long day. A group of seven retired men slept in tents outside the shelter.

"Where have you hiked in from?" they asked me.

"I left Delaware Water Gap yesterday morning," I said.

"That's seventy miles away!" They laughed.

"We've planned eight days to hike there!"

"Look, and he's done it in sneakers."

I overslept again the next morning. Fatigue had caught up with me and I was only able to rise and hike just twelve miles on the day to Wildcat Shelter. While that day's mileage was disappointingly low, at least a glance in my data book showed me that I had now left New Jersey behind and had entered New York. Eight states down, six to go.

Monastery Moments.

I had reached New York State, my birth state. It is surprising how near New York City this wilderness trail passes. On clear nights, hikers can see the lights of Manhattan from two different spots on the trail. The hiker's handbook mentions that here the trail has a *"tenuous search for accommodation as it skirts the New York City megalopolis."* Midday north of Wildcat Shelter, I crossed the New York State Thruway and entered Harriman State Park, following the trail through *The Lemon Squeezer,* which is a fifty-foot crack in a massive boulder that is so narrow you have to take off your pack and walk sideways to get through, pulling your pack behind you. I passed swimmer-filled Lake Tiorati Campground and slept alone at William Brien Memorial Shelter after 19.6 miles on the day. I had passed New York City.

I awoke and crossed Bear Mountain in the morning, descending northward down into Bear Mountain State Park which had playing fields, one hundred yellow school buses, and thousands of camp kids and councilors scurrying everywhere—hiking, playing softball, soccer, tag. I quietly followed the trail through this squealing, shouting, running, kicking, racing, kiddy crowd. It was Tuesday, June 15, my eighty-second day on the trail, and I had just 782 miles left to hike. I collected my PO #10 from the Bear Mountain post office in the park beside the trail; then I walked through the most noxious spot on the AT from Georgia to Maine: the *Bear Mountain State Park Trailside Museum and Zoo*. It was an old-fashioned zoo with animals in small cages the sizes of their bodies. The Appalachian Trail follows a sidewalk through the zoo, leading hikers just inches away from penned animals. There was a bobcat in a four-foot cage within reach of the sidewalk, and kids stood rattling the cage with a stick, frightening the animal to death. There were five black bears in a sunken holding pen—and these bears were so enormous that it forced me to reconsider the calm I had felt while bivied out that night at the edge of the field when I'd heard a big bear's nose snorts. But then, these bears got no exercise. Tales exist of through-hikers who walk through this zoo crying, tears rolling down their faces after having seen relatives of these same animals out in the wild. The zoo is on the Hudson River, and immediately out its eastern end the trail follows the highway over the Hudson on the Bear Mountain Bridge (New York City lies fifty miles downriver from here, and we could have rafted down). The high bridge stands twenty stories above the water, and I kept looking down over the railing as I went.

It is a geographic oddity that one can cross east of the Hudson River and still be in New York State; but that is what happens here, for a strange little thirty-mile wedge of New York State land is tucked east of the mighty Hudson but still west of New England. I knew from my handbook that there is a magical monastery here, one that it is open to through-hikers. Adding just a few more miles past the zoo and the bridge over the Hudson, I stopped after 14.9 miles on the day, having reached *The Graymoor Franciscan Friars of the Atonement Monastery,* in Garrison, New York. This was a place that I had been hearing about since my earliest days on the trail. East of the Hudson, I stepped off the trail and walked up the long drive to the monastery compound. It was not lost on me that this was quite probably the only chance in my life that I would get to sleep in a monastery, so I relished the moment. Through-hikers are welcome here. We are expected. I entered and signed in for a room and found bald-headed monks wearing long brown robes walking barefoot slowly down the corridors, exactly as you would expect. There were nuns here, as well, and there were nurses manning desks and supervising classroom courses in adult education, driving school, alcohol rehabilitation. They gave me a towel and a single small room upstairs and off in the old wing that was narrow, Spartan, quiet, and comfortable. Just a cot, a desk, and a bible. I ate dinner at a table with Brother Joseph in the monks' large cafeteria—tray, silverware, salad bar. After dinner, I read some books in the library, washed my clothes in the laundry room, then took a long hot shower down the hall. I ate M&M's, read my mail and wrote letters, surrounded by views out the windows of gardens and statues. I imagined my crystal ball fantasy—of how if long ago I could have looked into my future and seen myself lying on a small bed in a monastery, I would have screamed! The monastery has its own stationery, and I wrote to my friends on this logoed letterhead, carefully beginning each letter in the same manner: *"I'm sure that you would never have believed there would come a day when I would be writing to you from a monastery..."*

Next morning, having slept well, I continued on and hiked 28.2 miles to Morgan Stewart shelter, my sixth straight night sleeping without the company of a fellow through-hiker. The following morning I woke up knowing that I was now to reach precious New England. Near the Connecticut border stands a wooden platform railroad stop by a road in the middle of nowhere that has daily trains leading into New York City. I considered one instant that I might hop a train into New York City Port Authority and jump on the Hampton Jitney and ride out to Southampton to visit my friend Tinling, but I didn't go. I needed to keep making progress. I was moving. I had crossed the middle states. I had limped over Pennsylvania's rocks, had survived a pocket of creepy loneliness, had circumnavigated New York City, and enjoyed one night in a monastery. Now I would step into New England.

12

Into New England

The classification of the constituents of a chaos,
nothing less here is essayed.

—Herman Melville, *Moby-Dick*

My Territory Now.

I live in New England. This whole summer has been spent heading
for home. There is safety and comfort in home, in the familiar versus the
unknown. You enter New England knowing that you will be climbing again.
You rise a bit in Connecticut and Massachusetts; then you cross Vermont's ski
slopes and scale New Hampshire's White Mountains before finally reaching
the Maine wilderness. Sadly, reaching the New England border lacks dramatic
appeal because northbounders enter New England but then exit again for
seven miles before finally reentering (this time for good) as the trail snakes
back and forth across the New York StateñConnecticut line. The trail leads
only fifty miles in Connecticut and ninety miles in Massachusetts. You breeze
through these two states like chocolate candy. Entering New England, you
have only 707 miles left. This should have been such a celebration for me,
but I had begun to feel strange, unexplained emotions.

A 28.7-mile day took me out of New York and into Connecticut to the
Mt. Algo lean-to which I shared with an enormous fat man named *Baby Steps*.
At .3 miles the next morning, we came to a road crossing where a guy sacked
out in a rusted car offered us a ride into the town of Kent for the price of his

cigarettes. I rode in with Baby Steps and got cash from an automatic teller machine. Returning to the trail, we found the cigarette Kent dude asking if we wanted to get dropped off at River Road, five miles north on the trail, on the far side of a mountain beyond a steep climb. He said that's where he had dropped off *Water* on his return from Kent a week earlier. Water was yellow-blazing? The news affected me greatly. I was rapidly gaining ground on the three lead hikers ahead, but this news got me dejected. It wasn't a race; I knew that. I wasn't racing. Still it bothered me. I was lonely and feeling quite strange. I hiked through the *Red Pine Plantation* and made 17.6 miles on the day to Pine Swamp Brook lean-to, where I spent yet another night alone. The next morning (Saturday) I hiked 8.3 morning miles and crossed the Iron Bridge over the Housatonic River where dozens of inner tube riders were unloading vans, organizing, and hitting the rapids. I detoured off the trail and walked into the immaculate, antiseptic, tiny toy town of Falls Village, Connecticut (population five hundred), for my post office stop #11. The postmaster gave me my drop box, an additional letter from my parents, and a letter from my sister-in-law.

"Anything else?"

"That's all we have for you."

"No other letter? I'm expecting another letter."

He checked again.

"Nope. That's it."

"Look, can you check again? Is there any other separate pile? Is there any other place it could be?"

There was no letter from the Y. This was a first. At the time she had left for Germany I had only planned my PO stops up until Bear Mountain, New York. After that she was to mail her letters home to my parents for them to forward to me. Maybe the Y's letter was in my drop box from my parents. I checked every inch of the box: I opened containers, looked under the cardboard flaps. Nothing there. I had the postmaster check yet again. But no letter from the Y. I couldn't believe it. I needed that letter. She had spoiled me so much with such excellent letters that now I felt empty without one. My zeal was gone. Those letters had fueled me. Now what would I do without it?

Distraught, I packed up my food and walked outside in a daze only to find that my hiking stick had been stolen. I had left it outside, leaned against the post office front door. There had been kids on bikes in the parking lot when I had entered; now the kids were gone. One of them must have run up and swiped it. No letter, no hiking stick. I felt so fragile. I thought I might cry. I called home from a pay phone in front of that tiny town's little bank. My mother said she had just received a letter from the Y. She said she would mail it ahead to my next PO. I was glad for that, but how would I cope for the next eighty miles? I couldn't believe that one missing letter could get me so down. Yet here I was: I had crashed. I felt lousy. After three months on cruise control I had suddenly Hit the Wall. No letter from the Y; I could not continue. I had to get off the trail. I hadn't planned a stop here, but my aunt and uncle lived thirty minutes away so I called them. It was Saturday, June 19, at twelve noon.

I called and waited in a restaurant for my aunt to come pick me up. She took me home, fed me, and gave me a comfortable room. Still, I couldn't get comfortable. I couldn't relax. I couldn't eat much, which, for a through-hiker, was a great deal more than entirely odd. I drove to a movie theater that night and watched *Jurassic Park* ("You're going to engineer a bunch of prehistoric animals and set them on an island? Fine. A lovely dream. Charming. But it won't go as planned. It is inherently unpredictable, just as the weather is"). The movie's jungle scenes were appealing, but while driving home in the darkness I kept looking around expecting to see a dinosaur break through the trees and charge after me. I lay in a bed that night, but I slept fitfully. The following morning at 10 AM, I called Germany. It was 4 PM in Träunstein, and I called the pay phone in the tennis clubhouse knowing that the Y would be there on a Sunday afternoon. Sunday was match day, and Sunday afternoons everyone lingered at the clubhouse for hours eating and smoking and drinking. Heinze answered and he brought the Y to the phone. She said she was shaking it was such a surprise. I told her about the missing letter. I told her how I had crashed and had left the trail. She said that I should try to relax. I remained at my aunt and uncle's all day trying to focus, preparing myself to continue. My aunt drove me back to the trail Monday morning. She drove away and I stood at the edge of the woods outside Falls Village. Two days of rest off the trail had done nothing for me. I did not feel ready to continue. The woods held no appeal. I had no hiking stick. I still felt drained. Emotionally low. I had no motivation. I set out anyway.

Rejuvenated?

I didn't feel ready yet. I felt as if I was back on the trail too soon, as if the rest had done nothing for me. I had no enthusiasm. With my late start and constant search for a new stick, I made just 10.6 miles for a night alone in a wonderfully peaceful Riga lean-to with its view out over a valley. At 2.6 miles the next morning, I crossed Bear Mountain (yet another Bear Mountain; lots of mountains share the same name). This Bear Mountain has a small rock tower on top. It is the first elevation over two thousand feet that northbounders have stood upon since Pennsylvania. A half mile later I left Connecticut behind as I stepped across the state border into Massachusetts. Ten states down, four to go. Six hundred and sixty-four miles left. Twenty-four point four miles total that day brought me to Tom Leonard shelter where I slept with an old man who carried a stylish wicker backpack. Also there was *TC* with his younger adolescent brother *Hawkeye*. They cooked and ate in the shelter but slept down on a tent platform overlooking a mountain range and valley. The tenderness and patience which big brother showed little brother was an inspiration. The admiration and adoration which little brother showed big brother was palpable. I felt glad to see it.

Pushing on the next day, I hiked 21.5 miles for a bed at busy Upper Goose Pond Cabin, a two-story cabin beside the trail on a lake with a kitchen and canoes. There was a caretaker there named Andy, who had hiked the John Muir trail, which is part of the Pacific Crest Trail, in California. The next morning at 1.2 miles I crossed over the Massachusetts Turnpike on a footbridge. Looking down over the edge of the bridge I saw the small sign that reads APPALACHIAN TRAIL. It is visible to eastbound drivers, while on the other side is one visible to westbounders. Here was the very sign that I'd seen from my car years earlier, the first time I had ever heard of the trail. Now here I stood over that sign years later wearing a backpack.

North of the turnpike you have no more major roads to cross. You have now crossed all four big ones: *I-40, I-80, the New York State Thruway, and the Mass Turnpike.* There is nothing left; here you are north of it all, north of all civilization (not really, of course, but it's fun to think so). As if to support that theory, I saw two adult black bears on the trail by a stream thirty yards ahead of me just one mile north of the turnpike. These were the only wild bear I had actually seen on the trail the whole summer, except for the baby that I'd seen from a distance in the Smokies down south. These two large bears stood right before me. They glanced back and saw me; then one of them turned and jogged away while the other turned and grudgingly, unnervingly walked slowly away. That evening at 28.8 miles, I entered small Cheshire, Massachusetts (population thirty-five hundred). The trail brushes the edge of town. I left the trail, entered town, and walked to St. Mary of the Assumption Catholic Church, a modern brick building which puts up hikers in two small meeting rooms in the back.

Baby Steps was there in the Cheshire church. He had hitchhiked ahead. He showed me the pack of a through-hiker who had dropped off his things. It was Chinook's pack. Chinook returned later. We talked awhile. Chinook was a student at Middlebury College in Vermont. He had taken a year off from school to hike the trail. He was a tall, bruiser of a kid, terrifically strong. He laughed, telling me his story of how he had hiked naked one day in Virginia. He had developed a chaffing rash from his shorts that had grown so painful that one day he couldn't hike with them on. Heavy rain fell that day so he strapped on his backpack over his T-shirt and he hiked through the woods in the rain completely naked except for his T-shirt and hiking boots. He had passed by a group of three older women hiking southbound in the rain that afternoon. They all greeted him a hearty hello and they hiked on as natural as could be.

Chinook left the Cheshire church again later that night with his girlfriend,

137

who had driven down to visit him. He would now leave the trail to go home for five days. I tried to sleep on the stone church floor, but it was too hard. I was feeling sick and uncomfortable, so I moved outside with my sleeping bag and I bivied on a grass patch behind the church. I slept uneasily. I felt a bit off. Unusual.

I awoke in the morning and collected my drop box #12 at the post office. Again, no letter from the Y. I couldn't believe it. And yet I had almost expected it. I found a phone and called home again. My mother said that a second letter had arrived from the Y from Germany and that by the time she had gotten the chance to go to the post office it would have been too late for them to reach me at Falls Village so instead she had mailed them ahead to West Hartford, Vermont. I don't know. Perhaps it was my own fault. Perhaps I hadn't adequately expressed to my mother how important it was for me to get that first letter as soon as possible. But now there was no point explaining. I got off the phone. At least I was now heading toward those two letters with every step. But that knowledge somehow wasn't enough to revive me. I felt lower than ever—lousy, heavy, thick, dull, blunt, hurt. The damage was done.

Mt. Greylock (thirty-five hundred ft.) is the highest peak in Massachusetts. The trail runs directly over the summit. The mountain is nestled in the upper left (northwest) corner of the state just at the Vermont border. I had never climbed it, but this was a mountain that I knew very well. My younger brother had fallen in love with his wife on this mountain. They had spent four years in neighboring Williamstown, Massachusetts, where I used to visit them while they were in college there. From Cheshire, 12.8 miles took me up Mt. Greylock's summit with its parking lot, war memorial stone tower, and the Bascom Lodge. The lodge is a comfortable carpeted mansion on the wide, flat summit with a view out over the Berkshires. Inside there are sofas and chairs, pay phones, second-story bunk rooms and a cafeteria with homemade lemonade and cookies. I would have loved to sleep here in an upstairs bunk with company and cookies on hand, but I was eager to continue on and descend just two miles farther down the north side of the mountain to reach Williamstown. I reached Rte. 2 after 14.8 miles on the day out of Cheshire and I hitchhiked west two miles into Williamstown. I walked down main street past *Papa Charlie's* sandwich shop, and down to the outfitter store. I knew this town well, from visiting my brother at college here, and also from team tennis and squash trips. There was nowhere to sleep in town, but the outfitter store workers said I could sleep on the lawn behind the store by a stream. I watched *Like Water for Chocolate* in the single screen movie theater in town that evening. It was Friday, June 25.

My backpack sat in the aisle beside me on a theater floor sticky with spilled popcorn and dried soda. When the movie finished, two couples in front of me rose and a man said: *"It was a story about unrequited love."*

The others nodded agreement. They all seemed glad to have summed up that movie with a single phrase. I myself had no one to discuss the movie with. I left the theater while it was still light out. I bought a veggie footlong at Subway and I walked back down through town wearing my backpack, munching away. I was lonely. I lay down on the grass behind the outfitter store by its backyard stream. It was my second straight night sleeping outside on the ground in my bivy behind a building. Would anyone find me and harm me at night? I should have been happy here in this cozy town, here in this very familiar place; but it wasn't to be. I didn't feel good. I felt strangely sick. Feverish. Was something coming on? I felt anxious, worried, brown. I slept only fitfully at night once again.

Fading Fast.

I hitchhiked back to the trail in the morning. At 4.1 miles I reached the Vermont border and stepped into Vermont. Five hundred and seventy-six miles left. Eleven states down, only three states to go. Just three more states. Your first 103 Appalachian Trail miles in Vermont are also spent on *The Long Trail*. These two trails share the same turf for 103 miles, but then the Long Trail continues north up to Canada while the AT splits off taking a right-hand turn east toward Hanover, New Hampshire. The Long Trail predates the Appalachian Trail. The Long Trail runs 263 miles, for the height of vertical Vermont. Both trails are marked by signs at Vermont's southern border. A third sign on a little metal post there reads: *FUNERAL ROUTE*. It was almost prophetic. A father and son took my picture standing before that sign. After my late start out of town at only 14.1 miles on the day, I reached Congdon Camp shelter, an enclosed cabin which I shared with the father and son. They were through-hiking the Long Trail. It would take them three weeks. They asked me some questions. Flattered, I was eager to share my thoughts and experiences; but I couldn't force myself to be good company. I was feeling worse. I couldn't identify why. I had needed those letters from the Y. Now how did I know for certain that they would be waiting for me up ahead? What if they wouldn't be there at my next PO stop, either?

I pushed on that next day, hiking 23.3 miles to Story Spring shelter where I slept alone. The next day, 7.4 miles took me to the summit of Stratton mountain (3,936 ft.). This was the birthplace of the AT. Benton MacKaye had conceived his idea for a linked East-Coast footpath while here on Stratton mountain's summit. There was a beautiful young woman working alone for the summer as caretaker in the cabin on Stratton's peak. One sign of my weakness was that I lacked the energy to chat with her. I am certain that I was the only male hiker to pass over the mountain that summer who gave up the chance for her company. I climbed the metal fire tower on top of the mountain with an older married weekend couple and we stood on the high platform

139

looking out all around. Three miles beyond Stratton's peak I reached Stratton pond with two shelters and several tent platforms. At 18.4 miles on the day, I stopped at Spruce Peak shelter, another enclosed cabin, this one with a porch and an excellent view. I draped my sweat-drenched clothes over the porch railing and spent another night alone.

Vermont is the *Green Mountain State.* The French named it: *Verde* is green, *Mont* is mountain. You feel that you have hit wilderness once again here in Vermont. Here you see beaver dam ponds with stick-hut domes in the middle. You find chunks eaten out of wood shelters and picnic tables by porcupines that eat anything tainted with sweat or urine (both for salt). After Spruce Peak shelter I crossed Bromley Mountain, Styles Peak, Peru Peak, Baker Peak. Black flies bit me mercilessly. Grouse jumped into my path as I walked along. Early spring down south you heard grouse beating their breasts to attract mates. Now in the summer, they use crazy antics, leaping in front of you, flapping around in the trail pretending they are injured to try to lure you away from their nests. They hope that you will chase them instead of their chicks. They limp and spin and flap around all wobbly in the trail in front of you. It scares you at first. You wonder if perhaps they are drunk. Or brain damaged. You keep walking trying to ignore them, but they cannot be ignored: *"Oh my, OH MY POOR BROKEN WING!"* Spinning and falling, they stagger before you. Academy award winners, every one. After about twenty feet of this, they fly away and secretly circle back to their nests. Crazy survival skills. I met two southbound through-hikers whose water filter had broken. They were carrying just the one between them and they didn't have iodine pills, so now they could only purify water by boiling it. They begged me for iodine pills. I gave them half a container's worth. I met a southbound through-hiking Southerner named *Slimfast* who wore a Walkman. Slimfast was from Tennessee. I would learn only much later that this was a Frist from Nashville. But at the time I had no idea. He had his Walkman and I had my poor equilibrium, so we didn't stop to chat long.

Food hadn't been tasting good to me lately—not the food off the trail at my aunt's, not the sandwich from Subway in Williamstown, not the food in my little pot in the woods at night. I had lost my appetite; nothing was appealing. I met a weekend hiking couple who gave me an orange. I sat down, peeled it, and ate it. It would be the last solid food I could eat for five days. I reached Lost Pond shelter that evening after seventeen miles. Black flies surrounded me (at least *their* appetites were sound). The shelter floor felt too hard to sleep on. What was going on? What was my deal? Why was I feeling so sick? Had I eaten too many meals in the woods? Had I slept on too many hard shelter floors? What was wrong? Why was I down? Had I been bitten by too many black flies? Had I spent too many nights alone? Had I drunk bad water from too many beaver dam ponds? Or could this all be mental stress because I hadn't gotten a letter from the Y?

Inexplicably, I was still carrying my protein and mega-carbohydrate powdered power drinks even though I hadn't used them all summer. At every post office drop box I would repack my bags of power drink mixes and either throw away or mail home the new ones. Since I could now no longer eat solid food I thought that maybe these mixes would finally serve me well. Maybe at long last I had found a reason to keep them. Perhaps they could win me my strength back; perhaps they could nurse me back to health. I boiled water and stirred one up. I took a sip. Disgusting. I couldn't drink it. Why had I been carrying these powders all summer? The black flies never stopped biting. I stuck my head under my bug-screen head-dome (Mozyin' had included it in the deal for the bivy sack I had purchased from him back in Pearisburg). It was indispensable for just this reason. But maybe it was the problem. Was I not getting enough oxygen at night, sleeping with my head under my bug-screen head-tent? I hadn't seen black flies all trip, but for the past few days they were everywhere biting incessantly. People wrote shelter register entries about them:

> The black flies are devouring my flesh like a tiger ripping into
> a fresh zebra carcass. Even with ample bug solution I'm
> being dive-bombed by the hordes of black flies. The whole
> day is spent in a vertigo frenzy with arms waving and
> slapping. Even as I eat, bugs are landing in my hot dinner.
> Good protein I guess. The bugs are actually starting to
> taste good! The welts on my body are swollen and itchy. Is
> this fun? I ask. Is the scenery worth it? I wonder, ponder,
> and debate my frenzied dilemma. Did God make these flies?
> Did Satan? You choose. I'm staying the weekend at the
> platforms. Next time I'm bringing a scuba suit.

> (sung to the tune of the Bob Dylan classic):
> How many flies must a man swat off
> before he is driven insane?
> The answer my friend is sitting at Griff Lake
> The answer is sitting at Griff Lake.

The next day after eight miles, I broke the sub-five-hundred-mile mark. I now had fewer than five hundred miles left to Katahdin. I hiked up behind *Stinkfoot,* a section-hiker hiking half the trail this summer. He was young but confident, on summer vacation from college. Long-bearded, long-haired and mellow, he wore red gaiters, carried a purple Gregory backpack and was a strong hiker, a fast hiker, a good athlete. We kept passing each other alternately all day until we came to a road crossing. For me it made 17.4

141

miles. The hiker's handbook said that a one-mile walk right down the road led to Clarendon General store. We walked down together. Such tiny exits off the trail help you get through the summer. They are usually a treat. You buy Gatorade, lemonade, M&M's, ice slushes, candy bars. I didn't feel well, but I took the side trip for the company and also because I thought that I might find something that I could eat. To my dismay, I discovered that I couldn't even eat junk food.

Back on the trail, Stinkfoot stopped at Clarendon shelter. It was 18.6 miles on the day for me, but I pushed on another three miles farther, and at 21.6 miles I bivied on the ground by the trail. The next day at 5.4 miles I reached Cooper Lodge just below the summit of Killington mountain (4,235 ft.). All skiers have heard of the ski town of Killington. Killington's summit is just .2 away on a side trail, but I didn't go up. I felt too weak. At 10.3 miles I reached Pico Camp with its side trail up Pico Peak. This was yet another Vermont mountain ski resort, and yet another mountain of sentimental value to me. Pico Peak was forever associated in my mind with my friend Tinling. Tinling was born and raised in Malibu Beach, California. His family later moved into the Frank Lloyd Wright house in my hometown, Rochester, New York, where I met him. They sent him off for three years of high school to Pico Peak Ski Academy. Tinling had always told me they had never studied much there, but he had read voraciously and he listened to music. Tinling never went on to college. After high school he started pushing a vacuum cleaner over the tennis courts at the indoor club, beginning at 4:30 in the morning. At the end of his shift he would pick me up at my high school at 1 PM in his girlfriend's Camero and we'd drive around, drink beer, read greeting cards at the mall, drive back to the tennis club to hit balls, eat pizza, take Jacuzzis. Pico Peak had previously existed as merely a romantic notion in my head, an association with my old best friend Tinling. I had always heard of it, and yet I had never known where it was. Now here I stood upon it. But not even this close connection was enough to take me up the side trail to its summit. I felt so bad.

That afternoon beyond Pico Peak I met a boxer from New Jersey who gave me aspirin. It was the first medicine I had taken that summer. It would not be the last. My new friend told me all about amateur boxing. He said that I had to try it. He was very excited because we were fast approaching *The Inn at the Long Trail*. He was dying to reach there to have a Guinness. I told him how sick I felt, how unfortunately I wouldn't be able to have a beer with him. At 12.8 miles for me, we reached the inn. The Inn at the Long Trail is a landmark stop. Rte. 4 runs through this place, which is called Shelbourne Pass. It is a central road in Vermont, and Killington skiers eat at the inn. The Inn at the Long Trail was built into the side of a cliff. It has rooms with bathtubs for rent upstairs, but its greatest feature is a posh bar on the ground floor which has boulders for walls and boulders for tables. You sit in the bar and you set your drink on a boulder. You stand at the bar and you lean back against a boulder. There was tennis on the large screen TVs. It was the finals of Queens Club in England; grass court serve-and-volleyers. I thought that here at the inn I could find a meal I could eat. Hikers dream of finding restaurants directly on the trail. You relish having someone else prepare your meal and set it before you. I ordered a simple noodle dish, but I couldn't even eat this. I wasn't eating at all now. I hadn't eaten in days.

I left the inn, left the boxer behind. I couldn't handle company. Like my first day in the woods on the access trail with my seventy-five-pound pack, I wanted to suffer alone. I had enough to worry about myself. I had no energy for conversation. I could not be responsible. *"Sorrow can take care of itself, but to get the full value of happiness it has to be shared."* This was sorrow. Exiting the inn, I picked up the trail and I climbed a vertical dirt scramble up the cliff, up into the hills. At the top of the cliff above the inn lies the split with the Long Trail. I followed the AT's right-hand 90-degree turn and headed east toward the large trail town of Hanover, New Hampshire (population sixty-three hundred), home of Dartmouth College. Hanover was just 43.5 miles away. I had been there many times, so I felt some comfort in approaching that town, in approaching that somewhat-familiar place. I now knew that I would need to find a doctor there. That was my plan. I was making decisions now based on the way that I felt. Another six miles past the inn, I stopped at 18.1 miles on the day. There was no shelter, but I was exhausted and the sky was clear, so I stopped and lay down in my bivy sack in some ferns beside the trail. The shelter floors had grown too hard for me to sleep on now. Yet even here in the soft ferns I slept poorly. I woke up throughout the night. *Fever. Chills. Sweats. Bad dreams.*

I woke up in the ferns that next morning with a pinched nerve in my neck. Each day I had felt worse. Now I couldn't turn my head. The joints in my hips ached. I stood up and felt dizzy. I threw on my backpack and set out. I was weak from not eating. Standing upon a boulder, preparing to climb down a wooden ladder, I suddenly thought I might faint. I made it down the ladder, but after hiking just three miles that morning, I reached the side trail turnoff to Stony Brook shelter and I couldn't go on. I crashed. I staggered halfway down the side trail to the shelter before I stopped and flopped down on the ground. It was 9 AM. I thought I might nap for an hour or so, to gain back my strength. But I wouldn't budge for six hours.

"Get Me to a Doctor."

At 3 PM Stinkfoot walked up. I had been lying motionless since 9 AM, a bandanna over my head to shield my face from the sun. Even so, all day I'd had the intention of rising to hike. I didn't care how bad I felt. I couldn't hike *just* a three-mile day, after all. Stinkfoot sat beside me for thirty minutes there on the ground by the side of the trail. *"You look like shit,"* he said. He finally helped me gather my things and carry them a hundred more yards down the side trail to Stony Brook shelter. I knew that I wouldn't be able to sleep inside it on the hard shelter floor, so I lay in my sleeping bag in the dirt in front of the shelter beside a fire pit. I now knew for certain that I had to find a doctor. I was now thirty-five miles shy of Hanover. I checked the data book to see if I had to hike all the way in or whether there were roads that I could hitchhike in on if need be. There were minor roads at 13, 14, 17 and 25 miles. I also discovered in the hiker's handbook that there was a hospital in Hanover. I decided to try to head there.

Unleashed and *Homeward Bound* showed up. They had been chasing after me ever since I had passed them when they got off at Delaware Water Gap. Now they had caught me. *"You're* Sneakers?" they asked, surprised. I knew that I wasn't much to look at. These two had been high school football teammates. They painted houses now. Homeward Bound ran their company. They were tough. On the trail there are many hard people. There are strong athletes, marathon runners, trail runners, retired military officers; but these two were the only two truly crazy guys that I would meet on the trail that summer. They hiked shirtless under their backpacks, muscles bulging. Homeward Bound had red hair tied back in a ponytail—you have to be tough to look scary with red hair. Homeward Bound was the brains of their operation. I lay in the dirt in front of the shelter with a bandanna over my head doused in cold water to keep my fever down. I tried to make conversation.

"What do you do?" I asked Unleashed, to learn of his occupation.

"What do I *DO?* I smoke, I drink, I fight, I fuck…"

Here he was hard-pressed to think of more. Again, I couldn't eat that night. Stinkfoot gave me a prescription codeine painkiller to help me sleep. I didn't care what it was. I was out like a light.

Unleashed was having a manic swing. I hiked with him all that next day, listening to his life story. He was having a fight with his girlfriend, and he chattered away covering every detail. It was perfect for me as I never had to utter a word. His story grew worse with every detail. His girlfriend was separated from her husband. The husband had just gotten out of jail and now he wanted his wife back. The husband had abused her before and he threatened her now with violence. He showed up at her house with a gun. She was upset. She wanted Unleashed to come home. There were kids involved. Unleashed wasn't sure what to do. He wanted to leave the trail to beat up the ex-con. Or leave the trail to beat up his girlfriend, the wife. Or something like that. And on and on. And what did I think about it? *"No guns. Definitely, positively no guns,"* I said. The miles ticked by. We paused frequently. At every stop Unleashed lit up a cigarette. He had quit for a while, but now he was smoking again.

Unleashed knew I was sick. He slowed his pace and hiked with me now

144

out of charity. Unleashed was the one who had carried Peripidus four miles out of the woods in the middle of the night to get him to a road when he thought he was dying. He walked with me now and gabbed away because he knew that I lacked the energy to. He said that I probably had Lyme disease. I took off my sweat-drenched shirt as we broke for lunch and he noticed a circular red mark that had developed on my chest that I hadn't even known was there. So now it wasn't a guess any longer. Unleashed pointed at the mark. He said with certainty: *"You have Lyme disease."*

We crossed two small roads where I could have exited, but I continued. The sleep and the company had done wonders. Also, I wanted to reach a busier road. We passed three northbound weekend warriors who said that they had a car parked just up ahead, just 6.6 miles north on the trail at Rte. 14 in West Hartford, Vermont. They said that if I met them there at the bridge that next day, they would give me a ride to Dartmouth's hospital in Hanover. At 19.6 miles on the day, we reached Cloudland shelter. There was no room inside as it was occupied by an enormous group of weekend Canadians. Homeward Bound, Unleashed, Stinkfoot and I all slept in a clearing out back behind the shelter. I had only 6.6 more miles left to reach Rte. 14, a major road leading ten minutes into Hanover and the hospital. Just 6.6 more miles that next day and I would get help. I felt okay. I would make it. Still, I couldn't eat or sleep. Stinkfoot couldn't spare his second and last painkiller, but Unleashed gave me one of his. I was out like a light, sleeping on the ground in my bivy sack for the fourth straight night.

I woke up wet. It had rained during the night, but I hadn't noticed. I had slept right through it due to the painkillers. My things were wet. Everyone was gone. I began my 6.6 mile hike. I hadn't eaten in five days. I hadn't slept in five days except by the help of painkillers taken on an empty stomach. And yet, strangely, I felt okay. I experienced nothing like the romantic vision I had of needing to stagger heroically, tragically those last few final miles to get help. This was nothing like that. My morning hike was no challenge. Instead, I felt in a dream state. I walked very slowly. Comfortably. I distinctly noticed all my surroundings. I appreciated all that I saw. I stopped and looked at flowers. I paused and ate wild strawberries. It actually was a lovely walk. I felt serene and content, approaching the hospital. The wild strawberries tasted delicious. I couldn't remember the last time I had eaten anything.

I passed Bunker Hill Cemetery and gazed at the peaceful graves. At 6.6 miles I reached Rte. 14 and the small bridge over the White River in West Hartford, Vermont. It was Friday, midday. It was the Fourth of July. Some kids were jumping off the bridge into the river. Others were seated down below on the rocks, watching and smoking cigarettes. I sat and watched the jumpers on the bridge. I taught a kid how to do a backflip. I sat waiting for the three hikers to emerge from the woods and taxi me away in their car, but they never showed. I walked to the general store down the block and telephoned the Y's parents. The Y was due to arrive back from Germany in two days. I told them how I thought I had Lyme disease and how I would be checking into the Dartmouth hospital in Hanover. I said I would call again from there. The hikers still hadn't shown, so I left the store and stood by the road with my backpack, hitchhiking. It took me fifteen minutes to get a ride. A gentleman picked me up and drove me ten miles into Hanover, depositing me at the hospital—the Dartmouth College Hitchcock Medical Center.

I stood at the emergency room entrance.

13
Hospital Care

Tick, n. Bloodsucking mite-like animal.

Hitchcock Medical Center—Hanover, New Hampshire.

July 4, 1993. Sunday. Day #101.

The funny thing was, that there had been tick warning posters stapled to trees all through New Jersey and New York and I had walked by ignoring every one. I always think nothing bad will ever happen to me. I approached the emergency desk wearing my backpack. A receptionist looked up blankly. I wasn't quite sure how to handle this.

"I'm sick," I said. "What do I do?"

I expected the usual hospital wait, but within two minutes of scribbling down information on forms I found myself sitting back in an examining room with a doctor. It was fast service (emergency service?). I was very impressed. And grateful. I was glad to be here, glad to be able to speak with a doctor. I felt safe and secure. Saved. The doctor asked for my story. I told him how I had been out on the trail for three months and how I had suddenly fell sick. I told him how I had been hiking sick, how I hadn't eaten in five days. How I hadn't been sleeping much, either. The doctor felt my glands. He shone light in my eyes. He bent my arms and legs to test my joints.

"What are your symptoms?" he asked.

"My symptoms? I don't know," I said: "Everything: weakness, headache,

147

chills, fever, dizziness. Really just feeling funny. I've felt really weak. Achy."

"Any nausea? Diarrhea?"

"No. I don't think so. Neither one. Not really."

The poking continued.

"Oh yeah," I said suddenly, remembering the mark. "Yesterday I discovered *this.*"

I lifted my T-shirt and showed the doctor the red circle that had developed below my left breast. It had grown in size since the previous day and there was now a dark red inner circle the size of a dime like a bull's-eye in the middle of the fainter large circle.

"I think it's Lyme disease," I said. "Is that what it is?"

The doctor examined the mark. He scribbled some notes on a chart. He spoke with a nurse who walked over and stuck a needle into my arm for a blood sample. The nurse left the room, but she came back shortly and gave me two pills. The doctor said they were starting me on antibiotics to treat Lyme disease immediately. The blood sample would tell for sure, but it was a safe enough bet to start the pills in the meantime.

"We're going to admit you," he said. "You're going to be here for a few days. But the first thing we have to do is get something inside you. You haven't eaten, but you're also completely dehydrated."

"Dehydrated?"

"Completely dehydrated. We're going to give you an IV to fill you up." The doctor took two steps toward the door; then he turned back and said: "You're empty."

The nurse stuck a needle and tube into a vein in my right arm. The tube led up to an IV bag of clear liquid hanging on a peg above me. This was a fill-up.

Lyme Disease.

The nurse wheeled my stretcher into an elevator to cart me downstairs to my room. I lay on my back on the stretcher with an IV in my arm, a little bag of fluid overhead. My backpack lay on the stretcher by my feet. I had been hiking for one hundred days. A tick had bitten me giving me Lyme disease. I was weak and dehydrated. I had lost five pounds in five days. An old woman sat hunched in a wheelchair inside the elevator beside me. Her face was bruised. She looked at the IV cart with the fluid bag hanging above me and the tube leading down into my arm. She looked at my backpack and finally stared up at me. She rasped:

"Been out hiking?"

Yes I had.

148

"How long?" she asked.

"Three months," I answered.

"Three months? In the *woods?"* She tilted her head and squinted hard to see what this maniac looked like.

"Yeah," I said calmly. Our conversation might have ended there, too, except that I suddenly found humor in this. I grinned slightly, deciding that I just couldn't pass up this opportunity; I couldn't let this chance slip by. I turned my head toward the old woman and I whispered, quite meekly this time: *"Yeah...three months in the woods...and look where it got me!"*

My room was a small single behind a busy, nurse-monitored, medicine-stocked counter at the end of a hallway. I had a television set, telephone and bathroom. To any hiker considering a break off the trail in a comfortable spot, I recommend a hospital stay. There is every conceivable luxury at your disposal—remote control for your television, a comfortable, adjustable, reclining bed, meals brought to your room, constant attention, instant companionship one second away at the press of an emergency button. It was nice not to have bugs all over; not to be sick and have black flies biting my neck, arms, head, and behind my ears; not to be sick while lying in the dirt getting blown by the wind and fried by the sun. I lay back in bed and slept.

I awoke in the evening when the doctor came in. I did indeed have Lyme disease. But I would be okay. I would have to rest and take antibiotics for three weeks, but I would live. The doctor said that Lyme disease is increasingly common; nearly 75 percent of New Jersey State Park workers get it. The problem comes when you don't diagnose it on the first wave of sickness. The disease then goes into remission only to reappear later at which point it is serious (arthritis, brain damage). I asked where I could have gotten it. He said that I probably got bitten by the tick anywhere from two to three weeks ago. Looking back through my journal, I realized that I had passed through New Jersey and New York three weeks earlier. My 45.7-mile day was twenty-two days earlier—almost three weeks to the day. That long day had taken me through New Jersey, and that night I had slept naked in my bivy sack in the weeds at the edge of a field. I had slept naked and had crawled one yard through the weeds to urinate. It was then that I must have gotten bitten by the jabberwocky, when I was too exhausted to feel anything. And that next day I had hiked on, too exhausted to notice anything on my body.

I thought back to when I had first felt sick, for everything seemed to make sense now. I had felt sad and lousy at the Bear Mountain Park Zoo and then felt exceptionally low in Falls Village, where I'd gotten no letter from the Y. I remembered how hard I had crashed at Falls Village, and how very fragile I had felt. It wasn't the missing letter that had gotten me sick; no, it must have been early affects of the sickness. After that it had been all downhill—I'd felt strange in the woods, felt strange at my aunt and uncle's, felt strange in Cheshire, and felt strange in Williamstown. Then I had truly fallen sick. It all made sense now.

The doctor left. I called my parents and explained that I was okay. I called my two brothers and a few of my friends, but no one was in. It was Fourth of July evening and everyone was out watching fireworks. I couldn't reach a soul. I only got telephone answering machines. But that was okay. It was actually better this way. I left funny, cryptic messages: *"I'm in New Hampshire. I'm in the hospital. I'm not kidding. Call me back."* A nurse had me fill out a meal order for the following day. She gave me more pills. She unplugged my empty IV bag and hung up a second one. I hated having that needle and tube in my arm. It gave me the willies. I felt that if I moved I might yank it out. I had to wheel the IV cart with me every time I went into the bathroom. That night I watched MTV. All the music videos were new to me. The Proclaimers sang a song called "Wanna' Be 500 Miles": *"I would walk five hundred miles and I would walk five hundred more, just to be the man who walked a thousand miles to fall down at your door."* (So what if they had the mileage wrong?) Then a small young woman on the television stepped up to a microphone at a sparse poolside set and belted out in the most powerful voice I had ever heard. It was 4 Non Blondes singing "What's Up":

> *And I try,*
> *oh my god do I try*
> *I try all the time, in this In-sti-tution.*
> *And I pray,*
> *oh my god do I pray*
> *I pray every single day, for a REVOLUTION!*

I awoke in the dark at 4 AM. Disoriented. I noticed that my second IV bag was empty. I guess I'd been thirsty (or did that mean I'd been hungry?). I buzzed the night nurse and asked if he could take the needle and tube out of my arm. I was thinking about it so much that it started to hurt (or at least itch a lot). The nurse said no, that he had to wait for the doctor to make that call because they might want to give me a third unit. I got out of bed and I had him take a photo of me standing beside my IV cart in my little hospital gown. At 8 AM the doctor came in and said they could take out the IV. Freedom! No more willies. I felt like a new person in the morning. My temperature had dropped. My fever had disappeared. My appetite returned. The doctor brought in a photographer to snap shots of my chest for future medical text books. He said that my mark was an excellent specimen. I showered and shaved. Ate breakfast. That day the phone calls poured in. My older brother called back. He is a surgeon.

"Are they treating you like a street person?" my brother the doctor, asked.

"No," I said, "they're treating me like a celebrity."

It was true. An assortment of doctors came in through the course of the day to sit and ask about the trail. These doctors worked in New Hampshire because they loved the woods. One doctor sat and told me about the cross-country bicycle trip she had taken with her husband. It was heaven for me, lying there talking about the trail. My appetite back, I ate rice, bread, noodles, potatoes (brown foods, white foods, green foods). The Y was returning from Germany that next morning. I slept well that second night knowing that I would see her shortly. My third day in the hospital, I no longer felt sick. The doctor said that it would be my last night there. "You have become a boring patient—just a guy lying in bed with a headache."

The doctor gave me a prescription for Doxycycline. He said that I could get out of bed, that I should walk down the hall to the pharmacy to get the prescription filled. I walked along the hospital corridors. That clean new hospital had everything. I walked into a gift shop and bought Newsweek and an old Bjorn Borg tennis video. I mailed a letter from the hospital's post office. I got my prescription filled at the hospital pharmacy. For my last conversation with the doctor I had saved the ultimate question, one that I had been avoiding, one that I had been afraid to ask—CAN I RESUME MY HIKE? The doctor said that I could try, but that I needed at least seven more days off the trail first. He said not to overexert and to avoid direct sunlight. I spent the rest of that fourth day lying in my room, and that evening I called the Y. She was back. She would drive up three hours the following morning to pick me up at the outpatient house in town they were releasing me to. I gave her the address. She would meet me there at twelve noon. That next morning I packed up, put on my backpack, and said good-bye to the nurses and doctors. I walked down the corridor and out of the hospital, out through the doors I'd only recently staggered in through. I rode the hospital shuttle bus to the outpatient clinic house in town.

Cape Cod.

The Y to the rescue. The Y showed up at twelve noon and collected me from the outpatient house. We got a hotel room and we napped through the day. That next morning, we drove down to her family's summerhouse on Cape Cod, stopping first at the post office back in West Hartford, Vermont, to pick up my drop box #13 and the Y's two missing letters. At long last I had the letters, but now here I was opening them while she sat beside me. What a strange fate! How badly I had needed them earlier. I wondered if anything would have been different if I had gotten that first missing letter in Falls Village. Would I not have left the trail? Would I not have felt depressed? Would I have kept motivated, surging ahead, hiking straight through the first wave of my sickness, only to have it resurface later as a deadly disease?

151

Those five days in Cape Cod were heaven for me. The Y spent her mornings lying on the beach while I slept in. I was an invalid, on antibiotics, keeping out of the sun. I was weak and needing extra sleep. Those afternoons we sat on the porch sipping iced tea, eating Welch's frozen fruit bars, looking out over the ocean. The sand dunes, the magical smell of salt water. Wind, waves, wild grass, seashells, seaweed, sand, and horseshoe crabs. Mollusks. Beach balls. Beach towels smelling of coconut suntan oil. I read and reread the Y's two missing letters. I never told her the thoughts I'd had in Delaware Water Gap, New Jersey. Was this to be my wife? I took my medicine twice a day. I ate to gain strength. We rented movies at night. We bought CDs and listened to music. We showered outdoors in the sunshine in the wood shower beside the house with St. Ives Apple Mint Finishing Shampoo. The Y's parents came down for the weekend, Saturday morning. Weeks earlier they had taken a two-day hike for charity on the Appalachian Trail in Massachusetts with friends. They were an athletic family, but not a hiking family (not even the Y liked to hike). The Y's father had hated his time in the woods. He couldn't understand why I did it: *"All the bugs...and it's just walking along...there's nothing to see...what's the point?"* That's the GREEN TUNNEL, of course. The Y's mother was funny and had a jokey, inventive way of putting things. She said that I should not eat any more wild strawberries, for she didn't want me to catch "Harry Carry."

After five days on Cape Cod, I rode back to Hanover alone on a bus. Sunday, July 11, I found Panarchy, having learned earlier from the Dartmouth Outing Club office on the college's campus that Panarchy, on School Street, is a Greek social house which hosts hikers for free. I got myself a room and set out to run errands. Hanover has everything. It is the greatest trail town on the AT. It has a movie theater, outfitter store, twenty-four-hour Laundromat, food co-op, free place to stay, and all the restaurants and bars you could want. I ate vegetarian tofu hot dogs at a diner in town and washed my sleeping bag in a Laundromat for the first time all summer. At the outfitter store, I bought an ATC trail map of New Hampshire, simply because I wanted to know where I was in case something else went wrong and I needed to get to a doctor again. I felt ready to resume my hike, but I was nervous about overexertion. In Panarchy that night I found a large dehydrated sheep dog dying of thirst who drank without pausing four bowls of water that I put before it. Who knew when this dog had drunk last? I went to sleep that night planning to pick up my missing ten miles of trail that next morning.

My body was in Hanover, but my hike had left off ten miles back in West Hartford, Vermont, from where I'd hitchhiked the ride to the hospital. So that next morning I rode back to West Hartford in a taxi with only my hiking stick, water bottle, and a hat, and I slowly slackpacked my ten missing miles through pine trees, over gentle hills and finally across the bridge that leads out of Vermont, over the Connecticut River, and into New Hampshire. Now, on the trail, I was twelve states down, two to go. Only two more states. The trail led up through the center of town, straight down Main Street with white trail blazes painted on the sidewalk, on post office boxes, stop signs, fire hydrants, and the sides of buildings. I returned to Panarchy knowing that now I still hadn't missed an inch of trail in the woods. That second night sleeping in Panarchy I knew was my last in town. I would set out north toward the White Mountains with my backpack to resume my hike the following morning. I felt nervous and apprehensive; still I was glad to be where I was. I felt eager to hike for the first time in weeks. I was glad to be okay, glad to have had a vacation, glad to have seen the Y. I would not have changed a thing. I was now approaching the Whites and the most beautiful, awesome, difficult stretch of the trail. Through everything, no matter what, I was doing it.

14
High Peaks Again

*It had long occurred to him that the woods only
prepares you for woods.*

—Jim Harrison, *Westward Ho*

The Can-Can.

I carried my little bottle of antibiotics, taking two pills a day. It was
a humbled, timid me. I hadn't felt strong for twenty days. I thought back
to when I was chasing Water, hiking thirty-mile days. At my usual pace I
would have been farther up the trail alongside the one or two earliest hikers.
I wondered where everyone was, who was ahead of me now and who was
still behind. In all this time since Harpers Ferry I had seen no sign nor heard
any word of Hydro. Ghost-hiker or not, I had long suspected that he was off
the trail. I would later learn that I was right, Hydro had indeed unexpectedly
gone home to Florida to see his wife just beyond Harpers Ferry. Home for
a month, he would later return to finish his hike. I wondered who had gone
by. The shelter register entries later told me the answer: Homeward Bound,
Unleashed, Easy Stryder, Heel and Toe, Mozyin', Chinook, Mighty Mike,
Mercury Mark, Just Chris, Sidetracker, and section-hikers Stinkfoot and
Baby Steps were ahead now along with the three lead hikers, Water, J-Zero,
and Peaked in High School (Eddie-B not included). Hydro and Blazer had
gone home. Everyone else that I'd met that summer was still behind.

Twelve states down, two to go.

Months earlier, down in Tennessee, we had heard the story of an aspiring northbound through-hiker from some previous year who had hiked sixteen hundred miles all the way to Vermont and then quit. We had laughed at that seemingly inconceivable story. How could a northbounder quit in Vermont? We had thought that from there one could limp to the end, or at least fall forward and reach out and touch the end. But now here we were in New Hampshire and we could understand how it could happen. The trail leads 160 miles in New Hampshire and 283 miles in Maine, so it isn't over yet. And I wasn't kicking out twenty-mile days any longer. Everything changed for me after my Lyme disease. I cared only about comfort now. Early on, Big Miles had spelled happiness; now comfort spelled happiness. Now I only wanted to pamper myself. I altered my diet. I stopped carrying the power drinks and began carrying Tang, lemonade, and Hi-C grape mix to flavor my drinking water for the first time all trip. I still ate PowerBars for breakfast and vegetarian beef jerky for snacks, but now I quit carrying the dried fruit pouches I'd eaten all trip (I'd never liked them much anyway), and instead carried Pop Tarts and Fig Newtons. For lunch, instead of merely eating peanut butter straight out of the jar with a spoon as I'd done for three months, I now carried Saltine crackers and a tube of grape jelly for regal peanut butter and jelly cracker lunches. For dinner, instead of boiling noodles and using a knife to slice in hard tomato paste chunks as I'd done all trip (ever since my initial short-lived canned-tomato fiasco), I now carried packets of Lipton's spicy vegetarian Cajun rice and beans, dried mixes which I added to noodles to make gigantic, seasoned, delicious dinners. My appetite returned with a vengeance. My meals all tasted better now. It made such a difference.

I walked along slowly at first, afraid to raise my heart rate, nervous because of my medicine. I walked out of Hanover midday and hiked 11.2 miles to Moose Mountain shelter where I spent the night with a '92 through-hiker named *Old Nick* and with Baby Steps. They had read of my Lyme disease in the Dartmouth Outing Club register (I had written that entry with the Y before heading down to Cape Cod). I pushed on that next day hiking 17.8 miles to Jeffers Brook shelter for a night alone interrupted only by a welcome visit from some twelve-year-old summer camp girls who came over from their nearby tent area to perform a Can-Can routine they were practicing, singing: *"Oh yes, I can do the Can-Can, yes I can, I can, I can do the Can-Can!"*—over and over, arms around each other, legs kicking high!

Immediately that next morning began my five-mile climb up over streams, up through cow fields, up over fence stiles, higher and higher, up through forest hills and up over New England's four- thousand-ft. tree line on an endless climb up Mt. Moosilauke (4,802 ft.). A southbounder coming down had warned: *"It isn't vertical, but you have to lean into it."* You can see five states from the summit as well as the Franconia Ridge to the north which you are soon to cross. But I saw nothing. I stood on the summit in clouds and

155

rain on July 16, so cold and windy on top that I had to wear my hat and gloves while the wind pushed me off the trail twice. I continued four additional miles down into Kinsman Notch (Rte. 302) at the border of New Hampshire's White Mountain National Forest. Hiking five miles after that into the park, I stopped after 14.7 miles on the day for a night alone deep in the woods in Eliza Brook shelter. I took my pills. I laughed to myself imagining Easy Stryder's reaction to my Lyme disease:

> *"You don't need food any longer!" he would have said. "All you*
> *need is a couple IV bags every day. Just leave the tube hole*
> *in your arm and hook up an IV bag for dinner! No stove,*
> *spoon, pots or pans. No cooking or cleaning—no mess!*
> *Think of the time you save! Think of the clutter you avoid in*
> *your pack! You've got your sleeping bag with the arm holes*
> *and leg holes—and you hike with your arms and your legs*
> *sticking out, with your backpack on, and with your IV bag*
> *hooked up while you walk—it's the perfect way to hike!"*

We would have laughed hard over that. Memories of my trail friends lingered with me. I lay quietly listening to the wonderfully soothing sound of rain plunking down, swooshing water rushing by in an adjacent stream. White noise. I was glad to be back in the woods. I drifted to sleep.

The Presidentials.

Vermont has the Green Mountains; New Hampshire has its Whites. New Hampshire's White Mountains are higher, steeper, more rugged and rocky, have greater temperature fluctuations and get more snow. It can snow any month of the year in the Whites. People die in the Whites on top of Mt. Washington because they aren't prepared for the weather. The weather station on top of Mt. Washington is famous for having recorded 231 mile-per-hour winds—for a long while the fastest surface wind speed ever recorded on Earth. Traveling north on the AT through the Whites, you hit first the Franconia Range (thirty-eight-miles long) and then hit the Presidential Range (twenty-five-miles long) which leads to the end of the park near the Maine border. The Presidential Range is home to the highest mountain in the northeast, Mt. Washington (6,288 ft). These White Mountains are home to the largest crowds you will see on the trail. The Appalachian Mountain Club (different from Appalachian Trail Conference) maintains the trails in the park and runs seven enormous huts in the high ranges. The huts are spaced about eight miles apart and usually stand on high mountain ground. The largest AMC hut sleeps ninety guests. Weekend warriors call for reservations. The huts have bathrooms, kitchens, and bunk beds with pillows and blankets. Summer work

156

crews of college students man the huts and fix breakfast and dinner for the paying guests. Lodging with breakfast is $38, while lodging with breakfast and dinner is $50. Through-hikers can't afford this, which puts you in a jam because the trail is a narrow high ridge and park rules prohibit camping closer than two hundred feet to the trail, or closer than one-quarter mile to the huts. This doesn't leave you with many options, so you meet strange times maneuvering through the White Mountains, navigating past the expensive AMC huts. Unless you plan carefully, you end up staying in at least a few of the crowded huts where weekend warriors bustle and bluster about. One loophole exists. As a through-hiker, you are allowed to sleep in AMC huts without paying money provided that you stay late in the mornings to help the summer work crews clean up. A double whammy—you encounter the largest crowds of your summer in the huts, and you must wait until after breakfast is eaten and until after all the relatively unorganized (no fault of their own) weekend warriors have packed up and cleared out in the morning before you can begin working for over an hour polishing silverware, sweeping floors, cleaning windows. Many through-hikers enjoy moving slowly through the Whites hopping from hut to hut. Through-hikers who get into the spirit of the AMC huts don't get very far, but they have substantial dinners served to them every night, they share stories with the lodgers, and they make friends with the summer crews while working late in the mornings.

From Eliza Brook shelter my trek through the Whites began with a climb over Kinsman mountain. I passed Lonesome Lake Hut after six miles and reached Franconia Notch (Rte. 3) at 11.4 miles. I continued on, climbing up over the four-thousand-ft. tree line, and I hiked halfway along the Franconia Range crossing Mt. Lincoln (5,089 ft.), Mt. Lafayette (5,249 ft.), and Mt. Garfield (4,488 ft.) before stopping after 18.7 miles on the day at Garfield Ridge shelter. Inside was a crowd including two women from Massachusetts who knew the Y's family. An AMC caretaker dropped by the shelter that evening to collect $5 cash from everyone: one of the women said, *"AMC stands for Appalachian Money Collectors."* Eighteen point three miles that next day took me to the end of the Franconia Range over South Twin mountain (4,902 ft.), Mt. Guyot (4,560 ft.), and past Zealand Falls Hut down into Crawford Notch by the Saco River. Beyond the Saco River, I climbed up the trail into the wooded mountains for a night alone in the undergrowth in my bivy sack. Lying two hundred yards off the trail in dense bushes, I hoped that I wouldn't die as I slept because they never would have found me. But at least this meant I didn't have to polish silverware.

That next morning I began hiking the Presidential Range, which runs up out of Crawford Notch, along a high ridge and then down into Pinkham Notch. I hiked over Mt. Webster (3,901 ft.) and Mt. Jackson (4,052 ft.), past Mizpah Spring Hut and over Mt. Franklin (5,004 ft.), reaching Lakes of the Clouds Hut *(Lakes of the Crowds)* at ten miles. I was in a strange mood and I ran the 1.5 mile stone step climb from the pond beside Lakes Hut up to Mt. Washington's summit, arriving on top red-faced and with my heart pounding. This is the highest point you will stand on for the rest of your hike. The summit is rocky, immense. Mt. Washington's summit has a large cafeteria with a souvenir shop and a post office. There is a weather station on top as well as a large parking lot just below the summit which people drive up to and walk about (bumper sticker: THIS CAR CLIMBED MT. WASHINGTON). There is a train called the Cog Railroad which chugs people slowly up the mountain, whistling and spurting out huge puffs of black coal smoke as it goes. There is even a car race up the mountain every summer—a pleasure for the animals that live nearby and must listen to it and a pleasure for the ozone layer, too. I ate lunch in the mountaintop cafeteria with three southbounders, including a Nashville woman who helped me figure out that southbound, Walkman-wearing Slimfast, whom I'd met in Vermont, was my distant cousin by marriage. You can always pick out a fellow through-hiker anywhere on the trail, but on top of Mt. Washington it is especially easy: you start by looking for anyone with a backpack or for anyone who isn't dressed in street clothes.

In the AMC huts it is more subtle than that because, with no roads up the other summits, everyone sleeping up in the huts is there with a backpack. So to find a fellow through-hiker you look for a beard, for gaiters, for dirt, for scarred and scraped legs, for deep suntans, for unkempt wild hair, for permanently sweat-stained T-shirts. You look for journal writers off quietly alone in a corner, for anyone visibly repelled by the crowds, for pairings of hikers of different ages who look spiritually but not biologically related, for anyone not fumbling with or swearing at their gear. You look for a gleam in the eyes, a glow on the face, a calm. One look tells you who has been living in the woods for four months.

Exiting *"Mt. Washingcrowd's"* cafeteria midafternoon, I looked out over the 5.8 mile semicircle ridge loop from Mt. Washington to Mt. Madison. My hike around the loop was awesome with black high clouds above (and some below), and rumbles of thunder. The entire ridge is an exposed rocky path above tree line. I could see miles ahead around the right-turning loop, but I only caught glimpses down through the clouds, down the cliffs at my sides. I looked down for escape routes to descend into in case of sudden lightning or more powerful wind. I hiked the ridge with my rain cover over my backpack. It was rocky, windy, dark, threatening, tremendous. Wonderful. The Himalayan Mountain range north of India runs east-to-west and thus shelters southern lands from the Arctic southward winds, but the Appalachian chain runs north-to-south and these White Mountains get blasted by polar winds dropping down from the Arctic which collide with Jet Stream air rising up from the south. In the Whites they say: *"Don't like the weather? Wait a minute"* (and it will change).

158

Many high paths in the Whites are bordered by stones to keep hikers from wandering off the trail into sensitive alpine foliage. The hiker's handbook explains that alpine lichen is so fragile that it can take twenty-five years for it to flower for the first time, but that it can be killed by the single step of an errant hiker straying off the path. Proximity breeds familiarity, and the path is so narrow on the high ridge here that you bump elbows with everyone you pass. Weekend warriors stop you to shoot the breeze. They ask you questions in reference to their own long-weekend tripping experience. They see you out hiking in the mountains on a Monday and they want to know if you, too, have taken that extra day off from work like they have, or if you, too, are on your vacation like they are.

"When did you start?" they ask you in July expecting your answer to be the name of a day of the week—Wednesday? Thursday? Friday? Instead you say:

"March."

"March? March, the month March?"

Or they ask:

"Where did you start from?"

"Georgia."

"Georgia? Georgia, the state Georgia?"

Questioners this confused can't even fathom what to say next so you jump in and bail them out.

"I'm hiking the Appalachian Trail," you say. "We're on it right now. The trail runs from Georgia to Maine. A lot of people do it. It's actually pretty popular."

Then the questions burst toward you in waves. You hang in there cheerfully, generously answering a few questions about guidebooks, white blazes, food drops, and the ATC—then you modestly bid farewell and slip away.

I passed a father and son, out for a week in the White Mountains. The father spied my running shoes and grew concerned.

"You're going to have to be very careful," the man told me. "You shouldn't be hiking in sneakers. You're in danger wearing sneakers on these rocks."

"I hiked here from Georgia wearing sneakers," I said.

"Yeah, but you're here in the Whites now. Are you going down to Pinkham Notch? I want you to go buy a pair of hiking boots right away."

I reached Madison Hut at 16.9 miles on the day. Through careful maneuvering, this was the first and only AMC hut I got trapped in. Of the small college crew working there, two of the workers attended the college where I worked and this was their summer job. I sat with two already hardened southbounders including *President Kennedy* who carried no camera and kept no journal. He kept no record of his hike whatever. He had only the present.

159

Very Zen. You need no stove in the AMC huts (they aren't allowed). You need fetch no water, either. All boarders in the AMC huts (including through-hikers) just sit around waiting to get served by the work crews, so no one identifies you as anything special there. Through-hikers have medium-sized backpacks without a lot of stuff hanging off them, and this fails to impress the untrained eye in the presence of so many big backpacks all around. The AMC crew workers can easily pick out the through-hikers. Through-hikers are the ones off on their own patiently, quietly waiting for dinner to be served. They know you because you are independent. You aren't obsessively struggling with your gear (you did that earlier!). You aren't asking them endless questions. You aren't begging for news of the weather because you will take what weather you get; whereas a weekend warrior out for three days is desperate not to encounter three days of rain.

But the crew workers don't bother to introduce through-hikers. In the AMC huts, the crew workers pretend through-hikers don't exist. Territoriality. You are in their domain. They want to remain the celebrities of the huts. They are the ones hiking up and down their mountain hauling up food and supplies. They have their own concerns, their own challenges, their own jokes (a scale and a grid sheet in the kitchen detailed a contest over which crew worker could haul up the heaviest amount of supplies on a single trip). The paying guests in the huts ask the celebrity crew workers questions about what it's like to stay up in the huts all summer. You sit quietly amongst them unnoticed, having walked across twelve states, having walked over mountains, through meadows, fields, bogs, swamps. You have slept in lean-tos, in churches, in bushes and weeds, on picnic tables. You have been treated kindly, poorly. You have been crawled on by mice, mistaken by nearsighted snakes, overflown by turkeys, spooked by grouse, delighted by turtles, saturated with rain. You have seen rainbows, dirt, boulders, animal bones, men with guns, satellite dishes outside trailer park homes. You have felt joy, loneliness, fatigue, pain, hot, cold, wet, hungry, eager, anxious, nervous, mesmerized, curious, bewildered, fragile, humbled, inspired. You have gazed at stars, far away. You have gazed at a bug on a small piece of tree bark. You have gotten lost and gotten hurt. You have closed your eyes and listened to the wind. You have climbed into strangers' cars. You have walked on, on, on, on, on, for many hundreds of miles.

The work crew put on a skit; then several boarders milled around outside the hut after dinner looking at the sky, trying to gauge the weather. We saw a fox on the side of Mt. Madison (5,636 ft.) whose peak rises the final short distance straight up directly beside the hut. I stayed late in the Madison hut that next morning, polishing silverware. Out the window I watched a young attractive couple stretching, posturing outside the hut. Free at last, I set out over Mt. Madison, the final peak in the Presidential Range, and I descended down into pine-tree-covered Pinkham Notch at 7.8 miles. I perused the

Pinkham Notch outfitter store. I ate lunch in the Pinkham Notch cafeteria. I picked up my post office drop box, #14, from the Pinkham Notch help desk—a colored construction paper letter from the Y cut in the form of a hiker: GET BETTER! written all over a thermometer in the hiker's mouth. I had passed the last AMC hut and I now stood just thirty-seven trail miles shy of the Maine border *(the final state)*. I tried to somehow find a way to send my things ahead to the nearby trail town of Gorham, New Hampshire, to slackpack for a day, but I could not find a way.

Exiting Pinkham Notch this downcast day, I climbed north up out of the gap, uphill into dense wet clouds on Wildcat Mountain. Higher and higher. Fog so dense. All clouds. Gray, drizzly day. And then like a dream, the moment I reached the summit of Wildcat Mountain (thirty-eight hundred ft.), the clouds parted, the blue sky shone above, and the sun peeked out. Trail Magic. I stood on the summit of that ski resort at 11.8 miles on the day. It was six o'clock in the evening. The break in the clouds lasted over an hour. I looked south back at Mt. Madison across the gap. I walked around the deserted ski lodge and found no one about. I sat on a terrace deck chair and fed Saltine crackers to a chipmunk. After thirty minutes, the chipmunk climbed up my leg, sat on my knee, and ate out of my hand. Living in the woods so long, you now smell like the woods, and perhaps this familiar smell allows trusting animals to accept you more freely. I took photographs of the lodge, of the chair lift, of Mt. Madison in the distance. I hadn't had too many views in the Whites. Southern through-hikers who anticipate the views in the Whites their whole trips feel cheated when it rains the entire week they pass through. I didn't feel cheated. I enjoyed the dramatic, threatening feel, the rocks and the glimpses of cliffs. I enjoyed the scramble climbs, the hurricane winds, and the cold mountain air.

I got drenched that night. Dark clouds had rolled back in once again, and I had elected to sleep under an awning of the ski lodge for shelter, instead of sleeping inside on the dirt floor of a minuscule tool closet that I'd found open, home to who-knew-what dangers inside. My bivy sack didn't protect me from the rain. Wind blew rain under the awning. I crouched tight and curled up like a ball. I barely slept. The morning dawned clear and bright. I wrung out my saturated sleeping bag. It was to be a town day so it didn't matter that I was wet. I hiked 16.2 miles to Rte. 2, where I left the trail and hitchhiked two miles into Gorham, New Hampshire, a trail town with laundry, restaurants, and a bed at *The Barn*. I had come through the White Mountains, the most beautiful part of the trail. Upcoming early Maine, however, is considered the most difficult terrain.

Gorham, New Hampshire.

I spent two days at The Barn in Gorham, New Hampshire, drying out and relaxing. Gorham lies just 16.5 trail miles shy of the Maine border. Gorham is the perfect place to relax, the perfect place for a zero day. Besides my sick stops off the trail in Falls Village and Hanover, I hadn't taken a zero day purely to relax since Delaware Water Gap, Pennsylvania. The Barn faces Main Street on the trail side of town. Attached to a bed and breakfast called the Gorham House Inn, it is a two-story garage-barn with few frills. Fifteen mattresses sit on the second-floor loft, while the ground floor is a cement garage with a refrigerator, table, sofa, hiker bulletin board, and a tremendous amount of junk. Through-hikers stay in the barn for $7 a night, walking through a side door into the B&B kitchen to use the bathroom and shower. The barn's best feature is a huge, swinging double-door window on the second-story loft which opens out over the street and provides air, smells, light, and view. The open doors give the loft the feel of an open-faced lean-to, but with plenty more space inside to settle your things. I walked into town, ate dinner, washed my clothes. My first night I shared the loft with a shy, eighteen-year-old southbound through-hiker named *Cooter*. I bought a maroon T-shirt for the Y which had the AT symbol on it and said: *THE BARN*. I called work (the college) on my zero day and found that the tennis coach had quit. They wanted to bring me in to discuss giving me the tennis teams in addition to the squash teams I coached. I called the Y, who said she'd drive up to meet me in five days in Rangely, Maine, seventy-eight trail miles north, to pick me up and drive me to the college. The Y's support was constant. She would have me finish the trail. Whatever it took. I felt eager to reach the Maine border.

Just north of the Maine border sits the most talked-about, feared place on the entire trail: *the Mahoosuc Notch*. I exited Gorham on Friday, July 23. As usual, with my very late morning exits from towns, I wasn't able to make it far. I hiked just 11.9 miles on an exhausting climb up out of town and along a roller-coaster, dipping, bobbing, rocky, tree-root trail to Gentian Pond shelter beside a pond with a great view out the front of the shelter down a cliff over a vast gully. I saw my first and only moose of my hike that night across the pond at dusk. Here in this shelter we were poised just 4.7 miles shy of the Maine border. There was no doubt that I would step out of New Hampshire into Maine that next morning. It was a special feeling. I had good company in the shelter that night. Inside were two older gentleman from Georgia— Harrison Ford and Steve—section-hikers from the south, completing their last section of the AT. These were lifelong career men not yet nearly ready to retire, so they chipped away at the trail hiking sections for two or three weeks each year. Swapping stories, they told of a hiker named *The Traveler*, whom they had met the previous year in Springer Mountain shelter. This was the same Traveler that Hydro had once told me about. They said they were in Springer Mountain shelter when a man strode up, having walked 30.7 miles south from Neels Gap that day to get there. He announced that he was The

Traveler and asked them to call the Hansens at Neels Gap to verify that he truly had made it there. He then turned around and walked back to Neels Gap that night making it 61.4 miles in a day over unbelievably tough terrain. The next morning I awoke early and walked alone to the Maine border.

Maine.

The Maine border has just a small sign deep in the woods: WELCOME TO MAINE. THE WAY LIFE SHOULD BE. I stepped into Maine at 4.7 miles on the day. Thirteen states down, one to go! I was in my home state. It was an emotional moment as the thought struck me that I really had done it. Past tense. I had done it. I was now in Maine. Vacationland. The Pine Tree State (the State Motto: DIRIGO—I lead). There are three thousand miles of coastline in Maine. There are over two thousand coastal islands. I had moved to Maine on an impulse, years earlier, without ever truly knowing why. *Blueberries for Sal* by Robert McClosky must have branded a spot in my child's brain. That book shows a hillside beside the rocky coast; ocean waves crash against the rocks; blueberry bushes cover the hill. There is a bear there, too. When I was a child reading that book, I must have looked at that picture and known even then that Maine was where I needed to be.

Maine's trail reputation: wet, boggy, deep, dark, rooted, secluded, rugged. From the border at my present rate it would take me eight hiking days to reach the Kennebec River, one day after that to reach the one-hundred-mile wilderness, and five days through the wilderness and up onto Katahdin. Incredibly, I had just fifteen hiking days left. I climbed Mt. Carlo and Goose Eye mountain, then stopped to rest and eat lunch at Full Goose shelter at 9.6 miles. This shelter is 1.5 miles south of the dreaded Mahoosuc Notch, the most infamous spot on the trail. I thought to myself how nice it would have been to spend the night here in this shelter so close to the landmark before hiking through it. At the time, though, I didn't even know that the Notch was something one hikes through. I didn't know what it was. All I knew is that southbounders (a regular sight now) had, to a hiker, some vicious comment or another about the Notch:

"There's nothing else like it."

"You better get your first-aid kit ready."

"Dude, that Notch *destroyed* me."

"I hope you're ready for the Notch, young man."

All along the trail you get warnings from southbound weekend warriors of how tough the next section of trail is, but then you hike along encountering nothing special and you wonder what it was that you had been warned about. But this was different. Mahoosuc Notch occupies a category all its own. We knew that. Still, despite all the warnings, no one had ever described it to me. All I could imagine was a steep and difficult climb. I was wrong. I noticed that the data book marked the distance between the north and the south end of the Notch at just over one mile. Once in, I finally discovered for myself what the Notch is. If you want a surprise, skip ahead and don't read this description—the Mahoosuc Notch is a one-mile-long level hike through a dark gully that is hemmed in tightly between two cliffs. The trick is that the gully is filled with over a million boulders, rocks and stones that are trapped in the crevasse. Some of the boulders are bigger than houses. You hike from one end of the gully to the other. It is impossible to get lost in the Mahoosuc Notch. You just start at one end and you pick your way through the boulders to the other end. It is an athletic feat. A stream runs through the Notch under the rocks which is so dark and hidden from sunlight that there is ice and snow under some of the boulders year-round.

Through-hiker Andrew Giger, in 1969, met a group of Boy Scouts who had just hiked the Notch. The Boy Scouts explained that they had seen ice inside.

"Ice?" asked the incredulous through-hiker. "You mean Ice, I-C-E?"

"Yes," said the Boy Scouts. "And rocks, too, R-O-C-K-S!"

White blazes guide you, but you pick your own way through the Notch. The hiker's handbook advises hiking through the Notch with a friend to take pictures, but I went through alone. I saw a thick sheet of ice, July 24, in the Notch. Bending down to touch the ice, I felt a chill winter air blow by. Several times I had to take off my pack and push it ahead so that I could squeeze through holes under the boulders. The only other place on the trail that I'd had to take off my pack to fit through an area was The Lemon Squeezer in New York, but that was only a fifty-foot crack in a rock while this was a boulder field of over one mile (I had heard that it took one old man eight hours to hike this mile). I smelled something funny in the Notch; something rotting, putrid. The stench grew stronger until I looked down between two rocks and discovered a dead deer, full antlers. That deer had wandered into the Notch and had never made it out (it never had a chance). I loved the Notch. I was sorry to reach the north end and leave it behind. I followed the trail out into the forest trees once again. Out the far end, I climbed 1.6 miles up Mahoosuc Arm mountain (3,777 ft.), a treacherous climb—much more strenuous than hiking the Notch ("The Notch hits your crotch but the Arm does the harm"). I spent that night with a crowd of weekenders in Speck Pond shelter (3,450 ft.) at 14.4 miles on the day. Here past the Whites, past the Notch, only one final natural obstacle remained—crossing the Kennebec River.

I had three days from here at Speck Pond shelter to hike fifty-two miles into Rangely to meet the Y, so there was no reason to push for big miles. I hiked 16.8 miles through Grafton Notch, over Wyman mountain, Moody mountain, Old Blue mountain and the Bemis mountain range to Surplus Pond, where I laid down my bivy sack and slept alone by the trail. The next day I hiked 20.2 miles to Bemis Stream where I caught up with Stinkfoot,

Pacman, and Pitstop. From the shelter registers I'd been reading, I was now only one day behind Mozyin'. I had gained ground rapidly. I would have given anything to hike up behind Mozyin' on the trail to surprise him, but now I had to get off the trail for two days to head to the college for my job interview. At Beavis Stream, the others slept in their tents while I lay outside in my bivy sack. It rained that night, and I got drenched again. With an early start that next morning, I hiked 14.8 miles to Rte. 4 where I hitchhiked nine miles into the town of Rangely on July 27. I sat at an intersection in town chatting with a confused navy flip-flopping dude when I looked down the street and saw the Y walking toward me.

She was dressed in blue. I stopped mid-sentence and ran down the street to greet her. We drove to the college. A job interview on the trail? This felt bizarre to me. After the interview, they hired me to coach four teams now instead of just two. It felt strange to walk around the college, to sit at my desk in my office. I was glad it was just for a day. I couldn't get too comfortable off the trail. I had too far to go. The truth is that by this time I just wanted the whole thing to be over. My thoughts were of life off the trail, of life after the trail. I had job thoughts, life thoughts. I was still enjoying the woods, but at this point I just wanted it to end. The Y drove me back to the trailhead in the middle of the desolate woods on Rte. 4, nine miles outside Rangely, July 29. She waved good-bye. I turned and I walked away down the trail disappearing into the woods. The Y would tell me later that watching me walk away into the woods all alone was the first time she had felt, truly *felt,* what my hike was about.

Kennebec Crossing.

I hiked just 1.2 miles into the woods that evening for a crowded night with summer camp boys in the Piazza Rock lean-to. The next day I hiked 16.3 miles to Spaulding mountain lean-to, catching up to Pitstop, Packman, and Chief Charlie. The day after that, I left those hikers behind, hiked past the Sugarloaf mountain trail, and made 17.9 miles on the day for a night shared with raucous poker players in Horns Pond lean-to. The next day, I hiked 16.9 miles catching up to Stinkfoot again. We hiked together over the Bigelow Range—West peak, Avery peak (4,150 ft.), East peak. We met two mellow Canadians on the East peak and we all sat together enjoying the view looking down to the west over Flagstaff Lake. Just beyond the Bigelows we stopped to chat with two young southbound through-hikers. One was *Cro-Magnon,* a weight-lifter who proudly displayed a skinned chipmunk impaled on the end of his hiking stick. Chipmunks near the shelters grow so bold that they will sit on your hiking boot to eat nuts when you feed them. I fondly remembered my chipmunk friend who had crawled up my leg to eat a cracker out of my hand on the Wildcat mountain ski resort.

165

Cro-Magnon had encountered just such a chipmunk and bonked him with his hiking stick. He then cut open the chipmunk, emptied out the insides and stuck the emptied skin on his hiking stick—tail, body, arms, legs, head and all. He thought it was funny. I have never understood why people feel the need to kill things, why a photograph isn't enough to capture a moment, why hunters refer to themselves as sportsmen. Who sees a living being and feels the need to kill it? Cro-Magnon laughed. He continued hiking south, the impaled chipmunk tail wafting up on a light breeze while the little eyes, still in the sockets, stared out and saw nothing.

I spent that night with an old northbounder, plus Mighty Mike and Stinkfoot at West Carry shelter, just 13.7 miles shy of the Kennebec River, the greatest physical obstacle on the trail. The river is nearly half a mile wide at the AT crossing. The dammed river at low "tide" is only about five feet deep, even in the middle, but you don't want to be walking halfway across when the dam opens—so there is a canoe service which ferries hikers across at 11 AM every day. Mighty Mike and I leapt up early at 6 AM that next day and we set out to reach it. We reached the Kennebec River in plenty of time to meet the canoe. We enjoyed our ride across the water. A gondola ride in Venice. A taxi ride in New York City. Once across, we had before us a clear, easy path to Katahdin. A group of hikers including Just Chris plus the Chuck Wagon were camped out on the north side of the river. Chuck Wagon told the story of how Mozyin' had forded the swift, chest-deep river, carrying his backpack over his head. Here, north of the river, lies Caratunk, Maine (pop. four hundred), home to my post office drop box #15—my final PO. I retrieved my drop box and some letters, and I sat with my stash in front of the little general store. The Y wrote a note saying: *I CAME, I CONQUERED, I LYME-DISEASED IT!* My friend Amy, who had sent me articles all summer (including one about eight Princeton students who had summited Mt. McKinley), had sent me a Calvin and Hobbes: Calvin, undressing, preparing to take a bath, tells Hobbes:

> *My elbows are grass-stained, I've got sticks in my hair, I'm
> covered with bug bites and cuts and scratches. I've got
> sand in my socks and leaves in my shirt, my hands are
> sticky with sap, and my shoes are soaked! I'm hot, dirty,
> sweaty, itchy and tired.*

Hobbes replies: *"I say consider this day seized!"*

My last PO drop box. Such signs kept popping up to remind me that my trip was nearly done. I continued north out of Caratunk with Mighty Mike, making 16.9 miles on the day to West Carry Pond lean-to. An airplane landed on the pond that evening. We slept there with a group of Boy Scouts, a hiker named *Pacov* and with the Portland-Four who had popped up on the

trail in the north to spend some time in the woods. Mighty Mike and I left
the others behind, hiking 28.9 miles together that next day to the town of
Monson, Maine. Along the way that very long day, we forded the west branch
of the Piscataquis River. Then we forded the east branch of the Piscataquis
River, taking photos of ourselves crossing the rapids, trying to look poised
while trying not to slip. It was a beautiful, sunny day. We saw no one. I hadn't
known Mighty Mike, but after these two days hiking together I now found
that I liked him well. We hiked along, chattering away, when suddenly out of
the blue we found ourselves inventing *The Appalachian Trail Board Game.*

"It's like Monopoly."

"Or like Life."

"Yeah, but it has to have a long, long board."

"Like the large maps of the trail."

"It should be a really long map-board that folds down out into thirds."

"And you have to make it from one end to the other."

"It doesn't matter if you go north or south."

"Okay. So each player gets a little pewter hiking piece, and everyone
gets a trail name. You pick a card that tells you to either invent your own trail
name, invent one for somebody else, or pick a premade name from a pile of
names. Yeah?"

"Yeah. Okay. So then you take your turn by spinning a dial to determine
the mileage you make on your turn—four miles, eight miles, twelve miles,
sixteen miles, twenty, twenty-four, twenty-eight. Or it could be a really large
dial with one four, two eights, three twelves, three sixteens, two twenties, two
twenty-fours, one twenty-eight, and one thirty-two. Or something like that."

"So you spin the mileage dial and you move your piece along the
board."

"Yeah, that's good, that's good. Okay. But here's a question. How do
you win?"

"You don't win. You can't win. You just try to make it to the other
side."

"So everyone wins."

"Everyone that doesn't leave the game and walk away."

"Right."

"Okay, so everyone wins. The fun of the game is in playing it. You see
what different things can happen to everyone else."

"Kids learn geography."

"Sure."

"And the interest lies in seeing how all the little things affect everyone's
trip."

"Great."

"Okay, so you spin the dial for your daily mileage."

"Yeah."

"And let's say you can stop any number of spaces short of your mileage to stay in a lean-to or in a town. Or you can use your whole mileage and sleep out by the trail. Let's say that each space on the board has a color, and each time you land on a space you have to pick a card corresponding to the color you landed on from a pile filled with some good things, but filled mostly with things that can go wrong."

"Like what?"

"Good things are a slackpacking card, which means you double your mileage on the next turn."

"Bad things?"

"Anything—a full shelter, blisters. A blister card means that you have to stay put for one day so you lose your next turn. A broken hiking stick card means that you have to look for a new one so you hike only half your mileage next turn. A broken stove card means you lose strength from eating less so you hike only half your mileage next turn."

"Yeah but really if you broke your stove and you couldn't fix it, you wouldn't slow down. Instead you'd speed up, to reach town faster."

"So we should have cards like that—*Trail Magic* cards, *night-hiking* cards, *slackpacking* cards, *surge-hiking* cards that propel you forward lots of spaces."

"Great. And there have to be four or five red squares on the board, so if you land on a red square you have to pick a card from a special red card pile filled with things that go seriously wrong—break a bone and you lose five days off the trail in the hospital, get Giardia and you miss seven turns."

"Get Lyme disease and you miss ten turns!"

"A funeral off the trail?"

"You miss five turns."

"A wedding off the trail?"

"You miss five turns."

"Rattlesnake bite?"

"Seven turns."

"Somebody steals your backpack?"

"Five turns."

"I like it. I love it. But what about money? What about horrible weather? What about food and post office drop boxes?"

On and on, we figured it out, laughing, jarring our memories, remembering all we had been through.

That was a long, long day. We limped toward Monson, exhausted. Just as we thought we'd collapse, we emerged from the woods onto a dirt road after 28.9 miles. Salamander sat there by the trail. He had hitchhiked ahead from Gorham to be able to leave the woods in time to start his junior year of college with a semester abroad in Tibet. He had partied off the trail at Rusty's, partied off the trail back at Trail Days, and he'd lost so much time partying everywhere that he now needed to hitchhike a few hundred miles ahead in order to make his deadline (so much for hiking the trail).

Reaching the small town of Monson, we walked to crowded Shaw's boarding house, deer antlers over the front door, inside the house on the walls, everywhere. *Hunter Magazine, Hunter's Library of Sporting Books* on the coffee table. Wonderful articles inside: *"Shot Gun Trends in Transition," "Anti-'s Hunt Disruption," "Hunt of a Large-Maned Lion in Botswana," "Mozambic Ivory."* "You *need* meat," Linus Shaw told me. He sat in his chair at the dinner table while his wife carried his food to the table. So here was a host who laughs at his guests. I thought back to Elmer's, fondly. Elmer's Inn. That was long ago. Mighty Mike and I walked down the street and ate pizza for dinner. Mighty Mike would rest that next day and take a zero day here, but I would continue on. Here in Monson you stand poised at the edge of the one-hundred-mile wilderness. Here is the last town. Here you have just a few pages left in the hiker's handbook, just a few pages left in the data book. Through-hikers make phone calls from Monson to arrange for their families and friends to meet them at Katahdin in seven days. Unwisely, I made no such plan.

15
Special K

You can walk the straight and narrow,
but with a little bit of luck you'll run amok!

—Lerner Loewe

ONE-HUNDRED-MILE WILDERNESS.

Maine's one-hundred-mile wilderness is the longest stretch of wilderness on the trail. You believe you are entering true wilderness here, but instead inside you find cars parked on logging roads and day hikers dressed in street clothes milling about. Large crowds fill every lean-to, which surprises you. *Backpacker Magazine's* 1992 article called "100 Wild Miles" drew attention to this stretch and people have flocked here ever since. Camp groups, church groups, Boy Scouts, through-hikers, section-hikers, day hikers, even tourists sidle through. You enter the one-hundred-mile wilderness knowing that you have passed your last stop, knowing that you have 114 miles left to reach the summit of Mt. Katahdin. Through-hikers emerge out the north end of the one-hundred-mile wilderness at a bridge over the West Branch of the Penobscot River in Baxter State Park. Beyond the river is a road where sits a convenience store. From there, only fourteen trail miles remain to Katahdin's summit. Katahdin is what we'd been heading toward for so long. It was just ahead. I would spend four nights in the one-hundred-mile wilderness, hiking 15.2-, 20.5-, 29.4-, and 29.1-mile days.

Four miles outside Monson, on Rte. 15, I stood at the trailhead leading into the woods, leading into the one-hundred-mile wilderness. Here a sign reads: *"YOU SHOULD NOT ATTEMPT THIS SECTION UNLESS YOU CARRY A MINIMUM OF TEN DAYS' SUPPLIES."* A crazy sign. Ironically, anyone heeding the advice and heavily laden with that amount of food could do no more than merely inch slowly along so that it would indeed take them ten days to hike through. My plan (ever since Connecticut) had been to slackpack through the one-hundred-mile wilderness—to hike it in two days, packless, carrying only a water bottle, nylon tarp, and dry snack food. I changed my mind only after I got my pack weight down to twenty-four pounds in Caratunk, which really was like carrying nothing at all, so what was the difference?

Wednesday, August 4, day #132, I stepped into the one- hundred-mile wilderness alone. One hundred miles left. I wanted my hike to be over. I wanted to get to the end. Having been in the woods so long now and with merely this small stretch left, it felt somehow like taking a funeral march. The terrain is dark, wild, wet, rooty. Deep, moist smell. A chill in the air. It feels nothing like the woods in the south. There are twelve lean-tos in the one-hundred-mile wilderness. Shelter options out of Monson are at 3, 10.4, 15.2, 19.2, and 25.9 miles. I had a late start on the day. I wanted to fly, to try to catch Mozyin' again, but I wouldn't be able to get far this day. At six miles I reached Little Wilson Falls, a picnic spot of waterfalls cascading over smooth black slate down into pools of water on layers and layers of smooth black slate below. At 15.2 miles, I stopped for a night in Long Pond Stream lean-to with a church group of eighteen teenagers in tents. The trip leaders slept in the lean-to with me. A teenage girl in the group had horrible blisters, but they wouldn't let me drain them with a safety pin to air them out. Instead they smothered the blisters with Newskin, convincing the girl that they knew best. I could only imagine the continued pain that girl must have had for the rest of her trip.

My second day, I met four Georgians who had driven up just to hike through the one-hundred-mile wilderness. They had begun northbound, but I met them hiking south, backtracking out, returning to Monson because one of them had injured his knee and couldn't go on. Now they didn't have enough time to start again to try to make it through. They were terribly disappointed. The prospect of cutting their losses, driving north and climbing Mt. Katahdin, was not enough to lighten their spirit. Forget the Smokies, forget Mt. Washington, forget Katahdin; they had driven all the way up from Georgia just to hike through this stretch. At seventeen miles, I reached a side trail leading to Gulf Hagas, *"The Grand Canyon of the East."* I didn't detour. I lived in Maine. I would return one day at my leisure. That gave me something to look forward to. At 20.5 miles I stopped at Carl A. Newhall lean-to, where someone had written: *"EXPECT NOTHING. ENJOY WHAT YOU HAVE."*

Third day, at 4.7 miles, I reached the exposed rocky summit of White Cap mountain and looked out at my first glimpse of Katahdin, seventy-three miles away. I could look out and see the mountain, the very spot that I would be standing on just four days hence. The ground from here to Katahdin is low and flat—just a valley walk remained straight to the great mountain at the end. The Maine Woods. Descending White Cap's north side, I knew—because I had looked out and *seen* it—that there remained only one last mountain to climb. Inspired (and still trying to catch Mozyin'), I turned up the mileage. Big Miles. I hiked 29.4 miles the next day, stopping at Potaywadjo Spring lean-to with its thirty-foot spring of crystal clear ice cold water. Here I reached the last page in the Data Book, which had been a good friend for so long (another small sign that your trip has come to a close).

Next day, at twenty-seven miles, I reached Rainbow Ledges, where I picked some blueberries, enjoyed sunlight, and looked out at Katahdin. Adding two evening miles, for 29.1 total miles on the day, I stopped at Hurd Brook lean-to where inside sat Chinook, two southbounders, and Mighty Mike with his younger brother Brian who had joined him so that they could hike the state of Maine together. They had a roaring fire going. Darkness had already fallen. I approached the shelter, stepping out of the darkness.

"SNEAKERS?!"

It was a satisfying moment. I told my Lyme disease story. That next morning we hiked 3.5 miles, to where we stepped out of the one-hundred-mile wilderness in crossing the Abol Bridge over the West Branch of the Penobscot River. Here is the grocery store on the wide dirt road that leads through Baxter State Park. Here we had just fourteen miles left to Katahdin's summit. We continued another 6.4 miles to Daicey Pond campground with its ranger station where we signed in and chatted with park rangers. Daicey Pond has a library, parking lot, lake, and the best view of Mt. Katahdin that exists. We looked across the lake at the giant granite mountain which rises up across the water. We had been catching glimpses of the mountain for days. From here it is only 7.6 miles to the summit, but we had walked slowly all day and it was already midafternoon, so the park rangers sent us one hundred yards down the road and off on a side trail another one hundred yards into the woods where two small lean-tos that are reserved just for through-hikers sit in a clearing. Most through-hikers sleep here their last night on the trail, poised to rise and hike seven miles to the summit of Mt. Katahdin the following morning. That was our plan. It was the four of us, along with an old southbound man named *Little David.* We took photographs. Conversation was light and natural.

"What are you having for breakfast?" younger brother asked Mercury Mark.

"Tomorrow? I'm having some Special-K."

Why, Why, Why.

Sleeping here, north of the one-hundred-mile wilderness in this shelter below Kathadin, proves to be nearly impossible. Here your trip has nearly come to an end. At night you lie still, trying to sleep, knowing that this is your last chance to reflect, your last chance to remember the trademarks of your summer—the familiar whoosh of your stove, the powerful cravings you had while deep in the woods for Fresca, root beer, Tang, orange juice, sesame cold noodles. You remember the people who had treated you right. You remember scribbling down names, addresses, phone numbers in the margins of your guidebooks; scribbling down names of songs, names of books, and lists of things like the top-ten things you wish you could do instead of returning to your job. You remember how your feet enlarged, how a certain song had once gotten randomly lodged in your brain for an entire day nearly driving you insane: *"Frosty the Snowman, was a very merry soul."* On and on and on. You remember how you smeared palmfuls of Vaseline under your armpits to ease the unbearable pain of an underarm rash from your arms swishing forward and back day after day after day. You remember how strange you had felt seeing that first road at Neels Gap knowing that you were no part of it. You remember how you picked up a stick that looked like a duck, how you picked up an acorn that looked like an owl, how you picked up a twig that looked like a golf tee. You remember how you picked up a stone from the ground for no other reason except that you liked the look of this particular little one more than every other million-billion stones you saw all summer. You remember the sight of moose pellets. You remember how you set your spoon on a cow patty on a hillside in Vermont and took a photograph. You remember the retired banker you met who explained how entire cultures once lived on bread, how bread was once a complete meal in this country before big agriculture began extracting protein out of wheat during WWI to send protein-rich "wheat germ" to soldiers overseas. You remember the young woman you met who detailed the incredible ecological benefits of using Hemp as our source for paper products instead of trees. You remember shapes and swirls of green and brown. And rocks. Individual trees, branches, bushes.

I wondered about the future of the trail—hikers with cell phones and computers. Applications and reservations. Not enough room for everyone. Perhaps Easy Stryder's dream of helium-filled backpacks will one day come true. Perhaps pills will replace GORP, IV bags will replace stoves. The way we through-hike today is vastly different than it was in the early days back before the hiker's handbook, the data book, internal frame backpacks, trail names, and trail maps existed. The forty-six stories of the first men and women who hiked the trail from 1936 to 1972 are all detailed in the Rodale Appalachian Trail books, Volumes I and II. Two thousand pages tell their tales. The early through-hikers ate sardines, made wood fires, baked corn meal and buried food by the trail in caches. They called animal "game," horses "stock," and they forded the Kennebec River by hanging on to logs. The early hikers got bit by dogs, wore belts, wore pants, had long road walks. They got their maps from the library. They researched post offices through the U.S. government, and they called each one to learn if they would hold packages. They boiled their drinking water, killed rattlesnakes, called women "not-too-young ladies," and got invited into people's homes. They got newspaper articles written about them every step of the way. In 1964, TV, radio and newspaper crews all stood waiting for through-hikers Chuck Ebersole, his son, and their beagle at trail's end while the Town Council of Millinocket, Maine, presented them with an oil painting of Mt. Katahdin. In the old days through-hikers were mostly men, mostly old. Early through-hikers drank coffee with the postmasters. They were continually offered rides. One man carried a pedometer, another carried a ball of string in the woods to use in case he got lost. One hiker left three rings in a tub after taking a bath, another got a letter from his boss firing him. There was Embryo Beard, and there was Casanova Hiker who stopped to talk to every woman he saw. There was a man who counted the number of times he fell down. There was a couple who became unable to sleep indoors. A woman saw a rabbit sniff a chipmunk, a man saw ten rabbits emerge from the cold snowy woods to sit around his campfire. A through-hiker surprised a moose by hiking so close that the moose froze, staring at the hiker in horror, its mouth overflowing with grass but unable to chew.

The best title of the forty-six Rodale stories goes to James Wolf: *"From Springer's Peak in Spring I Sprang."* Worst title, Gene Espy: *"I Enjoyed It!"* There was the man who wrote to the ATC for information in 1971, inquiring if anyone had ever hiked the whole trail. Section-hiker Charles Konopa gives a course in AT packing: *"Make two piles: those absolutely needed items and those which might be needed. Now throw away the second pile."* There was the young man who walked through the woods with his "Friends of the Trail" journal asking every single person he met all summer to sign it. Two through-hikers' wives got told a tall tale by local people in a town that the woods their husbands had just entered were "infested" with mountain lions. A group of young boys down south couldn't help giggling while telling a through-hiker that the mountains he was heading up into were positively slithering with rattlesnakes. There was the kid seen dragging his sleeping bag through the woods tied to a string behind him. A bearded, ragged through-hiker was in a town and got asked: *"Are you an old man or a young man?"* Andrew Giger, through-hiking in 1969, lost half a pound of weight a day for thirty-five days, writing: *"The motel room mirror reflected an emaciated character whose ribs stuck out. My buttocks were noticeably smaller. I had literally walked my ass off."* Every hiker describes the Mahoosac Notch. Every hiker describes the crazy antics of grouse. Someone used the word "zillion" to refer to the number of black flies. And then, more than now, the early through-hikers got asked the question, *"WHY?"* Why, why, why? They found that their true answers were never accepted so they invented answers—to collect flowers, to test foot gear; and for some reason these false answers seemed to work better. But there wasn't always an answer, as there still isn't today. Dorothy Laker, a three-time through-hiker (1957, 1962, 1964), wrote: *"I cannot even fathom my own motives."* Benton MacKaye understood the value of long, solitary walks for introspection. That's why he planned the trail. Knowledge gained on the trail can be simple, James Rutter in 1971 wrote:

> *When we parted company the last comment the girl made*
> *was that I would certainly be experienced by the end of*
> *my hike. My mind was busy with what the girl had said.*
> *According to her reasoning, I would be an expert by trail's*
> *end—worthy of being heard, of writing in books, of giving*
> *advice. But as the trip progressed through the weeks of*
> *flies, the weeks of rain, and the days of hot roads, it seemed*
> *that about all I learned was that I got up in the morning,*
> *ate some, walked some, talked some, and went to bed at*
> *night to sleep some.*

And me, what knowledge had *I* gained? How had my life changed? What from this hike would I remember forever? Two things, mainly: that quiet matters, and that nature matters. So much time alone with your thoughts. It is humbling. Suddenly there isn't so much to say all the time anymore. You learn the basic elements of survival: water, food, shelter. Perspective. Gaining perspective gives you the ability to measure the importance of all the little daily happenings in life off the trail. All the little things just wouldn't rattle me much anymore. I learned that if I had to walk somewhere I could do it. And I learned that I could sleep anywhere now. I had learned how simple life is, how few are true necessities. I learned to live simply. I had gained a feel for the size of the country (of course, an airplane ride can provide the same thing). I had cleaned my stove by taking it apart. I had met a kid who didn't know how to pick blueberries. I had learned the sound of snorts from a bear in darkness at the edge of a field. I had learned the sound of light airy tinkling rain and the sound of a drumming cascade of rain on a lean-to roof. And I had learned that a little jabberwocky insect, one hundred thousand times smaller than I am, is a dangerous foe. I had touched trees, had brushed against plants. I had learned the pleasure of living life without an eye to the clock, an eye to the watch, without dissecting the day into minutes, seconds. I had learned what it's like to step on a slippery root and fall in a creek while alone deep in the woods. I had learned what it's like to step carefully and to choose my footsteps wisely.

I had learned to feel elemental in the woods. I had longed to find an arrowhead. I felt awed by the legacy of those who had come before. The AT parallels the greatest of Native American Indian trails, the Great Indian Warpath, which ran from Alabama to Pennsylvania. I was touched by the Native American Indian names for the places we hiked: Watauga, Nesuntabunt, Pemadumcook, Winturri, Chateauguay, Schaghticoke, Wawayanda, Piscataquis, Katahdin. I felt like an Indian myself—proud, independent. Artifacts of the Abenaki Indians of Maine date back eight thousand years. The Maine Indians living southwest of the Kennebec River grew maize, beans, squash, and tobacco, and they hunted and gathered. The Maine Indians living northeast of the Kennebec River hunted, fished, and collected shellfish. European diseases decimated the Native American Indian population beginning when the Pilgrims landed at Plymouth in 1620. Settlers ravaged the East Coast trees. Very few virgin tree stands remain, so total and massive was their destruction by settlers for houses, grazing land, ship masts. I had learned that stepping off the trail while deep in the woods will teach you the greatest lesson of your life.

Years earlier, bushwhacking down Tabletop Mountain in the Adirondacks with Toot, we had lost the herd path and were forced to descend the mountain through utter wilderness. That is the only way to learn what the woods are really like. Without constant attention from work crews, the trail gets swallowed up and recaptured by the woods (as roads and even buildings will, too). With trails or without, these forests are worth preserving. That is the Great Paradox of the trail: in order for people to care to preserve wilderness they have to spend time in the wilderness to feel how valuable it is. But if all civilized people on Earth rush into the wilderness to gain that appreciation, there won't be any wilderness left.

Worth gained from time on the trail is a glimpse of nature. On the trail you learn the natural cycle of things. You see death all around you. And you see new life. You witness the struggle for survival everywhere that you look. You see mountains and rocks. You see old things. You look off in the distance. See beauty. You see time at the speed of a creeping glacier. Then a bird flies past. And you continue on.

Katahdin.

Monday, August 9, 1993. Day #137.

The others set out early to meet their families. I woke up at 7 AM, packed and hiked 2.4 miles from our hidden Daicey Pond Campground shelters to the Katahdin Stream Campground where the Hunt Trail to the summit of Mt. Katahdin begins. There are three trails up Katahdin. The Hunt Trail (on the Appalachian Trail) is the most popular route and most scenic. Here I found a large volume of hikers. But the mountain is so large that no matter how many people are on it, it never feels crowded. And there is no road to the top.

Katahdin rises straight up from nothing. It is the most spectacular mountain on the trail, the most spectacular mountain east of the Mississippi River. Here at Katahdin Stream Campground is another ranger station, picnic tables: multiple parking lots and a small pond. I walked inside the screen porch at the ranger station and signed one last register. I read that Mozyin' had climbed Katahdin the day before. I had missed him by one day. But as far as he knew I had left the trail in Hanover with Lyme disease never to return. Mozyin' wrote in the final register that he had gotten his job back at work at Mobil Chemical. In four months, they hadn't found anyone to replace him. He wrote: *"I'm going back to my office job, to spend some time polishing a chair with my ass."* Easy Stryder had summited a week before Mozyin'. Easy Stryder had climbed up Katahdin with his girlfriend. He proposed to her on top. As I mentioned before, the trail gets you all sentimental like that. Hydro had left the trail to visit his wife in Florida, but he would return to complete his through-hike. Ponder Yonder, Kilgore Trout, Coyote would all complete their through-hikes. Blazer never would. Homeward Bound, Beauty and the Beast, Heel and Toe, Wrong-Way Peripidus, Low Rider, Stone, Big TR and Little TR would all complete their through-hikes. Unleashed, Jersey and Maddog would not.

I emptied everything but food and snacks out of my pack and left the pile in a corner in the ranger station screened porch. Then I set out. At the base of the Hunt Trail I reflected that I was at that moment already a section-hiker, as I had climbed up Katahdin's AT Hunt Trail once before.

"I don't think you'll be able to make it up there wearing those," a man volunteered, sidling over, pointing down at my running shoes.

"You don't think they'll work?" I asked.

"Not up there," he said. "It's awfully tough."

Holy prophecy, Batman—here it had come to pass exactly as Hydro had prophesized. On my last day, here was someone telling me that I'd never make it!

It was a clear, sunny day. The climb was familiar. I passed several people. I climbed over the tree line that lies on this mountain at just above two thousand feet, and began the rock scramble up the Dragon's Back. I thought of the woman who had carried a watermelon to the top. Through-hikers are often handed champagne bottles by their families at Katahdin Stream Campground which they carry to the top to pop open. I caught up to Chinook who was hiking slowly up the mountain with his family. I met them the moment his family decided to turn back. They had intended to climb the mountain, but here they stood at the spot where iron rungs in the mountain are the only handholds to hoist oneself up over several house-size boulders. That wasn't what they had bargained for. I continued on, catching up to Mercury Mark and Brother Brian a short while later.

177

Nearing the top of the Dragon's Back, we looked up at what appeared to be the summit high above. I knew that it wasn't the summit but I kept quiet for my companions' sake because the surprise view from over the false peak ("The Gateway") is astonishing. We gained the high ridge and my two friends' jaws dropped as they found themselves staring out across the Tablelands with the actual summit of Katahdin rising like a pimple so far off in the distance that we all had to laugh. The Tablelands is a mile and a half long. Flat ground. Northbounder Elmer Onstott had climbed up as high as the Tablelands in late October, 1968, having hiked 2,140 miles, all the way from Georgia only to be turned back by severe weather a few thousand feet from the summit—never to complete his through-hike. It was here on the Tablelands in July, 1939, that twelve-year-old Donn Fendler got lost in the fog from his family and hiked down the backside of the mountain. The National Guard, Millinocket mill workers, thousands of people searched for the boy for five days to no avail. Finally they scaled down the search, believing him dead. Fendler walked out of the woods at the East Branch of the Penobscot nine days after getting lost, pantless, shoeless, bug-bitten, dehydrated, with part of one toe missing, and weighing fifty-eight pounds. Fendler's incredible story is chronicled in the still-published story: *Lost on a Mountain in Maine.*

We had no such fog or bad weather. We hiked past Thoreau Springs. Henry David Thoreau had climbed Mt. Katahdin in 1846 during the two years he was living on Walden Pond. Thoreau said: *"In wilderness is the preservation of the world."* He had gotten up to the tablelands in a storm but never summited, and he thought that this was a cursed, impossible mountain. Of course, there were no trails back then. He wrote the story "KTAADN" about his trip. Maybe if he'd had a nice sunny day and nice views he would never have returned to that pond!

We made the final gentle ascent. There are stories of through-hikers who stand upon Katahdin at the end of their journey with tears streaming down. I felt no emotion. I knew very simply that it was now time to go home. I could go home now. And that was okay. I was ready to go home.

Summit. We touched the wood summit sign on Mt. Katahdin and our trip was over. We touched the giant cairn of rocks twenty feet beside it. There were many people about (mostly non-through-hikers). It is a spacious summit. Some gazed down at Chimney Pond. Others explored the Knife's Edge. Others sat amongst the rocks eating, resting, talking, smiling, laughing. There is always room for everyone on that rocky summit. Chinook made it up, having run the entire way upon leaving his family. We gave each other high-five's. A couple loud whoops. Many photographs. Then we quieted down and spent some time gazing at our surroundings. I thought of all that I knew about this mountain. How Maine's Governor Percival Baxter had given as a gift his purchase of Mt. Katahdin and the land in Baxter State Park to the state designating it as *"Forever Wild."* On some days of the year, depending

178

upon the tilt of the Earth's axis, the wooden summit sign on Katahdin is the first object in America touched by the sun. An old woodsman named LeRoy Dudley lived for thirty years at Chimney Pond behind Katahdin, entertaining visitors with his tales of *Pamola,* who was a mythical moose with an eagle's beak, eagle claws, and bat wings which the Native American Indians believed lived on the mountaintop. Pamola changed the weather, hurled boulders, and generally harassed passers-by. Dudley's stories are chronicled in *Chimney Pond Tales.* Pamola wasn't evil, but he was a Trickster.

Hiking legend Warren Doyle happened to be on the summit this day with his seven-year-old son, Forest. We chatted. Then quite rapidly dark clouds rolled in. Everyone hurried off the mountaintop, although our little group lingered longer. Soon we were under black clouds. We descended the summit, recrossed the Tablelands. The rain crashed down. We passed the Doyles who had taken cover under a rock. We hiked slowly down the Dragon's Back in the rain. Then for no great reason we started to run. The storm burst around us. We reached the dirt path that was muddy and slick. But we only ran faster... storm, running down, super heroes, Spider Man, twisting, leaping, shrieking in the rain...we ran down uncontrollably, slipping, crashing into rocks...utter abandon. Someone yelled:

"I'm Yo-Yoing! I'm starting my through-hike south!"

Mercury Mark and Brian were from Chicago, where Bears football coach Mike Ditka had become deified. The brothers, in racing down the mountain, yelled back and forth, launching into a comedy routine:

"Ditka through-hiking?"

"Seventy-three days."

"Ditka through-hiking without a pack, no stove, carrying a busload of cheerleaders on his back?"

"Fifty-five days!"

Back at the base of the mountain, sweating, soaked, out of breath, we huddled together dripping wet under a picnic area wooden tent, rain cascading down around our dry island. I stood in northern Maine having never arranged a way to get home, back to my car in New York. It would end up taking me two hitchhikes, two bus rides, a night outside on a hill behind a gas station, and an airplane ride to do it.

But that was another adventure.

CPSIA information can be obtained at www.ICGtesting.com
Printed in the USA
LVOW040856090212

267865LV00001B/529/P